Where to Stay and What to Do in London

MW01672349

Contents

London Tourist Board and Convention Bureau, Glen House, Stag Place, London SW1E 5LT
Tel: (0171) 932 2000 Fax: (0171) 932 0222

Editor: **Jennifer Boyes** Managing Editor: **Diana James**

London Tourist Board and Convention Bureau (LTB) is the official tourist organisation for Greater London, financed by membership subscriptions and certain commercial activities. In addition LTB receives financial support from the Department of National Heritage, the English Tourist Board and the London Boroughs Grants Scheme.

Funded by LBG

Published for London Tourist Board and Convention Bureau by:
Book Production Consultants PLC, 25-27 High Street, Chesterton, Cambridge CB4 1ND
Tel: (01223) 352790 Fax: (01223) 460718 E-mail: ltbpubs@bpccam.demon.co.uk

Advertisement sales:
Mongoose Communications Limited, Victory House, Leicester Square, London WC2H 7QH Tel: (0171) 306 0300

Printed in Great Britain by: The Burlington Press, Cambridge

Distributed by the publications divisions of the Automobile Association, Fanum House, Basingstoke, Hants RG21 2EA.

ISBN: 0 946837 51 1

Please mention "Where to Stay and What to Do in London" when contacting organisations featured in this publication.

For a copy of *London Capital Breaks*, London Tourist Board's free guide to London, giving details of opening hours, admission prices of many attractions and much more, write to LTB at the address given above.

LONDON

Don't miss this! New in London...

IMAX cinema, Trocadero

Below: Trafalgar Square

London is a city where there is always something new, something different and exciting to see. So even if you have been here many times before, there's sure to be a new gallery, a different exhibition, a ground-breaking show or a state-of-the-art attraction to see in this ever-changing city.

The **British Library** has been re-housed in St Pancras. The new building, designed by Professor Sir Colin St John Wilson, holds the UK's National Library and a staggering 150 million items – a veritable treasure house of the written word! There are three exhibition galleries, which display rare and unique items like the Lindisfarne Gospels (c700 AD), the Gutenberg Bible – the first Western printed book using movable type – and Shakespeare's First Folio (1623). Visitors can use the latest computer technology to 'turn the pages' of famous literary and historic documents. For details of events call Visitor Services on (0171) 412 7332.

Swords Gallery, National Army Museum

Aerial view of British Museum

The Estorick Collection of Italian Art opened in Canonbury Square in early 1998, showing a collection of Italian futurist art in a renovated Georgian building. There are six galleries, an art library, café and shop. Information about the collection and exhibitions is available on (0171) 704 9522.

A new **IMAX 3D cinema** has arrived at the Trocadero in Piccadilly Circus. The seven-storey high cinema screen shows 11 screenings daily. Audiences wear special headsets and listen in surround-sound. Another 500-seater IMAX cinema is due to open outside Waterloo Station in spring 1999 and a third is planned within the Science Museum. (No IMAX cinemas in London … and then three come along at once!)

The **National Army Museum** has a new gallery looking at the modern army from 1945 to the present day. In this interactive gallery, visitors are presented with a series of challenges and given an insight into the Army's activities in recent hot spots. There are lots of other interesting exhibits within the museum – such as Florence Nightingale's lamp, meagre wartime rations and not-so-meagre regulation ladies' underwear!

The award-winning **Natural History Museum** has added four new galleries which invite you to see the world's oldest rock – over four billion years old – sparkling diamonds and gemstones and much more. See under 'Must sees for families' and 'London's Winners' for more information.

London has a staggering 300 different museums and galleries – a taste of some of the best follows.

'Must sees' for Culture Vultures

• The **Victoria and Albert Museum** – for the greatest collection of decorative arts from 3000 BC to the present day – Naomi Campbell's platform shoes are on show!

Natural History Museum

• The **British Museum** – a treasure trove of objects (over six million of them) from all over the globe. Everything from mummies to Ming – highlights include priceless antiquities like the Elgin Marbles, Rosetta Stone and Mildenhall Treasure.

• The **Institute of Contemporary Arts** – the centre for international contemporary arts in Britain, with three galleries of changing exhibitions, two cinemas, a theatre and bookshop. Call (0171) 930 3647 for details of what's on for 1999.

• The **Museum of London** for the history of the Capital. From the Great Fire Experience and reconstructed Victorian shops to the *London Now!* gallery, the museum tells the city's fascinating story.

Don't miss this! New in London…

Five Fantastic Free Museums …

Some of the best things in life are free – and the following London attractions do not levy admission charges (except for special events and exhibitions):

Bank of England Museum – bank notes, gold bars and the chance to try your hand at being a trader!

Bethnal Green Museum of Childhood – toys, dolls' houses and lots of nostalgia.

British Museum – see the description on page 3.

Geffrye Museum – domestic interiors from 1500 through to Art Deco and the Fifties.

National Army Museum – see the description on page 3.

… and Five Great Galleries

Courtauld Gallery – the finest collection of Impressionist paintings in Britain, reopen after major refurbishment.

Hayward Gallery – four major exhibitions each year, on both contemporary and historic art.

National Gallery – from Leonardo to Rembrandt and Renoir, one of the best art collections in the world (free).

National Portrait Gallery – likenesses of the famous and infamous, from sportsmen to pop stars (free).

Tate Gallery – National Collection of British Painting, including some fabulous Turners (free).

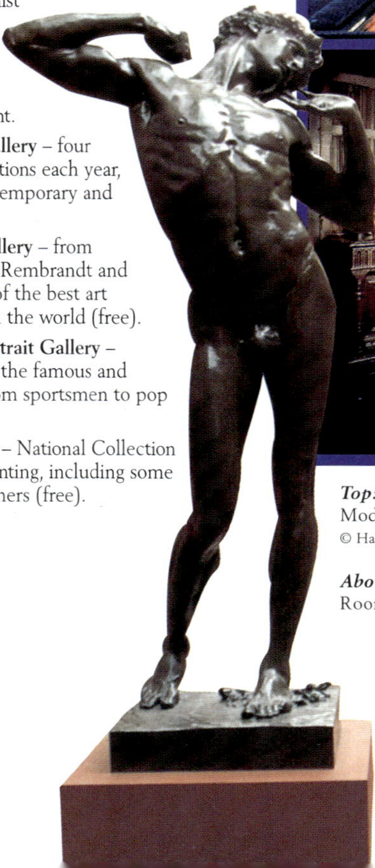

Top: Proposed Tate Gallery of Modern Art, Bankside Power Station
© Hayes Dividson

Above: Elizabethan and Jacobean Room 1580-1640, Geffrye Museum

acific Tank, the London Aquarium

Best for big kids:

• **Trocadero Centre** – includes delights like the Pepsi Max Drop indoor white-knuckle ride, plus all sorts of computer and virtuality games.

• **Segaworld** – 1998 saw the introduction of the new *Power* virtuality centre with 400 video games – including a virtual bobsleigh ride and *Max Flight*, Europe's only virtual roller-coaster. Open until midnight daily (0100 Fridays and Saturdays).

• **Rock Circus** – all the great rockers and latest ravers are here in waxwork and stereo sound, celebrating 40 years of rock and pop. Maybe put your hands where Ant and Dec did on the Wall of Hands!

Wellcome Wing at the Science Museum
© MacCormac Jamieson Prichard, Ove Arup & Partners, Davis Langdon & Everest

'Must sees' for Families

Visit the *Earth Galleries* in the **Natural History Museum**, which tell the story of our planet from its formation. Live the Earthquake Experience, see creepy-crawlies magnified hundreds of times and hear the roar of a dinosaur. Don't miss the huge dinosaur skeletons and animatronic displays.

The **Science Museum** is crammed full of information on science, technology, industry and medicine, but with plenty of interactive exhibits and fun things to see. There's a special-priced family ticket and kids' events in the school holidays.

Good for all the family:

• **BBC Experience** – how the famous British Broadcasting Corporation works, with plenty of amusing archive material and hands-on activities.

• **London Zoo** – 8,000 animals live in this wildlife park and conservation centre. Meet the animals, watch feeding time, encounter the spiders, visit the children's zoo, penguin pool and much more!

• **London Aquarium** – hundreds of species of fish and marine life, plus a 'beach' area where you can stroke friendly rays.

Changing the Guard

'The Beatles' at Rock Circus

New in London... Don't miss this!

'Must see' Sights

Changing the Guard – a splendid spectacle, every other day, but daily April to July. Call London Tourist Board's 'Changing the Guard' information line on 0839 123 411*.

Trafalgar Square – fountains, Nelson's column and, of course, the pigeons. Take your camera.

Get a great view of the River Thames from **Tower Bridge** or follow the Jubilee walkway along the South Bank.

See London from a balloon! The **London Balloon** rises to 400 feet every day until dusk – and until midnight on Fridays and Saturdays.

Try climbing the **Monument**, London's memorial to the Great Fire of 1666. It is 202ft high – and there are 311 steps and no lift – but you will receive a souvenir if you make it to the top!

Walk the parks – St James's for the lakes, Hyde Park for people-watching and Hampstead Heath for lots of wild parkland.

Head for the **Royal Observatory** in Greenwich Park and stand with one foot in the eastern and one foot in the western hemisphere. Watch out for a terrific party here on New Year's Eve 1999!

Right Royal Attractions

Buckingham Palace will reopen its State Apartments from August to October, daily. If you miss it, see a little of the Queen's art collection in the **Queen's Gallery** instead.

Kensington Palace State Apartments have re-displayed the glorious Court Dress Collection. You won't be able to see where the late Diana, Princess of Wales lived, but you can see where the memorial may be in Kensington Gardens. There are now several tours of London featuring the life of Diana – and you can visit **Spencer House** which was owned by her family.

Other places with a royal connection include the fabulous **Hampton Court Palace**, with its gardens and maze and the **Queen's House** at Greenwich.

Special Places for those with Special Needs

The National Maritime Museum in Greenwich was the winner of the *Tourism for All* (accessibility for disabled visitors) sector in the 1998 London Tourism Awards. Highly commended were the London Transport Museum and the Mount Royal Thistle Hotel.

For a free copy of *London for All*, London Tourist Board's newsletter for those with special needs in the Capital, write to London Tourist Board and Convention Bureau, Glen House, Stag Place, Victoria, London SW1E 5LT.

National Maritime Museum, Greenwich

BBC Experience

**Calls are charged at 49p per minute at all times (as at October 1998), plus any hotel/payphone surcharges.*

Hyde Park

Coming soon – in Millennium City!

A 170-metre high Ferris wheel will be built in Jubilee Gardens and should be giving rides by autumn 1999. The **Royal Opera House** is scheduled to reopen for December 1999 and the much-publicised Millennium Dome at Greenwich will be open for the whole of 2000. You will have to wait until spring 2000 for the new **Tate Gallery of Modern Art** at Bankside. Come and see the city for *the* new millennium!

The London Balloon

Cutty Sark, Greenwich

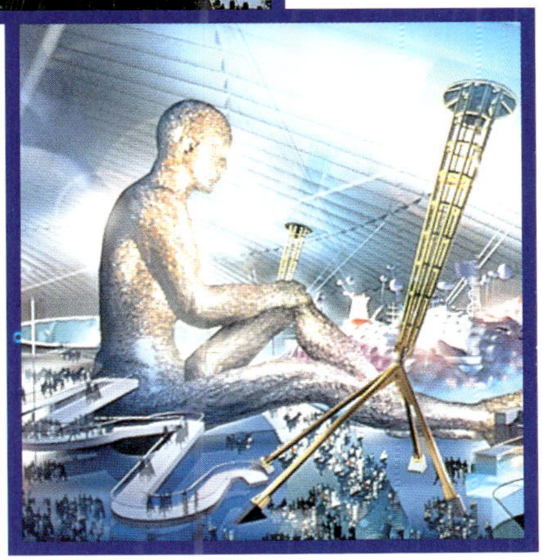

Millennium Experience Body Image
© NMEC/Hayes Davidson

What's in Store?

Whether it's fashions or furnishings you're after, boots or books, jeans or gems, London's dizzying range of shops will have the answer.

Oxford Street

⊖ Oxford Circus, Marble Arch, Bond Street

London's longest shopping street is always busy, so don't under-estimate the time it takes to shop-hop; jump on a bus to get from one end to the other. It appeals to all the family, with a great mix of medium-priced clothes and shoe shops, record shops, department stores like Selfridges, Debenham's and John Lewis, and bumper branches of British chain stores – including the giant Marks and Spencer near Marble Arch.

Bond Street

⊖ Bond Street, Green Park

Timelessly classy and chic, Bond Street boasts glittering jewellers, art galleries and auction houses and the cachet that attracts the top designers' flagship stores. Check out Donna Karan, Georgio Armani, Calvin Klein, Gucci and Tommy Hilfiger, and call into the Fenwick department store for a host more men's and women's high fashion labels.

Tottenham Court Road

⊖ Tottenham Court Road, Goodge Street

Londoners know to head here when they want the most competitive prices on computers, hi-fis and the latest electronic gizmos and gadgets. Shop around and you're sure to find a good deal. It's also an inspiration for design-conscious home-makers, with stores such as Heal's and Purves and Purves stocking contemporary furniture straight from the pages of the glossy style magazines.

Old Bond Street

Regent Street, Piccadilly, Jermyn Street

⊖ Oxford Circus, Piccadilly

Grand and elegant, Regent Street has bags of style and shopping landmarks like Liberty, Hamley's world-famous toy shop and the Lillywhites sports store. Afternoon tea in sumptuous Fortnum and Mason, Burlington Arcade's graceful Georgian architecture, and the Jermyn Street shops that have been serving the aristocracy for 300 years, all smack of tradition and quality.

Charing Cross Road

⊖ Tottenham Court Road, Leicester Square

Books, books and more books; new, second-hand and antique. Name your specialist subject and you'll find it here.

Top: Liberty, Regent Street
Middle: John Lewis, Oxford Street
Right: Harrods, Knightsbridge

Kensington High Street

⊖ Kensington High Street

A wide choice of shops and chain stores for all the family, with well-known designer labels in Barkers department store and off-the-wall creations for young fashion victims at Hype DF and Kensington market. Just round the corner, Kensington Church Street is lined with antique shops.

Christmas Shopping in London

Christmas is the most exciting time of the year for London's shops and stores and the capital is packed full of unusual gift ideas. The West End embraces Christmas with enthusiasm, creating an atmosphere of fun and festivity. Stunning window-displays add the rich colours of the season to the streets.

The time available for shopping is increased in the weeks before Christmas as shops and stores extend their opening hours. All the major department stores in the West End open for Sunday shopping during December.

- Most shops and stores open by 0930 and close at 1800 from Monday to Saturday, though Covent Garden's usually open until 2000. Shops rarely close at lunchtime. Late night openings vary; in Oxford Street and Regent Street it's Thursday; in Knightsbridge Wednesday. Many open on Sundays, usually for six hours, from 1100 to 1700, or 1200 to 1800.
- Call London Tourist Board's Visitorcall shopping line on 0839 123 486* for store information and details of sales and Christmas shopping (information on Christmas shopping not available until November 1998).

Covent Garden

⊖ Covent Garden

The bustling old fruit and flower market, immortalised in the film 'My Fair Lady', has been replaced by a buzzing shopping and entertainment area that has definite youth appeal. Jugglers and mime artists, musicians and magicians add to the shopping fun of the crafts market, natural cosmetics stores and hip hunting grounds like Agnes B, Diesel and Red or Dead.

Knightsbridge, Chelsea

⊖ Knightsbridge, Sloane Square

Upmarket shopping for just about anything. From Harrods' wondrous food hall and Harvey Nichols' Ab Fab designer fashions on Knightsbridge to boutiques on the King's Road and homewares at Sir Terence Conran's style emporium – the Conran shop – on Fulham Road.

**Calls are charged at 49p per minute at all times (as at October 1998), plus any hotel/payphone surcharges.*

City Lights

Top: Royal Albert Hall
Above: Trafalgar Square

When daylight fades, another side of London comes to life in a blaze of neon. Hundreds of theatres, comedy clubs, night clubs and live music venues open up a vibrant entertainment scene.

London's theatre is unrivalled, with more productions and more star names appearing than anywhere else in the world – and that includes Broadway! Any night of the week (several major theatres now open on Sundays) you can choose between blockbuster musicals, comedy, cabaret and drama, from Shakespeare to controversial new writing by today's sparkiest playwrights.

The West End and beyond

The theatres themselves are just as richly varied as the shows they put on. Many have retained their ornate Victorian décor while others, like the *Royal National Theatre* (0171 928 2252) and the *Barbican* (0171 638 8891) are purpose-built, state-of-the-art homes for superb quality productions. Smaller 'fringe' theatres, often located in pubs beyond the West End, are renowned for their creative approach and low ticket prices – some of the most innovative being the *Bush Theatre* at Shepherd's Bush (0181 743 3388), the *Almeida* in Islington (0171 359 4404) and the *Orange Tree* at Richmond (0181 940 3633). In summer, there's open-air theatre in *Regent's Park* (0171 846 2431), and other city parks stage performances of drama and music.

You can catch the spirit of the Victorian Music Hall at the *Players' Theatre* (0171 839 1134) or step back to the Elizabethan era at *Shakespeare's Globe Theatre* (0171 401 9919) where the actors perform in the open air without microphones and the

Bar Italia, Soho

South Bank

Her Majesty's Theatre

audience jeers and cheers. A ticket to be a 'groundling', standing just yards from the stage, is one of theatreland's great bargains at only £5 – though there are under-cover seats, too, for softies. The Globe's season runs from May to September but you can take a fascinating, daytime, behind-the-scenes tour any time of year, just as you can at the Royal National Theatre and the *Theatre Royal Drury Lane* (0171 494 5000).

Star-studded shows

Such is the lure and kudos of the London stage that movie and TV megastars cannot resist treading the boards. In recent years Jack Lemmon, Dustin Hoffman, Peter O'Toole and Kevin Spacey have taken starring roles, while Judi Dench, Maggie Smith, Helen Mirren, Alan Bates and Michael Gambon are frequent performers. 1999 promises to be a thrilling year for theatre-goers, with acclaimed box-office hits like *Les Miserables* and *Chicago* playing alongside new musical productions of *Jean de Florette*, Disney's *The Lion King*, and Andrew Lloyd Webber's much-anticipated follow-up to *The Phantom of the Opera*.

From the classics . . .

London's thriving dance scene gets a boost in 1999 with the reopening of *Sadler's Wells*, one of the city's most famous theatres for ballet and contemporary dance (0171 314 8800). New world-class facilities will allow the best of British dance to be seen, plus new opera and exciting art exhibitions throughout the building. Opera and ballet are both on the bill at the *London Coliseum* (0171 632 8300) and the some of the world's top classical musicians will be playing at the three concert halls in the *South Bank Centre* (0171 633 0932) – where you can drink in stunning views across the Thames along with your interval refreshments. Most famously the venue for the summer Proms and family carol concerts around Christmas time, the lavish *Royal Albert Hall* (0171 589 3203) is also a memorable place to see a rock band in action.

. . . To the coolest nightlife

Whether your taste runs to folk or jazz, country or techno, you can hear it live in London. From supergroups strutting their stuff at *Wembley Arena* (0181 900 1234) to gigging pub bands ever-hopeful of being spotted by a record company talent scout, London's dozens of music venues are hopping every night. The choice of night clubs is even more bewitching and bewildering, as crazes come and go and DJ's take their trademark style of record-spinning from club to club on different nights of the week. If hip-hop, house and garage aren't for you, try a salsa club and learn some new steps. One thing's for sure: you'll be glad you packed some dancing shoes!

- See the extensive listings for clubs, bars and nightlife in the weekly *Time Out* magazine (available in London newsagents).
- Call London Tourist Board's Visitorcall theatre newsline on 0839 123 438* for the latest information on theatre shows and how to book.

**Calls are charged at 49p per minute at all times (as at October 1998), plus any hotel/payphone surcharges.*

Capital Food and Drink

Think of a country and it's a fair bet that London has a restaurant devoted to its cuisine. There's Chinese and Thai, of course, but what about Vietnamese or Korean? You'll find those too. South African, Moroccan, Brazilian and Lebanese are just a few of the global gastronomies waiting to be tasted.

Prospect of Whitby, Wapping

Cutting-edge cuisine

A new wave of stylish restaurants with exciting, inspirational menus devised by talented Michelin-starred and TV-starring chefs is making London the world's gourmet capital. Antony Worrall Thompson holds court at *Woz* (0181 968 2200), Gary Rhodes makes British food fashionable at *City Rhodes* (0171 583 1313), while Ruth Rogers and Rose Gray do their own take on Italian cooking at the *River Café* (0171 381 8824). That wild child of the kitchen, Marco Pierre White, is the force behind the fabulous food at several very grown-up eating places, including *Quo Vadis* in Soho (0171 437 9585) where the décor features works of art by the headline-making Damien Hirst.

Veeraswamy, Regent Street

The theme's the thing

London's newest theme restaurants are ideal for families, as they're a real hit with little ones and teenagers. Top choices include *Planet Hollywood* (0171 287 1000), *Hard Rock Café* (0171 629 0382), and the totally tropical *Rainforest Café* with its jungle sound effects, staff dressed as safari guides and meals enlivened by the antics of animatronic monkeys and elephants.

Exotic cheap eats

The choice of lower-priced eating options is moving way beyond pasta, pizzas and burgers, though these are as popular as ever in the Capital. Plump for something different at the Japanese noodle joint *Wagamama* (0171 323 9223), the Belgian-inspired *Belgo* with its hallmark mussels and chips (0171 813 2233), or the *Sofra* chain of good-value restaurants dishing up authentic Turkish flavours (0171 240 9995).

Take advantage of fixed-price lunchtime and evening (often pre-theatre) menus. Even perennial favourites like *Simpson's-in-the-Strand* (0171 836 9112) and

Above: Planet Hollywood, Piccadilly Circus

Rainforest Café, Shaftesbury Avenue © Steve Orino

Riverside restaurant, Oxo Tower

Veeraswamy (0171 734 1401), London's most famous and fashionable Indian restaurant, offer bargain feasts.

And all over the city you will find café fare, cheap and cheerful fish and chips, the cockney classic 'pie and mash' and filling pub grub that won't over-stretch your budget.

A taste of history

Pubs are just as much part of London life as they were in Shakespeare's or Dickens' day and some have changed little over the centuries. For a sense of history, try *Ye Olde Cheshire Cheese* in Fleet Street (0171 353 6170) with its warren of cosy rooms dating back to the 17th century, or the *Prospect of Whitby*, in Wapping (0171 481 1095), built in 1520 and still with the pewter bar used 400 years ago.

Points of view

A spectacular vista adds an extra dimension to a celebratory meal or drink. Go skywards to the *Windows* restaurant and piano bar on the 28th floor of the London Hilton on Park Lane (0171 493 8000) for a city-wide panorama. Marvel at St Paul's Cathedral and the Thames from the glass-fronted *Oxo Tower* restaurant and brasserie (0171 803 3888) or take a *Bateaux London* dinner cruise past the illuminated riverside landmarks (0171 839 3572) – the most romantic way to see London.

• The most fashionable and popular restaurants get booked up days if not weeks in advance – make your reservations early.

• Call London Tourist Board's Visitorcall line for information on eating out in London on 0839 123 485*.

**Calls are charged at 49p per minute at all times (as at October 1998), plus any hotel/payphone surcharges.*

Travel Information

TRAVELLING BETWEEN LONDON AND ITS AIRPORTS

Gatwick Tel. (01293) 535353
⇄ Trains leave every 15 minutes to Victoria Station, every 30 minutes at night. The journey takes about 30 minutes. There is also the Thameslink service to the City and King's Cross. Tel. 0345 484950.
Gatwick Airport Station is in the South Terminal, and linked to other parts by escalators and lifts. A Transit Shuttle runs continuously between the South and North Terminals.

Coach Flightline route 777 serves both terminals, Tel. (0181) 668 7261. National Express operates from the South Terminal, Tel. 0990 808080. The services operate to Victoria Coach Station, where there are connections to all parts of Britain.

Heathrow Tel. (0181) 759 4321
⊖ The Piccadilly line connects the airport to Central London and the rest of the underground system. The trains have special luggage areas. The journey to Piccadilly Circus takes about 47 minutes. There are trains every few minutes. There are two stations in the airport: Heathrow Terminals 1, 2, 3, and Heathrow Terminal 4. Check which terminal applies to your flight. Tel. (0171) 222 1234.

⇄ The Heathrow Express runs from Paddington Station to Heathrow Airport (stops for Terminals, 1, 2, 3 and for Terminal 4) every 15 minutes from 0510-2340. Journey time is 15-20 minutes. Tel. 0845 600 1515.

Airbus Airbus A1 goes to Victoria rail and coach stations, with stops in Cromwell Road and Knightsbridge. Airbus A2 goes to Russell Square, with stops at Notting Hill Gate, Bayswater Road, Paddington and Euston. Both are equipped for disabled passengers and luggage. Tel. (0181) 400 6655.

London City Tel. (0171) 646 0000
Coach Shuttle Bus departs from Liverpool Street Station (journey time 30 minutes) and from Canary Wharf Station on Docklands Light Railway (journey time 15 minutes).

⇄ Silvertown + City Airport is the nearest station.

Luton Tel. (01582) 405100
⇄ There is a combined rail and coach link from King's Cross Thameslink to the airport, via Luton Station. Journey time about 45-60 minutes.

Coach Luton & District's 757 operates from Buckingham Palace Road, Victoria, to the airport, taking about 75-90 minutes. Tel. (0181) 668 7261.

Stansted Tel. (01279) 680500
⇄ A direct service from Liverpool Street takes about 45 minutes. The train stops at Tottenham Hale, giving direct access to the Victoria line of the underground. Tel. 0345 484950.

Coach National Express operates from Victoria Coach Station, taking about 80 minutes. Tel. 0990 808080.

TRAVELLING IN AND FROM LONDON

Bus and Underground

For information about bus or underground services in Greater London, or the Docklands Light Railway, telephone (0171) 222 1234 at any time.

There are enquiry offices for personal callers at: each of the arrivals halls at Heathrow Airport; Victoria, Euston and Liverpool Street Rail Stations; West Croydon and Hammersmith Bus Stations; underground stations: King's Cross, Oxford Circus, Piccadilly Circus, Heathrow Terminals 1, 2, 3, and St James's Park.

Visitors should take advantage of inclusive tickets such as the daily or weekly Travelcards, available from stations or information offices.

Car

Numerous international and British car hire companies have offices at the airports and in London. Charges may be calculated by the duration of hire, by the mileage, or both.

Motoring clubs offer emergency services. For the Automobile Association, Tel. 0800 887766; for the Royal Automobile Club, Tel. 0800 828282.

On-street parking in Central London is expensive and difficult. Illegal parking is controlled by fines, towing away of vehicles, and wheel clamps. Restrictions are shown by yellow lines on the road and kerb, and yellow plates on lamp posts. Parking is particularly restricted between 0830 and 1830 Monday to Friday, and from 0830 to 1330 on Saturday. National Car Parks: Tel. (0171) 499 7050.

Coach
National Express operates to all parts of Britain. Most coaches leave from Victoria Coach Station, Tel. 0990 808080. Green Line and London & Country operate to many interesting places around London, such as Windsor and Hampton Court. Tel. (0181) 668 7261.

Rail
National train enquiries, Tel. 0345 484950
Continental train enquiries, Tel. 0990 848848

Taxis
Taxis may be hailed in the street; the doorman will do it for you at your hotel. Taxis may be booked by telephoning (0171) 272 0272 or (0171) 253 5000. Extra charges, such as for evening and weekend journeys, are displayed inside the cab.

Drivers are not obliged to accept a hiring of over six miles, or over 20 miles for a journey from London Heathrow Airport, but if they do, and the journey is wholly within the London area, the fare payable is as shown on the meter. If a driver accepts a hiring to a destination outside the Greater London area, the fare becomes negotiable, and should be agreed beforehand.

Do not use unauthorised drivers who offer their services at airports and stations.

ADVICE

Bureaux de Change
Banks are normally open from 0930 to 1530 or later, Monday to Friday. Some branches may open on Saturdays. Bureaux de Change are open longer hours than ordinary banks. Many are near railway stations and in shopping areas. You are advised only to use those displaying the official Tourist Board symbol and code of conduct. Check both rates and commission.

Lost Property
Rail
Enquire at station of arrival.

National Express
Enquire at Victoria Coach Station.

London Transport
Enquire at Lost Property Office, 200 Baker Street, NW1, open Mon-Fri 0930-1400. Recorded Tel. (0171) 486 2496 Fax. (0171) 918 1028.

Taxis
Contact: Metropolitan Police Lost Property Office, 15 Penton Street, London N1 9PU, or Tel. (0171) 833 0996. Open Mon-Fri 0900-1600.

Theatre and Concert Tickets
Tickets may be bought from the Tourist Information Centres in Victoria Station, Heathrow Underground and Liverpool Street Station. They may also be bought direct from the theatre box office, in person or by telephone. Most theatres accept credit card bookings. There are also many theatre booking agents. Always check for the amount of commission or booking fee. Do not buy from touts.

Tipping
Cab drivers expect to be tipped about 10 per cent of the fare. Restaurants sometimes add a service charge of 10-15 per cent. This should be shown on the menu. Tipping of staff such as chambermaids and porters is discretionary but it is usual to tip guides at the end of sightseeing tours.

Sightseeing Tours
One of the best ways to see London is on a guided tour. Tours may be booked at your hotel or at one of London Tourist Board's information centres. Members of London Tourist Board who operate sightseeing tours use registered 'Blue Badge' guides, who have passed a thorough examination. Such guides wear blue badges. Also popular are walking tours, and river or canal trips. Tourist Information Centres have leaflets with details.

PUBLIC HOLIDAYS IN ENGLAND AND WALES, 1999

New Year's Holiday	1 January
Good Friday	2 April
Easter Monday	5 April
May Bank Holiday	3 May
Spring Bank Holiday	31 May
Summer Bank Holiday	30 August
Christmas Day	25 December
Boxing Day	26 December
Additional Bank Holiday	31 December

Tourist Information Services

Visitorcall is the London Tourist Board's comprehensive range of recorded information services. It is available 24 hours a day and updated daily. Visitorcall has been created so that you can quickly and easily select the answer to your question or, if you prefer, listen to up-to-date listings of current and forthcoming events. See page 108 for a full listing.

Accommmodation reservations can be made throughout London. Call the London Tourist Board's Telephone Accommodation Booking Service on (0171) 932 2020 with your requirements and MasterCard/Visa/Switch details.

* Accommodation reservations

POINT OF ARRIVAL

*** Heathrow Terminals 1,2,3 Underground Station Concourse (LTB), Heathrow Airport**
Open: Daily 0800-1800.

*** Heathrow Terminal 3 Arrivals Concourse, Heathrow Airport**
Open: Daily 0600-2300.

*** Liverpool Street Underground Station (LTB)**
Open: Mon-Fri 0800-1800, Sat & Sun 0845-1730.

*** Victoria Station Forecourt (LTB)**
Open: Easter-Oct, daily 0800-1900; Nov-Easter, Mon-Sat 0800-1800, Sun 0830-1600.

*** Waterloo International Terminal, Arrivals Hall**
Open: Daily 0830-2230.

INNER LONDON

*** Britain Visitor Centre, 1 Regent Street, Piccadilly Circus, SW1Y 4NS.**
Open to personal callers only: Mon-Fri 0900-1830; Sat & Sun 1000-1600; Jul-Sep: Sat 0900-1700.

Canary Wharf TIC, Canary Wharf Station, DLR Ticket Office, E14 4QT.
Tel: (0171) 512 9800.
Open: Mon-Fri 0900-1800; Sat, Sun & Bank Hol Mon 1000-1700.

*** Greenwich TIC, 46 Greenwich Church Street, Greenwich SE10 9BL.**
Tel: (0181) 858 6376.
Open: Apr-Sep, daily 1015-1645. Reduced hours in winter.

*** Discover Islington Visitor Centre, 44 Duncan Street, N1 8BW.**
Tel: (0171) 278 8787.
Open: Apr-Oct, Mon 1400-1700, Tue-Sat 1000-1700 (closed Sat 1330-1430). Reduced hours in winter.

Lewisham TIC, Lewisham Library, 199-201 Lewisham High Street, SE13 6LG.
Tel: (0181) 297 8317.
Open: Mon 1000-1700; Tue-Fri 0900-1700.

*** Southwark Gateway TIC at London Bridge.**
Opening Winter 1998.

*** Southwark Heritage TIC, Unit 4, Lower Level, Cotton's Centre, Middle Yard, SE1 2QJ.**
Tel: (0171) 403 8299.
Open: Mon-Fri 1000-1700; Sat & Sun 1100-1700.

Tower Hamlets TIC, 18 Lamb Street, E1 6EA.
Tel: (0171) 375 2549.
Open: Mon-Fri 0930-1630; Sun 1100-1430.

OUTER LONDON

Bexley Hall Place Visitor Centre, Bourne Road, Bexley, Kent, DA5 1PQ.
Tel: (01322) 558676.
Open: Apr-May, Sat 1130-1630; Sun & Bank Hols 1200-1730; May-Sep, Mon-Sat 1130-1630; Sun & Bank Hols 1200-1730; Sep-Oct, Sat 1130-1630, Sun 1200-1730.

*** Bexley TIC, Central Library, Townley Road, Bexleyheath, Kent, DA6 7HJ.**
Tel: (0181) 303 9052.
Open: Mon, Tue & Thu 0930-2000; Wed & Fri 0930-1730; Sat 0930-1700.

*** Croydon TIC, Katharine Street, Croydon, CR9 1ET.**
Tel: (0181) 253 1009.
Open: Mon-Wed 0900-1800;

Holiday illness? Get well sooner

If you are taken ill on holiday, **medicentre** can offer the perfect remedy. With no appointment necessary, the doctor can provide on-the-spot diagnosis, advice, prescriptions and recommendations for further treatment if appropriate. The price of a basic consultation is £36.

We have centres at Euston, Victoria and Waterloo mainline stations which are open from 7am to 9pm weekdays and 9am to 9pm weekends at some sites and Oxford Street Plaza from 10am until 7pm most days.

If you need to speak to a doctor for a consultation over the phone, our GP direct 24 hour helpline is available at £15 per call. The helpline also offers information on services, locations and prices.

For more information on **medicentre** sites in London

PLEASE CALL

0870 600 0870

Medicentre also offers:

aromatherapy

blood tests

ear syringing

ECG

emergency contraception

mole removal

nurse/GP consultation

physiotherapy

prescriptions

reflexology

stress counselling

suturing

travel vaccinations

healthcare that lets you get on with your life

medi centre

Thu 0930-1800; Fri 0900-1800; Sat 0900-1700.

Harrow TIC, Civic Centre, Station Road, Harrow, HA1 2XF.
Tel: (0181) 424 1103.
Open: Mon-Fri 0900-1700.

Hillingdon TIC, Central Library, 14 High Street, Uxbridge, UB8 1HD.
Tel: Uxbridge (01895) 250706.
Open: Mon, Tue & Thu 0930-2000; Wed & Fri 0930-1730; Sat 0930-1600.

*** Hounslow TIC, 24 The Treaty Centre, Hounslow High Street, Hounslow, TW3 1ES.**
Tel: (0181) 572 8279.
Open: Mon, Wed, Fri & Sat 0930-1730; Tue & Thu 0930-2000.

Kingston TIC, The Market House, The Market Place, Kingston-Upon-Thames, KT1 1JS.
Tel: (0181) 547 5592.
Open: Mon-Fri 1000-1700; Sat 0900-1600.

*** Richmond TIC, Old Town Hall, Whittaker Avenue, Richmond, TW9 1TP.**
Tel: (0181) 940 9125.
Open: Mon-Fri 1000-1800; Sat 1000-1700; May-Oct; Sun 1015-1615.

Twickenham TIC, The Atrium, Civic Centre, York Street, Twickenham, Middlesex, TW1 3BZ.
Tel: (0181) 891 7272.
Open: Mon-Thu 0900-1715; Fri 0900-1700.

London's Winners

London Tourist Board's **LONDON TOURISM AWARDS** are presented annually to tourism businesses displaying exceptional quality and excellence. In 1998, the winners of these prestigious awards were:

Natural History Museum: *Large Visitor Attraction of the Year (award sponsored by Payne and Gunter)* For the museum's commitment to customer care and efforts to widen accessibility, as well as improving ways of interpreting its wide-ranging collection.

Two Willow Road: *Small Visitor Attraction of the Year*
Excellent use of limited space and resources have made this National Trust property – Britain's only Modern Movement house open to the public – a success with visitors.

Royal Lancaster Hotel: *Independent Hotel of the Year*
Staff attitude, service and extensive refurbishment resulting in a total transformation won the award for this Five Crown Highly Commended hotel.

Le Meridien Waldorf: *Hotel of the Year – chain of five hotels or more*
Awarded for modernisation that adds exciting new ideas but enhances the hotel's original features; also for investment in staff training.

Highfield House: *Bed and Breakfast of the Year*
In recognition of excellent value for money and the outstanding efforts made in everything it does.

Groupe Chez Gérard: *Training for Tourism (award sponsored by Courage Ltd)*
A consistent and cost-effective staff training programme across their 21 London restaurants impressed the judges.

South Bank Employers Group: *Tourism and the Environment*
For regeneration of an urban area, the 'Spine Route'. A good example of a previously back-water area of London which has now become an area of civic pride and visitor interest.

National Maritime Museum: *Tourism for All*
Awarded for commitment to accessibility and special events for people with disabilities.

Greenwich Tourist Information Centre: *TIC of the Year*
For excellent management and making the most of tourism opportunities that the millennium celebrations are bringing to the area.

Choosing and Booking Accommodation

USING THIS GUIDE

London's hotels span all price bands and range from the luxurious properties of international hotel chains to small private hotels and guest houses.

Check the number of rooms given for each hotel in this guide as an indication of its size and use the symbols (see explanation on page 29) to see what facilities it offers.

Serviced and self-catering apartments are also available throughout London at price levels from budget to luxury and a wide selection is listed in this guide.

Staying with a family is an increasingly popular option for visitors wanting to experience the real London lifestyle, so you will find information on agencies that organise this kind of accommodation on page 95.

If you are travelling on a tight budget, it is useful to know that London's universities and colleges make their halls of residence available to visitors of all ages throughout the vacation period (roughly July-September). See the Group and Youth section for details, page 96.

Accommodation in Central London is listed in this guide by postal area (WC2, SW1, etc), as shown on the map on page 26.

Remember, too, that London's excellent public transport system gives easy access to accommodation outside the central area, which can be less expensive and more relaxing than a city centre hotel. Suburban commercial centres such as Croydon, Greenwich, Bromley, Richmond, Kingston and Harrow provide a choice of accommodation for visitors who wish to explore central London as well as those doing business with local companies in those areas and are particularly suitable if you are arriving by car.

OFFICIAL CLASSIFICATIONS

The Crown and Key Classification schemes are designed to help visitors choose their accommodation with confidence. Any accommodation that displays a classification sign is confirmed as having met or exceeded minimum standards by a Tourist Board inspector, who makes annual visits to ensure that the appropriate level of service is maintained.

The number of symbols, either crown or key, denotes the range of facilities and services you can expect, while the grades indicate the quality standard.

Every classified place to stay has a Fire Certificate, where this is required under the Fire Precautions Act, and all carry public liability insurance.

Quality Grades

APPROVED, COMMENDED, HIGHLY COMMENDED and DE LUXE whether alongside the Crowns, Keys or Moons indicate quality standard provided.
APPROVED – Indicates an acceptable overall standard of quality.
COMMENDED – Indicates a good overall standard of quality.
HIGHLY COMMENDED – Indicates a very good overall standard of quality.
DE LUXE – Indicates an excellent overall standard of quality.

Crown Classification

(Serviced Accommodation)

Listed Clean and comfortable accommodation, cooked or continental breakfast, adequate heating at no extra charge, clean towels and fresh soap, bedding clean and in sound condition, hot water with no extra charge for baths or showers.

♛ Facilities and services as for Listed, plus: Your own bedroom key, shared lounge area, washbasins in bedrooms or in private bathrooms.

♛♛ Facilities and services as for One Crown, plus: Colour TV, early morning tea, minimum of 20% of bedrooms with en-suite/private facilities.

♛♛♛ Facilities and services as for Two Crown, plus: At least 50% of bedrooms with full en-suite facilities, evening meal, hairdryer, shoe-cleaning equipment, ironing facilities, tea and coffee making facilities.

♛♛♛♛ Facilities and services for Three Crowns, plus: At least 90% of bedrooms with full en-suite facilities, evening meal, choice of dishes and selection of wine, colour TV, radio and telephone in bedrooms, laundry services, toiletries, quiet seating room.

♛♛♛♛♛ Facilities and services as for Four Crown, plus: All bedrooms with full en-suite facilities, restaurant serving breakfast, lunch and dinner, night porter and room service, 24-hour lounge service.

Key Classification

(Self-Catering Accommodation)

🔑 Clean and comfortable accommodation with cooker (including oven and grill), fridge, TV, adequate table and seating provision, full inventory of crockery, cutlery and equipment.

🔑🔑 Facilities and equipment as for One Key, plus: Colour TV, automatic electric kettle, easy chair seating, electrical shaver point or adaptor.

🔑🔑🔑 Facilities and equipment as for Two Key, plus: The unit will be self-contained, vacuum cleaner, ironing facilities, linen and towels free or for hire.

🔑🔑🔑🔑 Facilities and equipment as for Three Key, plus: Washing machine and tumble dryer available, garden furniture where there is a patio or garden, coffee maker.

🔑🔑🔑🔑🔑 Facilities and equipment as for Four Key, plus: Washing machine and tumble dryer or laundry facilities, telephone, hairdryer, dishwasher, fridge freezer, food processor and microwave all available within the unit.

The Lodge Category

The special 'Lodge' category provides national ratings for purpose-built bedroom accommodation of the kind that is proving familiar along our motorways and trunk routes. As it seldom provides meals or public lounges it is not eligible for a Crown rating.

The facilities provided by 'Lodges' are classified using one to three Moon symbols.

DISABLED VISITORS

Schemes to check accessibility have been developed throughout the UK as part of the nationwide *Tourism for All* campaign in conjunction with the Hotel and Holiday Consortium, and are designed to provide disabled travellers with reliable information on standards and facilities.

The criteria used by inspecting agencies are standard. All properties denoted as being accessible for disabled visitors in this publication have been inspected by London Tourist Board.

There are three categories of accessibility:

Category 1 Accessible to a wheelchair user travelling independently

Category 2 Accessible to a wheelchair user travelling with assistance

Category 3 Accessible to someone with limited mobility, able to walk a few paces and up a maximum of three steps.

The Holiday Care Service can provide information on other accommodation that has been inspected using the same criteria of accessibility as the accessible accommodation contained within this Guide. They can be contacted at:
Holiday Care Service, Second Floor, Imperial Buildings, Victoria Road, Horley, Surrey RH6 7PZ
Tel. (01293) 774535.

DEPOSITS AND ADVANCE PAYMENTS

For reservations made weeks or months ahead a deposit is usually payable and the amount will vary according to the length of booking, time of year and number in the party. The deposit is then deducted from the total bill at the end of the stay.

Many hotels, particularly the larger ones, now require payment for the room on arrival if a prior reservation has not been made – especially when a guest arrives late and/or with very little luggage. Major credit cards are usually accepted. Regrettably this practice has become necessary because of the number of guests who have left without paying their bills. If you are asked to pay on arrival, it may be advisable to see your room first to ensure that it meets your requirements.

CANCELLATIONS

When you accept offered accommodation on the telephone or in writing, you may be entering into a legally binding contract with the proprietor of the establishment. This means that if you cancel a reservation, fail to take up the accommodation or leave prematurely the proprietor may be entitled to compensation if it cannot be re-let for all or a good part of the booked period. If a deposit has been paid it is likely to be forfeited and an additional payment may be demanded.

However, no such claim can be made by the proprietor until after the booked period, during which time every effort should be made to re-let it. Any circumstances which might lead to repudiation of contract may also need to be taken into account and, in the case of a dispute, legal advice should be sought by both parties. It is therefore in your interest to advise the management immediately if you have to change your travel plans, cancel a booking or leave prematurely.

COMMENTS AND COMPLAINTS

Accommodation establishments have a number of legal and statutory responsibilities toward their customers in areas such as giving information on prices, providing adequate fire precautions and safeguarding valuables. Like other businesses, they must also meet the requirements of the Trade Descriptions Acts 1968 and 1972 when describing and offering accommodation and facilities.

The establishment descriptions and other details appearing in this guide have been provided by proprietors themselves who have signed a declaration that the information conforms with the requirements of the Trade Descriptions Acts. Prices and other details should always be carefully checked at the time of booking.

We hope that you will not have any cause for complaint but problems do inevitably occur from time to time. If you are dissatisfied, make your complaint to the management at the time of the incident. This gives the management an opportunity to take action at once to investigate and to put things right without delay. The longer a complaint is left the more difficult it is to deal with it effectively.

In certain circumstances LTB may look into complaints. However, the Board has no statutory control over registered establishments or their methods of operation and cannot become involved in legal or contractual matters.

How to Book through LTB

Same Day Bookings LTB staff at the Tourist Information Centres at Victoria Station, Liverpool Street Station and Heathrow Airport are available to make on-the-spot bookings. Bookings can also be made at the EuroStar Terminal at Waterloo International.

Credit Card Bookings Dial direct on our hotline (0171) 932 2020 to make a booking. Mastercard, Visa or Switch.

Group Bookings Dial direct on (0171) 932 2020 to make a group booking. Mastercard, Visa or Switch required.

BABAS Book A Bed Ahead – to make a booking for accommodation in London from outside London go into the Tourist Information Centre closest to where you are currently staying, and the staff there will be able to assist. Similarly, bookings for accommodation outside London can be made from the Tourist Information Centres within the capital.

Reservations on Arrival LTB Tourist Information Centres at Victoria Station and Heathrow Terminals 1, 2, 3, Underground Station can help with reservations on arrival – as can staff at the Visitor Centre at the EuroStar Terminal at Waterloo International. Go to any of them on the day when you need accommodation. A deposit and communication charge is payable when making a reservation.

Good Value Accommodation in Central London

Central Reservations Telephone 0171 402 0202

Abbey Court and Westpoint Hotel

Central London hotel - two minute walk to Paddington and Lancaster Gate Stations. This hotel has long been a popular choice amongst tourists due to its pleasant central location, with easy access to London's major tourist attractions, museums, theatres, Oxford Street and Piccadilly Circus. Choice of rooms with en suite bathrooms, colour TV and radio/intercom.

200m from Paddington station for connection to Heathrow Express

Car Park - Bed and Breakfast

RATES	LOW SEASON	HIGH SEASON
Singles	from £30.00	from £46.00
Doubles *pp*	from £26.00	from £31.00
Triples *pp*	from £24.00	from £26.00
Family Room *pp*	from £19.00	from £22.00

Abbey Court and Westpoint Hotel
170-174 Sussex Gardens
Hyde Park London W2 1TP

***Tel* 0171 402 0704**
***Fax* 0171 262 2055**
*http//www.*westpointhotel.com
e-mail info@westpointhotel.com

***Tel* 0171 402 0281**
***Fax* 0171 224 9114**
*http//www.*abbeycourt.com
e-mail info@abbeycourt.com

Sass House Hotel

Central London hotel located within two minutes walk from Hyde Park. Most rooms with private showers/toilets. All rooms have colour TV and radio. Easy access to all tourist attractions – within 5 minutes walking distance of Lancaster Gate and Paddington underground/mainline stations and Heathrow Express.

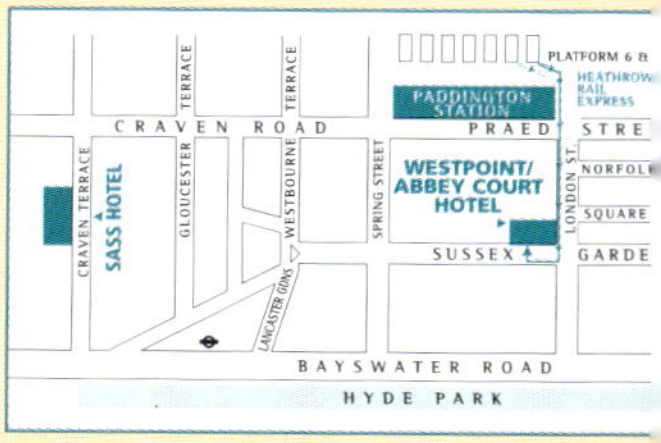

RATES	LOW SEASON	HIGH SEASON
Twin *pp*	from £23.00	from £28.00
Doubles *pp*	from £19.00	from £24.00
Triples *pp*	from £20.00	from £26.00

Sass House Hotel
11 Craven Terrace,
Hyde Park,
London W2 3QT

***Tel* 0171 262 2325**
***Fax* 0171 262 088**
*http//www.*sasshotel.com
e-mail info@sasshotel.com

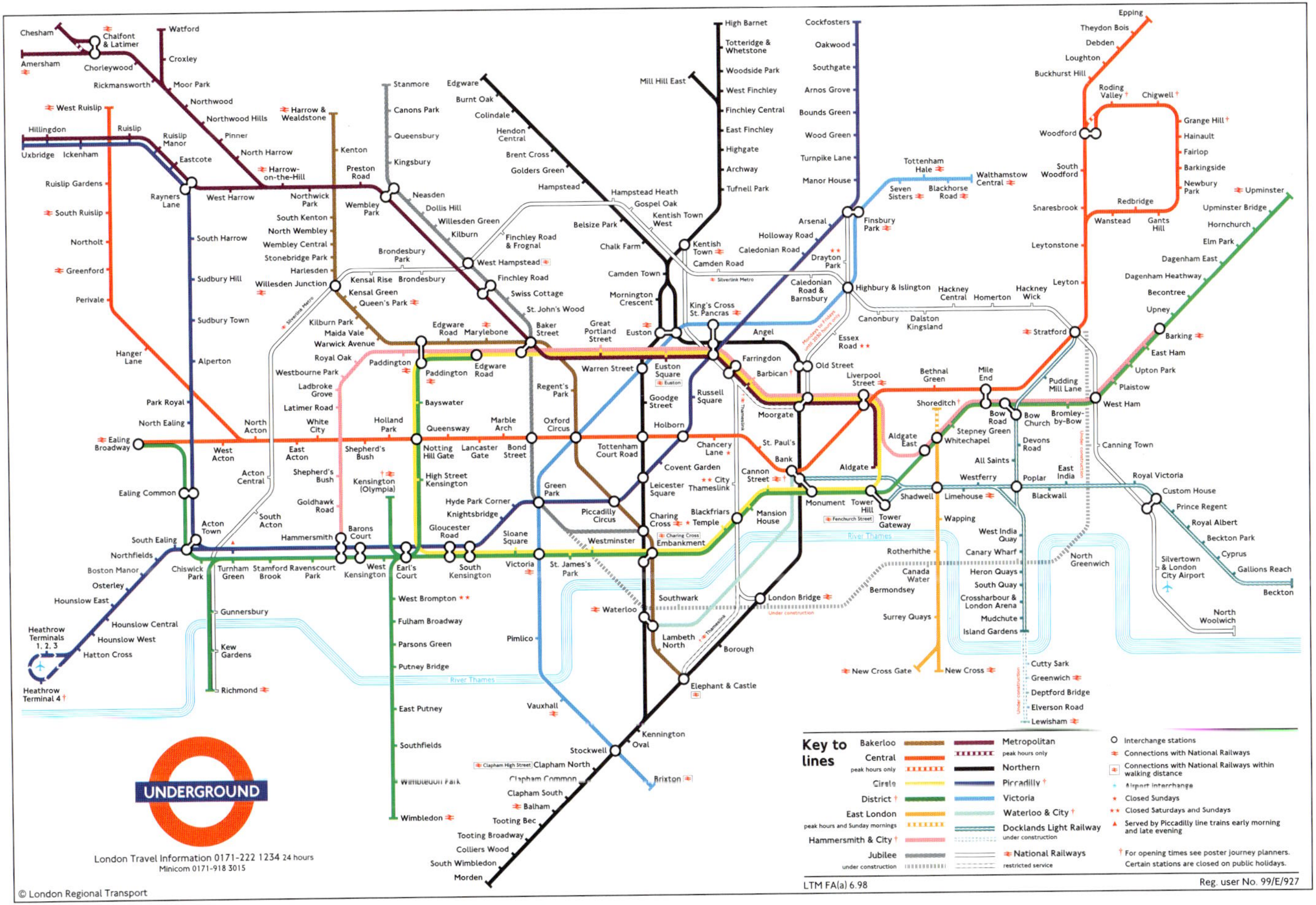
Chesham
Chalfont & Latimer
Amersham
Chorleywood
Rickmansworth
Watford
Croxley
Moor Park
Northwood
Northwood Hills
Pinner
North Harrow
Harrow-on-the-Hill
West Ruislip
Hillingdon
Uxbridge
Ickenham
Ruislip
Ruislip Manor
Eastcote
Ruislip Gardens
South Ruislip
Northolt
Greenford
Perivale
Hanger Lane
Rayners Lane
West Harrow
South Harrow
Sudbury Hill
Sudbury Town
Alperton
Park Royal
North Ealing
Ealing Broadway
Ealing Common
West Acton
North Acton
Acton Town
South Ealing
Northfields
Boston Manor
Osterley
Hounslow East
Hounslow Central
Hounslow West
Hatton Cross
Heathrow Terminals 1, 2, 3
Heathrow Terminal 4
Chiswick Park
Turnham Green
Stamford Brook
Ravenscourt Park
Gunnersbury
Kew Gardens
Richmond
Stanmore
Canons Park
Queensbury
Kingsbury
Harrow & Wealdstone
Kenton
Preston Road
Northwick Park
South Kenton
North Wembley
Wembley Central
Stonebridge Park
Harlesden
Willesden Junction
Wembley Park
Neasden
Dollis Hill
Willesden Green
Kilburn
West Hampstead
Finchley Road
Swiss Cottage
St. John's Wood
Brondesbury Park
Brondesbury
Kensal Rise
Kensal Green
Queen's Park
Kilburn Park
Maida Vale
Warwick Avenue
Royal Oak
Westbourne Park
Ladbroke Grove
Latimer Road
White City
East Acton
Acton Central
South Acton
Shepherd's Bush
Goldhawk Road
Hammersmith
Barons Court
West Kensington
Kensington (Olympia)
Earl's Court
West Brompton
Fulham Broadway
Parsons Green
Putney Bridge
East Putney
Southfields
Wimbledon Park
Wimbledon
Holland Park
Notting Hill Gate
High Street Kensington
Gloucester Road
South Kensington
Queensway
Bayswater
Paddington
Edgware Road
Marylebone
Baker Street
Lancaster Gate
Marble Arch
Bond Street
Oxford Circus
Regent's Park
Great Portland Street
Hyde Park Corner
Knightsbridge
Sloane Square
Victoria
Green Park
Piccadilly Circus
St. James's Park
Westminster
Pimlico
Vauxhall
Stockwell
Brixton
Clapham North
Clapham High Street
Clapham Common
Clapham South
Balham
Tooting Bec
Tooting Broadway
Colliers Wood
South Wimbledon
Morden
Edgware
Burnt Oak
Colindale
Hendon Central
Brent Cross
Golders Green
Hampstead
Belsize Park
Chalk Farm
Camden Town
Mornington Crescent
Euston
Hampstead Heath
Gospel Oak
Kentish Town West
Kentish Town
Camden Road
Finchley Road & Frognal
High Barnet
Totteridge & Whetstone
Woodside Park
West Finchley
Finchley Central
Mill Hill East
East Finchley
Highgate
Archway
Tufnell Park
Cockfosters
Oakwood
Southgate
Arnos Grove
Bounds Green
Wood Green
Turnpike Lane
Manor House
Arsenal
Holloway Road
Caledonian Road
Drayton Park
Caledonian Road & Barnsbury
Highbury & Islington
Finsbury Park
Seven Sisters
Tottenham Hale
Blackhorse Road
Walthamstow Central
Canonbury
Dalston Kingsland
Hackney Central
Homerton
Hackney Wick
King's Cross St. Pancras
Angel
Euston Square
Warren Street
Goodge Street
Russell Square
Holborn
Tottenham Court Road
Chancery Lane
Covent Garden
Leicester Square
Charing Cross
Embankment
Temple
Blackfriars
City Thameslink
Farringdon
Barbican
Moorgate
Old Street
Essex Road
Liverpool Street
St. Paul's
Bank
Cannon Street
Mansion House
Monument
Tower Hill
Fenchurch Street
Tower Gateway
Aldgate
Aldgate East
Shoreditch
Whitechapel
Bethnal Green
Mile End
Stepney Green
Bow Road
Bow Church
Bromley-by-Bow
Pudding Mill Lane
Stratford
West Ham
Plaistow
Upton Park
East Ham
Barking
Upney
Becontree
Dagenham Heathway
Dagenham East
Elm Park
Hornchurch
Upminster Bridge
Upminster
Leyton
Leytonstone
Snaresbrook
South Woodford
Woodford
Buckhurst Hill
Loughton
Debden
Theydon Bois
Epping
Roding Valley
Chigwell
Grange Hill
Hainault
Fairlop
Barkingside
Newbury Park
Gants Hill
Redbridge
Wanstead
Canning Town
Devons Road
All Saints
Poplar
East India
Blackwall
Westferry
Limehouse
Shadwell
Wapping
Rotherhithe
Canada Water
Surrey Quays
New Cross Gate
New Cross
West India Quay
Canary Wharf
Heron Quays
South Quay
Crossharbour & London Arena
Mudchute
Island Gardens
Cutty Sark
Greenwich
Deptford Bridge
Elverson Road
Lewisham
North Greenwich
Bermondsey
London Bridge
Southwark
Waterloo
Lambeth North
Borough
Elephant & Castle
Kennington
Oval
Royal Victoria
Custom House
Prince Regent
Royal Albert
Beckton Park
Cyprus
Gallions Reach
Beckton
Silvertown & London City Airport
North Woolwich
River Thames
Under construction
Silverlink Metro
Thameslink
Mondays to Fridays until 2030 hours only
Key to lines
Bakerloo
Central
peak hours only
Circle
District †
East London
peak hours and Sunday mornings
Hammersmith & City †
Jubilee
under construction
Metropolitan
peak hours only
Northern
Piccadilly †
Victoria
Waterloo & City †
Docklands Light Railway
under construction
National Railways
restricted service
Interchange stations
Connections with National Railways
Connections with National Railways within walking distance
Airport interchange
Closed Sundays
Closed Saturdays and Sundays
Served by Piccadilly line trains early morning and late evening
† For opening times see poster journey planners. Certain stations are closed on public holidays.
UNDERGROUND
London Travel Information 0171-222 1234 24 hours
Minicom 0171-918 3015
LTM FA(a) 6.98
Reg. user No. 99/E/927
© London Regional Transport

LONDON
A GLOBALVISION™ STREET PLAN
ST. JOHN'S WOOD
CAMDEN TOWN
PRIMROSE HILL
LONDON ZOO
REGENT'S PARK
QUEEN MARY'S GARDENS
MAIDA VALE
PADDINGTON
PADDINGTON STATION
MARYLEBONE
OXFORD STREET
MAYFAIR
HYDE PARK
KENSINGTON GARDENS
HOLLAND PARK
KENSINGTON
KNIGHTSBRIDGE
BELGRAVIA
CHELSEA
BROMPTON CEMETERY
BATTERSEA PARK
WESTWAY A40 (M)
HARROW ROAD
BAYSWATER ROAD
KENSINGTON ROAD
KENSINGTON HIGH STREET
CROMWELL ROAD
BROMPTON ROAD
KING'S ROAD
CHELSEA EMBANKMENT
SLOANE SQUARE
GLOBALVISION © Copyright Globalvision (Holdings) Limited, 1998. All Rights Reserved. +44 (0) 171 437 4370

The representation on this map of any road or track is no evidence of right of way.

Inner London Area Map

MAIN HOTEL AREAS IN CENTRAL LONDON

SW1 – Victoria/Westminster
W1 – West End/Mayfair/Oxford Street
WC1/WC2 – Bloomsbury/Strand/Leicester Square
W2 – Paddington/Bayswater
SW3/5/7 – Chelsea/Earl's Court/South Kensington

OTHER AREAS IN LONDON

EC1/2/3/4 – City of London
W8/11/14 – Kensington/Notting Hill Gate/Holland Park
W3/4/5/6/7/12 – Acton/Chiswick/Ealing /Hammersmith
North West London
North London
South West London
East London
South East London
London's Country

Good Value Accommodation in Central London

Central Reservations Telephone 0171 402 0202

Abbey Court and Westpoint Hotel

Central London hotel - two minute walk to Paddington and Lancaster Gate Stations. This hotel has long been a popular choice amongst tourists due to its pleasant central location, with easy access to London's major tourist attractions, museums, theatres, Oxford Street and Piccadilly Circus. Choice of rooms with en suite bathrooms, colour TV and radio/intercom.

200m from Paddington station for connection to Heathrow Express
Car Park - Bed and Breakfast

RATES	LOW SEASON	HIGH SEASON
Singles	from £30.00	from £46.00
Doubles *pp*	from £26.00	from £31.00
Triples *pp*	from £24.00	from £26.00
Family Room *pp*	from £19.00	from £22.00

Abbey Court and Westpoint Hotel
170-174 Sussex Gardens
Hyde Park London W2 1TP
***Tel* 0171 402 0704**
***Fax* 0171 262 2055**
***http//www.*westpointhotel.com**
***e-mail* info@westpointhotel.com**
***Tel* 0171 402 0281**
***Fax* 0171 224 9114**
***http//www.*abbeycourt.com**
***e-mail* info@abbeycourt.com**

Sass House Hotel

Central London hotel located within two minutes walk from Hyde Park. Most rooms with private showers/toilets. All rooms have colour TV and radio. Easy access to all tourist attractions – within 5 minutes walking distance of Lancaster Gate and Paddington underground/mainline stations and Heathrow Express.

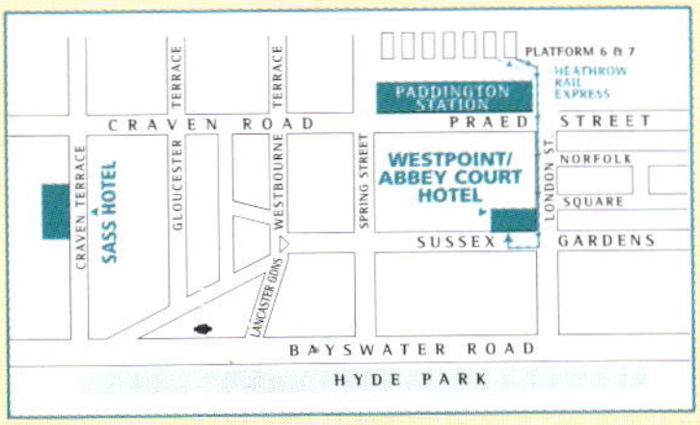

RATES	LOW SEASON	HIGH SEASON
Twin *pp*	from £23.00	from £28.00
Doubles *pp*	from £19.00	from £24.00
Triples *pp*	from £20.00	from £26.00

Sass House Hotel
11 Craven Terrace,
Hyde Park,
London W2 3QT

***Tel* 0171 262 2325**
***Fax* 0171 262 0889**
***http//www.*sasshotel.com**
***e-mail* info@sasshotel.com**

The Rhodes Hotel

Commended AA ratings QQQ

195 Sussex Gardens, Hyde Park, London W2
Tel Nos: 0171 262 5617 / 0171 262 0537
Fax No: 0171 723 4054
E-mail: chris@rhodeshotel.co.uk
Web page: http://www.rhodeshotel.co.uk

This elegant late Georgian House is 200 metres from the beautiful Hyde Park and Kensington Gardens.

For shopping it is close to Marble Arch and the famous Oxford Street and the West End.

For travelling it is conveniently situated between Paddington Rail Station for Heathrow Express and Lancaster Gate Tube - the Airbus A2 for Heathrow stops close to our door.

For your comfort, all our rooms have satellite TV, telephone, hairdryer, refrigerator and tea/coffee making-facilities.

For your budget, en-suite room rates from £50 single, £70 double. All rates inclusive of VAT and include a generous continental breakfast. Families are specially catered for.

CIVIC GUEST HOUSE

Tel: 0181 572 5107/570 1851
Fax: 0181 814 0203

AA Listed, Approved

87-89 LAMPTON ROAD, HOUNSLOW, MIDDX TW3 4DP

- Colour TV/Sky TV & Hot Drinks in all rooms
- En-suite facilities in most rooms
- Ample Car Parking
- Full English Breakfast
- 200 yds to Hounslow Central Tube Station (Piccadilly Line)
- 20 mins from Central London
- 10 mins from Heathrow Airport & M4 Junc. 3
- 15 mins from M25 Junc. 4B/M3 Junc. 1
- Close to Twickenham Rugby Ground, Hampton Court Palace, Kew Gardens & Osterley Park

www.LondonTown.com
The Official Internet Site for LONDON

HIGHFIELD LODGE HOTEL

"A Comfortable Bed & Breakfast All At Budget Prices"

We Are A Newly Refurbished Hotel Comprising:
- 19 Rooms all ensuite
- Full central heating
- Colour TV with satellite
- Direct-dial telephone
- Tea-making facilities
- Close to Tufnell Park Tube station
- Ample free parking facilities
- Easy access to West End and City
- Shopping complex close by

Prices from
Single £25 - £30
Double £40 -£45
Family £56 - £65

TEL: 0171 607 8889 FAX: 0171 607 6821
2 DALMENY ROAD
LONDON N7 0HH

Hunters Lodge Hotel

Budget Rates

Singles from £25 - 42,
Twin Doubles from £32 - £55, Family/triple from £30 - £55

- Clean and comfortable hotel situated in a picturesque neighbourhood, 3 mins from Earl's Court tube. Easy access to Gatwick and Heathrow Airports.
- All rooms with colour TV and direct-dial telephone. Open 24hrs.
- Good facilities.

38 Trebovir Road, London SW5 9NJ
Tel: 0171 373 7331 Fax: 0181 460 3524
E-mail: taher_tayeb@Compuserve.Com

LONDON MEMBER

Lord Jim Hotel

LONDON MEMBER

'We welcome school groups at very competitive rates'

An attractive Hotel well situated close to Earl's Court Station, which is directly linked to Heathrow & Gatwick Airports (via Victoria) and all major tourist attractions while Earl's Court & Olympia Exhibition Halls are within easy reach. Most rooms have private en-suite facilities and hairdryers. All rooms have a colour TV and direct-dial telephones. Lift to all floors. Open 24hrs.

Singles from £24-40. Doubles £30-52. Triples £36-65

23/25 Penywern Road, Earl's Court, London SW5
Tel:0171 370 6071 Fax: 0171 373 8919
e-mail: taher_tayb@compuserve.com

Key to Accommodation Symbols

HOTELS

- l.o. Last order for evening meal.
- Facilities for non-smokers.
- Passenger lift.
- Television in all bedrooms.
- Tea/coffee making facilities in all bedrooms.
- Unlicensed (alcoholic drinks not served).
- Conference facilities for 10 or more persons.
- Garage or parking.
- Ground floor bedrooms.
- Night porter on duty.
- Telephone in all bedrooms.
- Four poster bed(s).
- Indoor swimming pool.
- Lounge for residents' use.
- Ironing facilities.
- Central heating throughout.
- Dogs not accepted.

SELF CATERING

- Garage or parking.
- Washing machine.
- Daily cleaning service.
- Television in all units.
- LP Linen provided.

GROUP AND YOUTH

- Garage or parking.
- Television lounge.
- Central heating throughout.
- Games room.
- Children welcome.
- Lounge for residents' use.
- Public telephone.
- Ironing facilities.
- Ground floor bedrooms.

CARAVAN AND CAMPING

- Children welcome.
- Clothes drying facilities.
- Showers.
- Cooking facilities.
- Ironing facilities
- Unlicensed (alcoholic drinks not served).

Accommodation

Hotels and Bed and Breakfasts

SW1 Victoria/Westminster

Airways Hotel Nationlodge Ltd
Listed Approved

29-31 St George's Drive, Victoria, London SW1V 4DG
Tel: (0171) 834 0205
Fax: (0171) 932 0007
⊖/⇌ Victoria
Centrally located, close to Victoria underground, rail and coach stations and the Gatwick Express terminal.
Bedrooms: 8 single, 9 double, 11 twin, 10 family
Bathrooms: 38 en suite, 1 public
Bed only: single £50.00-£55.00, double £60.00-£65.00
Credit Cards: Mastercard/Eurocard/Visa/Barclaycard/American Express/Switch/Delta/Diners/Eurocheque

Astoria Hotel
Listed Approved

39 St George's Drive, London SW1V 4DG
Tel: (0171) 834 1965
Fax: (0171) 834 1977
⊖/⇌ Victoria
Clean, reasonably priced accommodation close to Victoria station. All bedrooms have en suite bathrooms.
Bedrooms: 1 single, 4 double, 5 twin, 6 family
Bathrooms: 16 en suite, 1 public
Bed & Breakfast: single £55.00-£60.00, double £65.00-£75.00
Credit Cards: Mastercard/Eurocard/Visa/Barclaycard/Switch/Delta/Eurocheque

The Berkeley

Wilton Place, Knightsbridge, London SW1X 7RL
Tel: (0171) 235 6000
Fax: (0171) 235 4330
E-mail: info@the_berkeley.co.uk
URL: **www.savoy-group.co.uk**
⊖/⇌ Victoria, ⊖ Knightsbridge
The elegant Berkeley in Belgravia provides traditional service while offering high standards of modern comfort.
Bedrooms: 14 single, 144 double
Bathrooms: 158 en suite
Evening meal: 1900 (l.o. 2245)
Parking for: 50
Credit Cards: Mastercard/Eurocard/Visa/Barclaycard/American Express/Switch/Delta/Diners/Eurocheque

Blair Victoria
Listed Approved

78-82 Warwick Way, London SW1V 1RZ
Tel: (0171) 828 8603/0468 660098
Fax: (0171) 976 6536
⊖/⇌ Victoria
Situated close to Victoria station. Behind a period facade, the Blair Victoria offers comfort and service in the heart of London.
Bedrooms: 12 single, 12 double, 16 twin, 7 family
Bathrooms: 47 en suite
Bed & Breakfast: single £59.50-£64.00, double £78.00-£88.00
Credit Cards: Visa/Barclaycard/American Express/Switch/Delta/Diners/Eurocheque

Brindle House Hotel
Listed Approved

1 Warwick Place North, London SW1V 1QW
Tel: (0171) 828 0057
Fax: (0171) 931 8805
⊖/⇌ Victoria
Small, quiet bed and breakfast, ideally located for Victoria bus, train and underground stations. Friendly atmosphere.
Bedrooms: 4 single, 3 double, 4 twin, 2 family
Bathrooms: 5 private showers, 2 public
Bed & Breakfast: single £32.00-£34.00, double £44.00-£48.50
Credit Cards: Eurocard/Visa/American Express/Diners/Eurocheque

Carlton Hotel
Listed Approved

90 Belgrave Road, Victoria, London SW1V 2BJ
Tel: (0171) 976 6634/(0171) 932 0913
Fax: (0171) 821 8020
⊖/⇌ Victoria
Small, friendly bed and breakfast, situated near Victoria station and within walking distance of Buckingham Palace. Within easy reach of Trafalgar Square and Piccadilly Circus.
Bedrooms: 4 single, 5 double, 2 twin, 6 family
Bathrooms: 11 en suite, 1 private shower, 1 public
Bed only: single £25.00-£35.00, double £45.00-£49.00
Bed & Breakfast: single £30.00-£39.00, double £49.00-£54.00
Credit Cards: Visa/Barclaycard/American Express/Switch/Delta/Eurocheque

Caswell Hotel
Listed Approved

25 Gloucester Street, London SW1V 2DB
Tel: (0171) 834 6345
⊖/⇌ Victoria
Pleasant, family-run hotel in a quiet location.
Bedrooms: 1 single, 6 double, 6 twin, 5 family
Bathrooms: 7 en suite, 5 public
Bed & Breakfast: single £30.00-£60.00, double £44.00-£72.00
Credit Cards: Mastercard/Eurocard/Visa/Barclaycard/Switch/Delta/Eurocheque

Cavendish Hotel
Commended

81 Jermyn Street, St James, London SW1Y 6JF
Tel: (0171) 930 2111
Fax: (0171) 839 2125
E-mail: 76213,171@compuserve.com
⊖ Piccadilly Circus
Located in Jermyn Street, the hotel is ideally positioned for business or leisure, a short stroll from London's major attractions. The 81 restaurant is on the first floor serving modern European cooking with a Spanish influence.
Bedrooms: 129 single, 45 double, 72 twin
Bathrooms: 246 en suite
Bed only: single £165.00, double £190.00

NAYLAND

Evening meal: 1800 (l.o. 2230)
Parking for: 51
Credit Cards: Mastercard/Eurocard/Visa/Barclaycard/American Express/Switch/Delta/Diners/Eurocheque

Central House Hotel
Listed APPROVED

39 Belgrave Road, London SW1V 2BB
Tel: (0171) 834 8036/ (0171) 828 0644
Fax: (0171) 834 1854
Victoria, Pimlico

Situated within a row of Victorian buildings minutes away from Victoria coach, rail and underground stations.

Bedrooms: 4 single, 17 double, 17 twin, 12 family
Bathrooms: 50 en suite, 1 public
Bed & Breakfast: single £56.00-£76.00, double £76.00-£96.00
Credit Cards: Mastercard/Visa/Barclaycard/Switch/Delta/Eurocheque

Chester House
Listed APPROVED

134 Ebury Street, London SW1W 9QQ
Tel: (0171) 730 3632
Fax: (0171) 824 8446
Victoria

Small, friendly bed and breakfast close to Sloane Square and convenient for public transport. Harrods is ten minutes' walk away.

Bedrooms: 3 single, 2 double, 5 twin, 2 family
Bathrooms: 6 en suite, 2 public
Bed & Breakfast: single £32.00-£55.00, double £50.00-£65.00
Credit Cards: Mastercard/Eurocard/Visa/Barclaycard/American Express/Diners/Eurocheque

Colliers Hotel
Listed APPROVED

97 Warwick Way, London SW1V 1QL
Tel: (0171) 834 6931/ (0171) 828 0210
Fax: (0171) 834 8439
E-mail: cmahotel@aol.com
Victoria

Friendly hotel convenient for all amenities.

Bedrooms: 4 single, 7 double, 5 twin, 2 family
Bathrooms: 2 en suite, 3 private showers, 3 public
Bed & Breakfast: single £30.00-£35.00, double £38.00-£42.00
Credit Cards: Mastercard/Eurocard/Visa/Barclaycard/American Express/Diners/Eurocheque

Collin House
COMMENDED

104 Ebury Street, London SW1W 9QD
Tel: (0171) 730 8031
Fax: (0171) 730 8031
Victoria

Conveniently located for Victoria rail, underground and coach stations. Ideal base for visiting London and the surrounding areas.

Bedrooms: 3 single, 4 double, 3 twin, 3 family
Bathrooms: 8 en suite, 3 public
Bed & Breakfast: single £45.00-£50.00, double £70.00-£75.00

Comfort Inn Westminster
APPLIED

82-86 Belgrave Road, London SW1V 2BJ
Tel: (0171) 828 8661
Fax: (0171) 821 0525
Victoria

Bedrooms: 4 single, 23 double, 16 twin, 15 family
Bathrooms: 58 en suite
Credit Cards: Mastercard/Visa/Barclaycard/American Express/Switch/Eurocheque

Dolphin Square Hotel
COMMENDED

Dolphin Square, London SW1V 3LX
Tel: (0171) 834 3800/ (0171) 798 8890
Fax: (0171) 798 8896
E-mail: dolphin-square-hotel@btinternet.com
Victoria, Pimlico

Centrally located complex consisting of suites and apartments; set among private gardens with its own extensive sports and leisure facilities.

Bedrooms: 19 single, 95 double, 35 twin, 2 family
Bathrooms: 151 en suite
Bed only: single £110.00, double £130.00-£145.00
Evening meal: 1800 (l.o. 2230)
Parking for: 16
Credit Cards: Mastercard/Eurocard/Visa/Barclaycard/American Express/Switch/Delta/Diners/Eurocheque

Dover Hotel
Listed APPROVED

44 Belgrave Road, London SW1V 1RG
Tel: (0171) 821 9085
Fax: (0171) 834 6425
E-mail: dover@rooms.demon.co.uk
URL: www.rooms.demon.co.uk
Victoria

Small, friendly bed and breakfast hotel with easy access to all major attractions and three minutes from Victoria station.

Bedrooms: 4 single, 9 double, 7 twin, 13 family
Bathrooms: 29 en suite, 4 private showers, 2 public
Bed & Breakfast: single £40.00-£55.00, double £50.00-£69.00
Credit Cards: Mastercard/Eurocard/Visa/Barclaycard/American Express/Switch/Delta/Diners/Eurocheque

Elizabeth Hotel
COMMENDED

37 Eccleston Square, Victoria, London SW1V 1PB
Tel: (0171) 828 6812
Victoria

Friendly, quiet hotel overlooking the magnificent gardens of this stately residential square, within five minutes of Victoria station. Special car parking arrangements.

Bedrooms: 6 single, 5 double, 4 twin, 23 family
Bathrooms: 35 en suite, 2 public
Bed & Breakfast: single £40.00-£55.00, double £55.00-£80.00
Credit Cards: Eurocheque

Georgian House Hotel
APPROVED

35 St George's Drive, London SW1V 4DG
Tel: (0171) 834 1438
Fax: (0171) 976 6085
E-mail: georgian@wildnet.co.uk
Victoria

Offers value for money in a good location. Extensive English breakfast and very warm service. Student rooms are also available.

Bedrooms: 8 single, 13 double, 2 twin, 11 family
Bathrooms: 29 en suite, 2 public
Bed & Breakfast: single £20.00-£44.00, double £33.00-£59.00
Credit Cards: Mastercard/Eurocard/Visa/Barclaycard/Switch/Delta/Eurocheque

Book your accommodation through London Tourist Board – from within Britain: (0171) 932 2020, from outside Britain: +44171 932 2020 (MasterCard, Visa or Switch required).

The Goring Hotel

15 Beeston Place, Grosvenor Gardens, London SW1W 0JW
Tel: (0171) 396 9000
Fax: (0171) 834 4393
E-mail: reception@goringhotel.co.uk
URL: www.goringhotel.co.uk
⊖/⇌ Victoria
Family-owned hotel with private garden, near Buckingham Palace and parks.
Bedrooms: 23 single, 38 double, 10 twin, 4 family
Bathrooms: 75 en suite
Bed only: single £170.00-£190.00, double £205.00-£230.00
Evening meal: 1800 (l.o. 2200)
Parking for: 7
Credit Cards: Mastercard/Eurocard/Visa/Barclaycard/American Express/Switch/Diners/Eurocheque

The Grosvenor Thistle Hotel

101 Buckingham Palace Road, London SW1W 0SJ
Tel: (0171) 834 9494
Fax: (0171) 630 1978
⊖/⇌ Victoria
Elegant and spacious in the great Victorian tradition, offering modern facilities. Ideal for London sightseeing.
Bedrooms: 96 single, 53 double, 206 twin, 11 family
Bathrooms: 366 en suite
Bed only: single £140.00, double £180.00-£203.00
Bed & Breakfast: single £151.50, double £190.00-£220.00
Evening meal: 1730 (l.o. 2200)
Credit Cards: Mastercard/Eurocard/Visa/Barclaycard/American Express/Switch/Delta/Diners/Eurocheque

The Halkin

5-6 Halkin Street, Belgravia, London SW1X 7DJ
Tel: (0171) 333 1000
Fax: (0171) 333 1100
E-mail: sales@halkin.co.uk
⊖ Hyde Park Corner, ⊖/⇌ Victoria
Set in a peaceful side street in Belgravia. The Halkin is a stylish and elegant, small, luxury hotel.
Bedrooms: 41 double
Bathrooms: 41 en suite
Bed & Breakfast: single £270.00, double £300.00-£375.00
Evening meal: 1930 (l.o. 2300)
Credit Cards: Mastercard/Eurocard/Visa/Barclaycard/American Express/Switch/Delta/Diners/Eurocheque

Hamilton House Hotel

APPROVED

60 Warwick Way, London SW1V 1SA
Tel: (0171) 821 7113
Fax: (0171) 630 0806
⊖/⇌ Victoria
Small hotel, conveniently located for Buckingham Palace and the West End.
Bedrooms: 6 single, 10 double, 23 twin, 2 family
Bathrooms: 18 en suite, 7 private, 5 public
Credit Cards: Visa/Eurocheque

Holiday Inn Express London Victoria

106-110 Belgrave Road, London SW1V 2BJ
Tel: (0171) 630 8888
Fax: (0171) 828 0441
⊖/⇌ Victoria
Grade II Listed building.
Bedrooms: 6 single, 18 double, 18 twin, 8 family
Bathrooms: 50 en suite
Bed & Breakfast: single £79.00-£85.00, double £79.00-£85.00
Credit Cards: Mastercard/Visa/Barclaycard/American Express/Switch/Delta/Diners/Eurocheque

Holiday Inn Victoria

2 Bridge Place, Victoria, London SW1V 1QA
Tel: (0171) 834 8123
Fax: (0171) 828 1099
⊖/⇌ Victoria
Modern, Scandinavian hotel with extensive leisure facilities, located adjacent to Victoria station.
Bedrooms: 22 single, 61 double, 118 twin, 11 family
Bathrooms: 212 en suite
Bed only: single £160.00, double £170.00
Bed & Breakfast: single £171.50, double £193.00
Evening meal: 1800 (l.o. 2245)
Credit Cards: Mastercard/Eurocard/Barclaycard/American Express/Switch/Diners/Eurocheque

Hotel Rama

APPLIED

43 Belgrave Road, London SW1V 2BB
Tel: (0171) 828 1166
Fax: (0171) 828 1167
⊖/⇌ Victoria
Hotel offering single, double and triple rooms, all with en suite facilities, telephone and TV. All prices include breakfast and VAT.
Bedrooms: 2 single, 8 double, 2 twin, 6 family
Bathrooms: 17 en suite
Bed & Breakfast: single £35.00-£45.00, double £50.00-£65.00
Credit Cards: Mastercard/Eurocard/Visa/Barclaycard/American Express/Switch

Hyatt Carlton Tower

DE LUXE

2 Cadogan Place, London SW1X 9PY
Tel: (0171) 235 1234
Fax: (0171) 235 9129
⊖ Knightsbridge
In the heart of London's Knightsbridge shopping area, the hotel is within easy reach of the City and tourist attractions.
Bedrooms: 6 single, 117 double, 38 twin, 59 family
Bathrooms: 220 en suite
Bed only: single £200.00-£380.00, double £200.00-£380.00
Evening meal: 1900 (l.o. 2315)
Parking for: 70
Credit Cards: Eurocard/Visa/Barclaycard/American Express/Diners/Eurocheque

Knightsbridge Green Hotel

HIGHLY COMMENDED

159 Knightsbridge, London SW1X 7PD
Tel: (0171) 584 6274
Fax: (0171) 225 1635
E-mail: thekghotel@aol.com
⊖ Knightsbridge
Small, family-run hotel close to Harrods.
Bedrooms: 7 single, 3 double, 5 twin, 12 family
Bathrooms: 27 en suite
Bed only: single £110.00, double £145.00-£170.00

CARLTON HOTEL
BED AND BREAKFAST
Excellence in Comfort and Service

For comfort and convenience, for business and pleasure - THE CARLTON HOTEL has a lot to offer at a moderate all inclusive price. Conveniently situated within walking distance of famous landmarks such as Buckingham Palace, Westminster Abbey, The Houses of Parliament, Trafalgar Square, Piccadilly Circus, Leicester Square and many more.

90 Belgrave Road, London SW1V 2BJ
Telephone: 0171 976 6634 Fax: 0171 821 8020

VISA · AMERICAN EXPRESS

Stay in the heart of London

Central House Hotel

39 Belgrave Road, London SW1V 2BB
Tel: 0171 834 8036 & 0171 828 0644 Fax: 0171 834 1854

Centrally located just minutes from Victoria rail, tube and coach stations and Buckingham Palace.
Newly refurbished hotel. 50 en-suite bedrooms with central heating, colour TV, hair dryers, telephone and tea/coffee facilities. Lift serving all floors.
Comfortable lounge and Breakfast room.

You can be sure of a warm welcome and service with a smile

LONDON S.W.1
ELIZABETH HOTEL 37 Eccleston Square, VICTORIA, London SW1V 1PB.
TEL: 0171-828 6812

Friendly, private Hotel, with English character and charm, in ideal, central, quiet location overlooking magnificent gardens of stately residential square (c.1835) on fringe of Belgravia and not far from Buckingham Palace, Westminster etc. Comfortable Single, Double, Twin and Family Rooms. Lift Good. ENGLISH BREAKFAST. MODERATE PRICES. Most highly recommended.
FREE COLOUR BROCHURE AVAILABLE | HIGHLY COMMENDED in the Considerate Hoteliers Of Westminster 1994 Awards

---

The Airways Hotel

-at the centre of things

All our 40 ensuite bedrooms have telephone, TV, hairdryer, refrigerator, tea/coffee making facilities. Underground parking facilities with concession fees.

Singles from £45
Doubles/twin from £59

All inclusive of Full English Breakfast and VAT

LONDON MEMBER

29-31 St George's Drive, Victoria, London SW1V 4DG
Tel: 0171 834 0205
Fax: 0171 932 0007

Blandford Hotel

80 Chiltern Street, London, W1M 1PS
Tel: 0171 486 3103 Fax: 0171 487 2786
e-mail: blandford@capitalhotels.co.uk
http://www.capitalhotels.co.uk/

- **Fully refurbished in 1998**
- **TV and Satellite**
- **Excellent transport links**
- **Marble Arch & Oxford Street 10 mins' walk**
- **24 Hour service**

Room rates from £35 per person inclusive of breakfast and VAT

The Blair Victoria

Tel: 0171 828 8603 Fax: 0171 976 6536

Part of the Blair Group of Hotels and Apartments, this is a modern townhouse hotel in the heart of London. 47 en-suite rooms with colour TV, tea/coffee-making facilities, direct-dial telephone and hairdryer. A short walk to Victoria station and within easy reach of all the top tourist attractions, theatreland and the best restaurant and shopping scene in Europe.

Bed & Breakfast: single £119.50, double £164.00-£189.00
Credit Cards: Mastercard/Eurocard/Visa/Barclaycard/American Express/Diners/Eurocheque

The Lowndes Hyatt Hotel

21 Lowndes Street, Belgravia, London SW1X 9ES
Tel: (0171) 823 1234/(0171) 823 0003
Fax: (0171) 235 1154
E-mail: lowndes@hyattintl.com
URL: www.hyatt.com
Knightsbridge
Located in quiet, residential Lowndes Square, close to Harrods and the West End. Easy access to the City. Prices are subject to change.
Bedrooms: 49 double, 24 twin, 5 family
Bathrooms: 78 en suite
Bed only: single £275.00, double £290.00
Evening meal: 1800 (l.o. 2300)
Credit Cards: Mastercard/Eurocard/Visa/Barclaycard/American Express/Delta/Diners/Eurocheque

Luna-Simone Hotel

Listed Approved

47 Belgrave Road, London SW1V 2BB
Tel: (0171) 834 5897
Fax: (0171) 828 2474
Victoria
Friendly, good-value bed and breakfast hotel within easy walking distance of Victoria rail, underground and coach stations.
Bedrooms: 3 single, 11 double, 11 twin, 10 family
Bathrooms: 19 en suite, 5 private showers, 4 public
Bed & Breakfast: single £30.00-£35.00, double £50.00-£70.00
Credit Cards: Mastercard/Visa/Barclaycard/Switch/Eurocheque

Melbourne House

Listed Commended

79 Belgrave Road, London SW1V 2BG
Tel: (0171) 828 3516
Fax: (0171) 828 7120
Victoria, Pimlico
Family-run bed and breakfast. Most rooms en suite. Tea and coffee facilities, TV, direct dial telephone, free luggage storage, hairdryers.
Bedrooms: 2 single, 5 double, 5 twin, 2 family
Bathrooms: 12 en suite, 1 public
Bed & Breakfast: single £30.00-£50.00, double £60.00-£70.00
Credit Cards: Mastercard/Eurocard/Visa/Barclaycard/Eurocheque

Melita House Hotel

Listed Approved

35 Charlwood Street, London SW1V 2DU
Tel: (0171) 828 0471/(0171) 834 1387
Fax: (0171) 932 0988
E-mail: reserve@melita.co.uk
URL: www.melita.co.uk
Victoria, Pimlico
Family-run, friendly, good-value bed and breakfast with well-appointed rooms. Close to Victoria station.
Bedrooms: 6 single, 10 double, 4 twin, 5 family
Bathrooms: 19 en suite, 2 private showers, 1 public
Bed & Breakfast: single £32.00-£45.00, double £50.00-£65.00
Credit Cards: Mastercard/Eurocard/Visa/Barclaycard/American Express/Switch/Delta/Eurocheque

The Millennium Chelsea

17-25 Sloane Street, London SW1X 9NU
Tel: (0171) 235 4377
Fax: (0171) 235 3705
URL: www.mill-cop.com
Knightsbridge
Located in the heart of Knightsbridge, close to Harrods and Hyde Park.
Bedrooms: 73 single, 80 double, 71 twin
Bathrooms: 224 en suite
Bed & Breakfast: single £240.00, double £255.00
Evening meal: 1800 (l.o. 2230)
Parking for: 9
Credit Cards: Mastercard/Eurocard/Visa/Barclaycard/American Express/Switch/Delta/Diners/Eurocheque

Oxford House Hotel

Listed Approved

92 Cambridge Street, Victoria, London SW1V 4QG
Tel: (0171) 834 6467
Fax: (0171) 834 0225
Victoria
Small, friendly, family-run bed and breakfast hotel within walking distance of Westminster. (Five per cent surcharge for Mastercard and Access bookings.)
Bedrooms: 2 single, 5 double, 4 twin, 6 family
Bathrooms: 4 public
Bed & Breakfast: single £36.00-£38.00, double £44.00-£46.00
Credit Cards: Mastercard/Eurocard/Visa/Barclaycard

Park Hotel

Listed Commended

64 Belgrave Road, London SW1V 2BP
Tel: (0171) 834 3118
Fax: (0171) 834 9328
Victoria
Newly refurbished, 18-room hotel. Breakfast of tea and coffee, freshly baked muffins and croissants available at any time on request. Friendly staff.
Bedrooms: 4 single, 2 double, 1 twin, 11 family
Bathrooms: 17 en suite, 1 private shower
Bed & Breakfast: single £49.00-£52.00, double £58.00-£67.00
Credit Cards: Mastercard/Visa/Barclaycard/American Express/Switch/Delta/Diners/Eurocheque

Quality Eccleston Hotel

Eccleston Square, London SW1V 1PS
Tel: (0171) 834 8042
Fax: (0171) 630 8942
Victoria
In a quiet location close to Buckingham Palace. Ideal for Victoria coach and rail stations. Hotel overlooks a garden square.
Bedrooms: 15 single, 43 double, 46 twin, 3 family
Bathrooms: 107 en suite
Bed only: single £76.00-£87.00, double £87.00-£99.00
Evening meal: 1800 (l.o. 2145)
Credit Cards: Mastercard/Eurocard/Visa/Barclaycard/American Express/Switch/Diners/Eurocheque

Royal Horseguards Thistle Hotel

Whitehall Court, London SW1A 2EJ
Tel: (0171) 839 3400
Fax: (0171) 925 2263
Charing Cross, Embankment

Located in central London, the Royal Horseguards Thistle is within easy reach of sights such as the Houses of Parliament, Buckingham Palace and Trafalgar Square.
Bedrooms: 9 single, 130 double, 141 twin
Bathrooms: 280 en suite
Bed only: single £190.00-£260.00, double £225.00-£290.00
Bed & Breakfast: single £200.00-£275.00, double £255.00-£305.00
Evening meal: 1800 (l.o. 2230)
Credit Cards: Mastercard/Eurocard/Visa/Barclaycard/American Express/Switch/Delta/Diners/Eurocheque

Royal Westminster Thistle Hotel

49 Buckingham Palace Road, Victoria, London SW1W 0QT
Tel: (0171) 834 1821
Fax: (0171) 931 7542
⊖/⇌ Victoria
Air-conditioned hotel close to Buckingham Palace, St James's Park, Victoria station and the Houses of Parliament. Prices subject to change.
Bedrooms: 8 single, 43 double, 14 twin, 69 family
Bathrooms: 134 en suite
Bed & Breakfast: single £180.00-£200.00, double £200.00-£250.00
Evening meal: 1800 (l.o. 2300)
Credit Cards: Mastercard/Eurocard/Visa/Barclaycard/American Express/Switch/Delta/Diners/Eurocheque

The Rubens at the Palace

39-41 Buckingham Palace Road, London SW1W 0PS
Tel: (0171) 834 6600
Fax: (0171) 828 5401
⊖/⇌ Victoria
Traditional hotel opposite the Royal Mews of Buckingham Palace and close to Westminster.
Bedrooms: 42 single, 74 double, 56 twin, 8 family
Bathrooms: 180 en suite
Bed only: single £130.00-£150.00, double £160.00-£175.00
Bed & Breakfast: single £142.50-£162.50, double £184.00-£209.00
Evening meal: 1800 (l.o. 2000)
Credit Cards: Mastercard/Eurocard/Visa/Barclaycard/American Express/Switch/Delta/Diners/Eurocheque

St James Court Hotel

41-54 Buckingham Gate, London SW1E 6AF
Tel: (0171) 834 6655
Fax: (0171) 630 7587
⊖ St James's Park
Traditional hotel close to Buckingham Palace and within easy reach of West End and City. Self-catering apartments also available.
Bedrooms: 67 single, 203 double, 106 twin, 13 family
Bathrooms: 389 en suite
Bed only: single £148.00-£203.00, double £223.00-£242.00
Bed & Breakfast: single £164.00-£219.00, double £255.00-£274.00
Evening meal: 1930 (l.o. 2230)
Credit Cards: Mastercard/Eurocard/Visa/Barclaycard/American Express/Switch/Diners/Eurocheque

Sheraton Belgravia

20 Chesham Place, London SW1X 8HQ
Tel: (0171) 235 6040
Fax: (0171) 259 6243
⊖ Knightsbridge
Intimate town house hotel tucked away in a leafy square in Belgravia. Close to Harrods and Knightsbridge shopping.
Bedrooms: 89 double
Bathrooms: 89 en suite
Evening meal: 1830 (l.o. 2230)
Credit Cards: Mastercard/Visa/American Express/Switch/Diners/Eurocheque

Sheraton Park Tower

HIGHLY COMMENDED

101 Knightsbridge, London SW1X 7RN
Tel: (0171) 235 8050
Fax: (0171) 235 8231
⊖ Knightsbridge
Conveniently situated hotel in the elite shopping area of Knightsbridge, four minutes from Harrods and opposite Hyde Park.
Bedrooms: 198 double, 44 twin, 23 family
Bathrooms: 265 en suite, 2 public
Evening meal: 1900 (l.o. 2230)
Parking for: 100
Credit Cards: Mastercard/Eurocard/Visa/Barclaycard/American Express/Switch/Delta/Diners

Sidney Hotel

68-76 Belgrave Road, London SW1V 2BP
Tel: (0171) 834 2738
Fax: (0171) 630 0973
⊖/⇌ Victoria, ⊖ Pimlico
Noted for its friendly atmosphere, in an ideal location for both tourists and corporate visitors.
Bedrooms: 24 single, 23 double, 17 twin, 18 family
Bathrooms: 82 en suite
Bed & Breakfast: single £40.00-£65.00, double £62.00-£85.00
Credit Cards: Mastercard/Eurocard/Visa/Barclaycard/American Express/Switch/Delta/Diners/Eurocheque

Stakis London St Ermin's Hotel

Caxton Street, London SW1H 0QW
Tel: (0171) 222 7888
Fax: (0171) 222 6914
⊖ St James's Park
An elegant Edwardian property. Traditional furnishings add charm in relaxing atmosphere. Prices on application.
Bedrooms: 53 single, 108 double, 118 twin, 4 family
Bathrooms: 283 en suite
Bed only: single £175.00, double £195.00
Evening meal: 1800 (l.o. 2130)
Parking for: 23
Credit Cards: Mastercard/Visa/Barclaycard/American Express/Switch/Delta/Diners/Eurocheque

Stanley House Hotel

Listed APPROVED

19-21 Belgrave Road, London SW1V 1RB
Tel: (0171) 834 5042/ (0171) 834 7292
Fax: (0171) 834 8439
⊖/⇌ Victoria
Located in elegant Belgravia only a few minutes' walk from Victoria station. Within easy reach of London's most famous sights and the West End for theatres and shopping
Bedrooms: 4 single, 23 double, 7 twin, 10 family
Bathrooms: 44 en suite, 4 public
Bed & Breakfast: single £30.00-£42.00, double £45.00-£55.00
Credit Cards: Mastercard/Eurocard/Visa/Barclaycard/American Express/Switch/Delta/Eurocheque

Surtees Hotel
Listed Approved

94 Warwick Way, Victoria, London SW1V 1SB
Tel: (0171) 834 7163/ (0171) 834 7394
Fax: (0171) 460 8747
Victoria
Bed and breakfast hotel located in the heart of London near many tourist attractions.
Bedrooms: 2 single, 3 double, 1 twin, 4 family
Bathrooms: 3 en suite, 4 private, 2 public
Credit Cards: Mastercard/Visa/Switch

Vegas Hotel
Listed Approved

104 Warwick Way, London SW1V 1SD
Tel: (0171) 834 0082
Fax: (0171) 834 5623
E-mail: VgasHotel@aol.com
Victoria
Close to Victoria coach and underground stations and 15 minutes from Buckingham Palace.
Bedrooms: 1 single, 3 double, 9 twin
Bathrooms: 11 en suite, 2 private showers, 1 public
Bed & Breakfast: single £49.00-£55.00, double £50.00-£69.00
Credit Cards: Mastercard/Eurocard/Visa/Barclaycard/American Express/Switch/Delta/Diners/Eurocheque

The Victoria Inn
Listed Commended

65-67 Belgrave Road, London SW1V 2BG
Tel: (0171) 834 6721/ (0171) 834 0182
Fax: (0171) 931 0201
Victoria
Modern hotel situated in the heart of Victoria within five minutes' walk of the coach and rail stations.
Bedrooms: 6 single, 11 double, 14 twin, 10 family
Bathrooms: 41 en suite
Bed & Breakfast: single £61.00-£64.00, double £83.00-£89.00
Credit Cards: Mastercard/Visa/American Express/Delta/Diners/Eurocheque

Windermere Hotel
Commended

142-144 Warwick Way, Victoria, London SW1V 4JE
Tel: (0171) 834 5163/ (0171) 834 5480
Fax: (0171) 630 8831
E-mail: 100773.1171@compuserve.com
URL: www.windermere-hotel.co.uk
Victoria
Small, well-maintained hotel with a restaurant and bar; welcoming atmosphere and home comforts in an elegant setting.
Bedrooms: 4 single, 11 double, 5 twin, 3 family
Bathrooms: 20 en suite, 2 public
Bed & Breakfast: single £59.00-£77.00, double £69.00-£99.00
Evening meal: 1800 (l.o. 2130)
Credit Cards: Mastercard/Eurocard/Visa/Barclaycard/American Express/Switch/Delta/Eurocheque

W1
West End/Mayfair/ Oxford Street

The Berners Hotel
Highly Commended

10 Berners Street, London W1A 3BE
Tel: (0171) 666 2000
Fax: (0171) 666 2001
E-mail: berners@berners.co.uk
Euston, Oxford Circus
Edwardian building restored to its original beauty and elegance, a few minutes' walk from Oxford Circus and Soho.
Bedrooms: 37 single, 135 double, 45 twin
Bathrooms: 217 en suite
Bed only: single £160.00-£230.00, double £195.00-£240.00
Bed & Breakfast: single £175.00-£245.00, double £225.00-£260.00
Evening meal: 1730 (l.o. 2230)
Credit Cards: Mastercard/Barclaycard/American Express/Switch/Delta/Diners/Eurocheque

The Bickenhall Hotel
Approved

119 Gloucester Place, London W1H 3PJ
Tel: (0171) 935 3401
Fax: (0171) 224 0614
Baker Street
Well-appointed Georgian house, in the heart of London's West End. Convenient for shops, theatres and sightseeing.
Bedrooms: 4 single, 5 double, 2 twin, 7 family
Bathrooms: 15 en suite, 1 public
Bed & Breakfast: single £45.00-£65.00, double £65.00-£89.00
Credit Cards: Mastercard/Eurocard/Visa/American Express/Diners/Eurocheque

Blandford Hotel
Listed Approved

80 Chiltern Street, London W1M 1PS
Tel: (0171) 486 3103
Fax: (0171) 487 2786
Baker Street, Marylebone
Located in the heart of London, convenient for Madame Tussaud's, theatreland and the West End. Harley Street clinics and London Zoo are also nearby.
Bedrooms: 9 single, 6 double, 8 twin, 10 family
Bathrooms: 30 en suite, 3 private
Bed & Breakfast: single £65.00-£70.00, double £85.00
Credit Cards: Mastercard/Eurocard/Visa/Barclaycard/American Express/Switch/Delta/Eurocheque

Brown's Hotel
Highly Commended

Albemarle Street and Dover Street, London W1X 4BP
Tel: (0171) 493 6020
Fax: (0171) 493 9381
E-mail: brownshotel@ukbusiness.com
URL: www.brownshotel.com
Green Park
In the heart of Mayfair, one of London's most distinguished hotels. Prices quoted are valid for 1998 and are subject to change.
Bedrooms: 21 single, 51 double, 30 twin, 15 family
Bathrooms: 117 en suite
Bed only: single £256.00, double £288.00-£323.00

Book your accommodation through London Tourist Board – from within Britain: (0171) 932 2020, from outside Britain: +44171 932 2020 (MasterCard, Visa or Switch required).

124/144 Warwick Way,
Victoria, London
SW1V 4JE
Tel: 0171 834 5163/5480
Fax: 0171 630 8831

E-mail: 100773.117@compuserve.com

An award-winning small hotel situated within minutes walk from Victoria station and Buckingham Palace. Individually designed rooms. Moderate rates inclusive of English breakfast and VAT. Licensed restaurant and bar.

**Winner of the 'BTA TROPHY', AA selected-QQQQ,
RAC Highly Acclaimed,
ETB 3 Crown Commended.
http://www.windermere-hotel.co.uk**

Sidney Hotel

74-76 Belgrave Road, Victoria, London SW1V 2BP
Telephone 0171 834 2738 & Fax 0171 630 0973

The Sidney Hotel is noted for its friendly atmosphere and impeccable cleanliness. Situated a few minutes' walk from Victoria railway, underground and coach stations giving easy access to the heart of London, Europe, Gatwick, Heathrow and City airports.

Totally refurbished, offering modern, comfortable, and tastefully decorated bedrooms and most bedrooms enjoying en-suite bathrooms. All rooms are equipped with colour television, radio, direct-dial telephone, tea/coffee-making facilities, hairdryer and ironing facilities.

Finally, we love old London and if we can help you enjoy it we will. Please book as far ahead as possible.

Are you looking for a Victorious stay in London?

Why not begin your conquest from the Victoria area and its famous surroundings and after a 'hard day of battles' you'll be welcomed and honoured like a great winner at

The Victoria Inn
65-67 Belgrave Road, Victoria,
London SW1V 2BG
Tel: 0171-834 6721/0182 Fax: 0171-931 0201

Best Bed & Breakfast in London

FROM £22.00

per person (minimum 2 nights stay)
www.bestbandb.co.uk

Excellent private homes

Friendly hosts

Full English breakfast

Central locations

Reservations Service

Fast, Efficient Computerised

Credit Card Facilities

**U.S.A. & Canada:
Toll-free 011 800 852 26320
Australia:
Toll-free 0011 800 852 26320
Tel: +44 (0)181 742 9123
Fax: +44 (0)181 749 7084
E-mail: bestbandb@atlas.co.uk**

Evening meal: 1800 (l.o. 2200)
Credit Cards: Mastercard/Eurocard/Visa/Barclaycard/American Express/Switch/Diners/Eurocheque

The Chesterfield Mayfair

35 Charles Street, Mayfair, London W1X 8LX
Tel: (0171) 491 2622
Fax: (0171) 491 4793
E-mail: reservations@chesterfield.viewinn.co.uk
Green Park
The 110-bedroomed Chesterfield is ideal for both business and pleasure and is centrally located in the heart of Mayfair.
Bedrooms: 27 single, 69 double, 8 twin, 6 family
Bathrooms: 110 en suite
Bed only: single £145.00-£220.00, double £175.00-£245.00
Bed & Breakfast: single £160.00-£235.00, double £199.00-£280.00
Evening meal: 1830 (l.o. 2300)
Credit Cards: Mastercard/Visa/Barclaycard/American Express/Diners/Eurocheque

Churchill Inter-Continental London

30 Portman Square, London W1A 4ZX
Tel: (0171) 486 5800
Fax: (0171) 485 1255
E-mail: churchill@interconti.com
URL: www.interconti.com
Marble Arch
Traditional, Regency-style hotel situated in the heart of the West End.
Bedrooms: 23 single, 281 double, 104 twin
Bathrooms: 408 en suite
Bed only: single £260.00, double £330.00
Bed & Breakfast: single £280.00, double £350.00
Evening meal: 1800 (l.o. 2300)
Parking for: 70
Credit Cards: Mastercard/Visa/Barclaycard/American Express/Switch/Delta/Diners/Eurocheque

Claridge's

Brook Street, Mayfair, London W1A 2JQ
Tel: (0171) 629 8860
Fax: (0171) 499 2210
E-mail: info@claridges.co.uk
URL: www.savoy-group.co.uk
Bond Street
In the heart of Mayfair with its fashionable boutiques. A favourite of London society and distinguished visitors for over 100 years.
Bedrooms: 45 single, 88 double, 6 family
Bathrooms: 136 en suite
Bed only: single £260.00, double £300.00-£370.00
Evening meal: 1730 (l.o. 2300)
Credit Cards: Mastercard/Eurocard/Visa/Barclaycard/American Express/Switch/Delta/Diners/Eurocheque

The Connaught Hotel

Carlos Place, Mayfair, London W1Y 6AL
Tel: (0171) 499 7070
Fax: (0171) 495 3262
E-mail: info@the-connaught.co.uk
URL: www.savoy-group.co.uk
Green Park
Set in a picturesque part of Mayfair. A haven of cosiness, tranquillity and supreme comfort; a gastronomic experience.
Bedrooms: 30 single, 60 twin
Bathrooms: 90 en suite
Bed only: single £270.00-£290.00, double £375.00-£400.00
Evening meal: 1830 (l.o. 2230)
Parking for: 3
Credit Cards: Mastercard/Eurocard/Visa/Barclaycard/American Express/Switch/Delta/Diners/Eurocheque

Cumberland Hotel

COMMENDED

Marble Arch, London W1A 4RF
Tel: (0171) 262 1234
Fax: (0171) 724 4621
Marble Arch
An internationally famous hotel overlooking Hyde Park and at the top of Oxford Street. With four international restaurants, four bars and conference and banqueting facilities for eight to 800.
Bedrooms: 167 single, 345 double, 373 twin, 21 family
Bathrooms: 906 en suite
Bed only: single £162.00-£189.00, double £183.00-£210.00
Bed & Breakfast: single £172.00-£200.00, double £205.00-£232.00
Evening meal: 1730 (l.o. 2400)
Credit Cards: Mastercard/Eurocard/Visa/Barclaycard/American Express/Switch/Delta/Diners

The Dorchester

DE LUXE

Park Lane, London W1A 2HJ
Tel: (0171) 629 8888
Fax: (0171) 409 0114
Hyde Park Corner
A Five Crown De Luxe, traditional English, country house-style hotel, with all modern facilities including a spa and three restaurants.
Bedrooms: 32 single, 120 double, 92 twin
Bathrooms: 244 en suite
Bed & Breakfast: single £285.00-£315.00, double £330.00-£390.00
Evening meal: 1800 (l.o. 2330)
Parking for: 24
Credit Cards: Mastercard/Visa/Barclaycard/American Express/Diners

The Edward Lear Hotel

APPROVED

30 Seymour Street, Marble Arch, London W1H 5WD
Tel: (0171) 402 5401
Fax: (0171) 706 3766
Marble Arch
Family-run Georgian residence, with an informal and friendly atmosphere, in a central location, one minute from Oxford Street and Marble Arch.
Bedrooms: 13 single, 4 double, 10 twin, 4 family
Bathrooms: 3 en suite, 1 private, 7 private showers, 6 public
Bed & Breakfast: single £39.50-£55.00, double £65.00-£89.50
Credit Cards: Mastercard/Eurocard/Visa/Barclaycard/Switch/Delta/Eurocheque

Forte Posthouse Regent's Park

COMMENDED

Carburton Street, London W1P 8EE
Tel: (0171) 388 2300
Fax: (0171) 387 2806
Great Portland Street
Situated just north of Oxford Street and to the east of Regent Street, close to Regent's Park and London Zoo. Business services available.
Bedrooms: 5 single, 203 double, 118 twin
Bathrooms: 326 en suite

LONDON CONTINENTAL HOTEL

88 Gloucester Place, London W1H 3HN
Tel: 0171 486 8670 Fax: 0171 486 8671
Email:reservation@london-continental.com
Website:http://www.london-continental.com

Central London location, off famous Oxford Street. 25 rooms, all en suite, with telephone, satellite TV, radio alarm, tea/coffee making facilities, hairdryer, fridge/ freezer. Singles, doubles, triples and quads. Lift to all floors. Five minutes from Baker Street underground.
Continental breakfast and dining room

AA Recommended · LONDON Tourist Board and Convention Bureau MEMBER · RAC Listed · English Tourist Board COMMENDED Listed · LES ROUTIERS

MARBLE ARCH INN

49-50 Upper Berkeley Street, London W1H 7PN
Tel: 0171 723 7888 Fax: 0171 723 6060
e-mail: marble@rooms.demon.co.uk

Small friendly B & B Hotel near Paddington Station, ideally located within 2 minutes of Marble Arch, Hyde Park and Oxford Street. London's theatres, museums and other tourist attractions are nearby.

Most rooms with Colour/Satellite TV Shower/WC, Telephone, Hairdryer, Tea/Coffee Bar.

Credit Cards: Visa, Access, Amex, JCB, Diners **(Very competitive prices)**

English Tourist Board APPROVED Listed

Colliers Hotel

A clean, budget priced hotel. Centrally situated in Victoria, close to railway, coach and underground stations. Central heating throughout. All rooms with TV and telephone. ETB Listed/Approved.

Singles from £28 Doubles/twins from £38

97 Warwick Way, London SW1V 1QL
Telephone: 0171 834 6931/828 0210

EDWARD LEAR HOTEL

www.edlear.com

30 Seymour Street, Marble Arch, London W1H 5WD
Tel: 0171-402 5401 Fax: 0171-706 3766
e-mail: edlear@aol.com
Singles from £45.00 p.n.
Doubles from £65.00 p.n.

PARKWOOD HOTEL

www.parkwoodhotel.com

4 Stanhope Place, Marble Arch, London W2 2HB
Tel: 0171-402 2241 Fax: 0171 402 1574
e-mail: pkwd@aol.com
Singles from £49.00 p.n.
Doubles from £70.00 p.n.

GEORGE HOTEL

www.georgehotel.com

60 Cartwright Gdns, London WC1H 9EL
Tel: 0171-387 8777 Fax: 0171 387 8666
e-mail: ghotel@aol.com
Singles from £46.50 p.n.
Doubles from £64.50 p.n.

PRICES INCLUDE FULL ENGLISH BREAKFAST, TAX AND SERVICE
Children sharing parents' bedroom from £9.50 p.n. (includes breakfast). FREE at weekends.

* Each hotel in a perfect central location in the heart of London. Parkwood and Edward Lear only one minute from Oxford Street. George Hotel close to British Museum and West End.
* All rooms with TV (free film and sports channels), radio, tea/coffee, telephone etc.
* Recommended in most guides, including *Frommers, Let's Go, Time Out* etc. Over 50% of the guests have stayed before or had the hotels recommended.
* Easy direct access by A2 Airbus to each hotel from Heathrow Airport.

AA · RAC · English Tourist Board · LES ROUTIERS

Evening meal: 1800 (l.o. 2200)
Parking for: 80
Credit Cards: Mastercard/Eurocard/Visa/Barclaycard/American Express/Switch/Delta/Diners/Eurocheque

Four Seasons Hotel

Hamilton Place, Park Lane, London W1A 1AZ
Tel: (0171) 499 0888
Fax: (0171) 493 1895
URL: www.fourseasons.com
Hyde Park Corner
Luxury hotel close to Hyde Park and convenient for shops and theatres.
Bedrooms: 63 single, 123 double, 34 twin
Bathrooms: 220 en suite
Bed only: single £317.25-£352.50, double £370.13-£381.88
Evening meal: 1800 (l.o. 2230)
Parking for: 55
Credit Cards: Mastercard/Visa/Barclaycard/American Express/Delta/Diners

Georgian House Hotel

Listed Approved

87 Gloucester Place, London W1H 3PG
Tel: (0171) 935 2211
Fax: (0171) 486 7535
Marylebone, Baker Street
Small, comfortable hotel providing personal service and convenient for the business, shopping and entertainment centres of London's West End.
Bedrooms: 4 single, 4 double, 7 twin, 4 family
Bathrooms: 12 en suite, 7 private
Bed & Breakfast: single £70.00-£75.00, double £85.00-£90.00
Credit Cards: Mastercard/Eurocard/Visa/Barclaycard/American Express

Glynne Court Hotel

Listed Approved

41 Great Cumberland Place, Marble Arch, London W1H 7LG
Tel: (0171) 262 4344
Fax: (0171) 724 2071
Marble Arch
Friendly, comfortable hotel in a prime location, convenient for shops, theatres and business. Two minutes' walk from Marble Arch, Hyde Park and Oxford Street. Budget hotel in the heart of London's West End.
Bedrooms: 1 single, 8 double, 1 twin, 3 family
Bathrooms: 10 en suite, 5 public
Bed & Breakfast: single £45.00-£55.00, double £50.00-£65.00
Credit Cards: Mastercard/Eurocard/Visa/Barclaycard/American Express/Switch/Delta/Diners/Eurocheque

Grosvenor House

De Luxe

Park Lane, London W1A 3AA
Tel: (0171) 499 6363
Fax: (0171) 493 3341
E-mail: ghmarketing_ed@dial.pipex.com
Marble Arch/Hyde Park Corner
This famous hotel is situated on Park Lane overlooking the 360 acres of Hyde Park.
Bedrooms: 75 single, 113 double, 176 twin, 73 family
Bathrooms: 437 en suite
Evening meal: 1800 (l.o. 2245)
Parking for: 120
Credit Cards: Mastercard/Visa/Barclaycard/American Express/Diners

Hallam Hotel

Applied

12 Hallam Street, Portland Place, London W1N 5LF
Tel: (0171) 580 1166
Fax: (0171) 323 4527
Oxford Circus
Quiet, friendly hotel five minutes from Oxford Circus.
Bedrooms: 15 single, 6 double, 4 twin
Bathrooms: 25 en suite
Bed & Breakfast: single £76.50-£81.50, double £92.50-£97.50
Credit Cards: Mastercard/Eurocard/Visa/Barclaycard/American Express/Diners/Eurocheque

Hotel Inter-Continental London

1 Hamilton Place, Hyde Park Corner, London W1V 0QY
Tel: (0171) 409 3131
Fax: (0171) 493 3476
E-mail: london@interconti.com
URL: www.interconti.com
Hyde Park Corner
In the heart of London, on Hyde Park Corner. Close to Piccadilly, West End shopping and theatres.
Bedrooms: 286 double, 118 twin
Bathrooms: 399 en suite, 3 public
Bed & Breakfast: single £248.00-£310.00, double £266.00-£330.00
Evening meal: 1800 (l.o. 2300)
Parking for: 100
Credit Cards: Mastercard/Eurocard/Visa/Barclaycard/American Express/Switch/Delta/Diners/Eurocheque

Hotel La Place

Commended

17 Nottingham Place, London W1M 3FF
Tel: (0171) 486 2323
Fax: (0171) 486 4335
URL: www.bit-byter.demon.co.uk/hlp.htm
Baker Street
West End hotel specialising in personal service and friendliness. Multilingual staff. Caters especially for women travelling alone.
Bedrooms: 7 single, 6 double, 3 twin, 5 family
Bathrooms: 21 en suite
Bed & Breakfast: single £82.00-£150.00, double £102.00-£155.00
Evening meal: 1800 (l.o. 2030)
Credit Cards: Mastercard/Eurocard/Visa/Barclaycard/American Express/Switch/Delta/Diners/Eurocheque

Kenwood House Hotel

Listed Approved

114 Gloucester Place, London W1H 3DB
Tel: (0171) 935 3473/(0171) 935 9455
Fax: (0171) 224 0582
E-mail: woutersz@mgr.com
Baker Street
A small, friendly bed and breakfast hotel in a central location, with budget prices.
Bedrooms: 4 single, 6 double, 4 twin, 2 family
Bathrooms: 11 en suite, 4 public
Bed & Breakfast: single £35.00-£50.00, double £60.00-£70.00
Credit Cards: Mastercard/Eurocard/Visa/Barclaycard/American Express/Switch/Eurocheque

The Langham Hilton

1c Portland Place, Regent Street, London W1N 4JA
Tel: (0171) 636 1000
Fax: (0171) 323 2340
Oxford Circus
A revival of London's first grand hotel restored to its Edwardian splendour.

The Langham Hilton overlooks Portland Place and Regent's Park and is five minutes from Oxford Street.
Bedrooms: 280 double, 99 twin
Bathrooms: 379 en suite
Bed only: double £305.50-£399.50
Evening meal: 1800 (l.o. 2245)
Credit Cards: Mastercard/Eurocard/Visa/Barclaycard/American Express/Switch/Delta/Diners/Eurocheque

Le Meridien Piccadilly

HIGHLY COMMENDED

21 Piccadilly, London W1V 0BH
Tel: (0171) 734 8000
Fax: (0171) 437 3574
Piccadilly Circus
Traditional, centrally located hotel with a unique leisure club and high standards of service and facilities.
Bedrooms: 71 single, 111 double, 49 twin, 35 family
Bathrooms: 266 en suite
Bed only: single £348.85-£374.32, double £374.32-£387.03
Bed & Breakfast: single £364.89-£390.25, double £405.10-£418.89
Evening meal: 1900 (l.o. 2230)
Credit Cards: Mastercard/Eurocard/Visa/Barclaycard/American Express/Switch/Delta/Diners/Eurocheque

The Leonard

HIGHLY COMMENDED

15 Seymour Street, London W1H 5AA
Tel: (0171) 935 2010
Fax: (0171) 935 6700
E-mail: the.leonard@dial.pipex.com
Marble Arch
Four 18th century town houses, elegantly restored. Twenty suites and eight bedrooms, all with air-conditioning, 24-hour room service and friendly staff.
Bedrooms: 22 double, 4 family
Bathrooms: 26 en suite
Credit Cards: Mastercard/Eurocard/Visa/Barclaycard/American Express/Switch/Diners/Eurocheque

Lincoln House Hotel

COMMENDED

33 Gloucester Place, London W1H 3PD
Tel: (0171) 486 7630
Fax: (0171) 486 0166
E-mail: reservations@lincoln-house-hotel.co.uk
URL: www.lincoln-house-hotel.co.uk
Marble Arch
Fully refurbished Georgian hotel, offering en suite rooms with admirable standard of facilities and services. Close to the shops of Oxford Street, theatres and nightlife.
Bedrooms: 6 single, 8 double, 4 twin, 4 family
Bathrooms: 20 en suite, 2 private, 2 public
Bed & Breakfast: single £42.00-£69.00, double £65.00-£99.00
Credit Cards: Visa/American Express/Switch/Diners/Eurocheque

London Continental Hotel

Listed COMMENDED

88 Gloucester Place, Marble Arch, London W1H 3HN
Tel: (0171) 486 8670/0860 642345
Fax: (0171) 486 8671
Baker Street
Centrally located hotel ideal for both businessmen and tourists. Close to Hyde Park and Marble Arch.
Bedrooms: 8 single, 8 double, 5 twin, 4 family
Bathrooms: 23 en suite, 2 private showers, 1 public
Credit Cards: Mastercard/Eurocard/Visa/Barclaycard/American Express/Switch/Delta/Diners/Eurocheque

London Hilton on Park Lane

HIGHLY COMMENDED

22 Park Lane, London W1Y 4BE
Tel: (0171) 493 8000
Fax: (0171) 208 4136
E-mail: sales_park-lane@hilton.com
Hyde Park Corner, Victoria
Built in 1963. The flagship hotel of Hilton International. All bedrooms have magnificent views of London. The hotel has one of the largest ballrooms in London, three restaurants and four bars.
Bedrooms: 269 double, 124 twin, 53 family
Bathrooms: 446 en suite
Bed only: single £334.88, double £334.88
Credit Cards: Mastercard/Eurocard/Visa/Barclaycard/American Express/Switch/Delta/Diners/Eurocheque
Parking for: 300

London Marriott Hotel Grosvenor Square

10-13 Duke Street, London W1A 4AW
Tel: (0171) 493 1232
Fax: (0171) 491 3201
URL: www.marriott.com/marriott/londt
Bond Street
In the heart of Mayfair. Close to shopping, theatres, art galleries, antique shops, restaurants and Hyde Park.
Bedrooms: 2 single, 116 double, 86 twin, 17 family
Bathrooms: 221 en suite
Bed & Breakfast: single £275.00-£320.00, double £290.00-£320.00
Evening meal: 1730 (l.o. 2200)
Parking for: 50
Credit Cards: Eurocard/Visa/American Express/Diners/Eurocheque

London Marriott Hotel – Marble Arch

134 George Street, London W1H 6DN
Tel: (0171) 723 1277
Fax: (0171) 402 0666
Marble Arch/Edgware Road
Located centrally a short walk from Oxford Street, Hyde Park and Marble Arch underground. Paddington station is one mile away, giving access to Heathrow via the Heathrow Express.
Bedrooms: 145 double, 95 twin
Bathrooms: 240 en suite
Bed & Breakfast: single £165.70-£269.00, double £178.70-£269.00
Evening meal: 1700 (l.o. 2230)
Parking for: 80
Credit Cards: Mastercard/Eurocard/Visa/Barclaycard/American Express/Switch/Delta/Diners/Eurocheque

London Mews Hilton

2 Stanhope Row, Park Lane, London W1Y 7HE
Tel: (0171) 493 7222
Fax: (0171) 629 9423
E-mail: Info_Mews@Hilton.Com
URL: www.Hilton.com/Hotels
Hyde Park Corner
An intimate town house hotel situated in the heart of Mayfair. Close to Piccadilly, Oxford Street and many major attractions. Direct link to Heathrow.

Bedrooms: 19 single, 32 double, 20 twin
Bathrooms: 71 en suite
Bed only: single £185.00-£227.00, double £200.00-£242.00
Evening meal: 1730 (l.o. 2130)
Parking for: 5
Credit Cards: Mastercard/Eurocard/ Visa/Barclaycard/American Express/ Switch/Diners/Eurocheque

Marble Arch Inn

Listed APPROVED

49-50 Upper Berkeley Street, Marble Arch, London W1H 7PN
Tel: (0171) 723 7888
Fax: (0171) 723 6060
E-mail: marble@rooms.demon.co.uk
URL: www.rooms.demon.co.uk
Marble Arch
This friendly hotel is located near Marble Arch, within minutes of Hyde Park and Oxford Street and within easy reach of other major attractions.
Bedrooms: 2 single, 8 double, 9 twin, 10 family
Bathrooms: 25 en suite, 4 private showers, 2 public
Bed & Breakfast: single £30.00-£60.00, double £40.00-£70.00
Credit Cards: Mastercard/Eurocard/ Visa/Barclaycard/American Express/ Switch/Delta/Diners/Eurocheque

May Fair Inter-Continental London

HIGHLY COMMENDED

Stratton Street, London W1A 2AN
Tel: (0171) 629 7777
Fax: (0171) 629 1459
E-mail: mayfair@interconti.com
URL: www.interconti.com
Green Park
Situated close to Green Park and Piccadilly. Facilities include informal restaurant, May Fair café, May Fair theatre, crystal ballroom, spa health club, business centre and two bars.
Bedrooms: 79 single, 163 double, 45 twin
Bathrooms: 287 en suite
Bed only: single £229.00-£279.00, double £239.00-£299.00
Evening meal: 1900 (l.o. 2100)
Credit Cards: Mastercard/Visa/ American Express/Diners/Eurocheque

Mermaid Suites

Listed COMMENDED

4 Blenheim Street, London W1 9LB
Tel: (0171) 629 1875
Fax: (0171) 499 9475
Oxford Circus/Bond Street
Centrally located for shops and sightseeing. Five minutes away from Piccadilly and Leicester Square.
Bedrooms: 15 double, 12 twin, 2 family
Bathrooms: 29 en suite
Bed & Breakfast: single £55.00-£70.00, double £70.00-£90.00
Credit Cards: Mastercard/Eurocard/ Visa/Barclaycard/Eurocheque

The Metropolitan

Old Park Lane, London W1Y 4LB
Tel: (0171) 447 1000
Fax: (0171) 447 1100
E-mail: sales@metropolitan.co.uk
Hyde Park Corner
Opened in 1997, the Metropolitan is contemporary in style and attracts a fashionable market. Nobu, the Japanese restaurant and the chic Met Bar are on-site.
Bedrooms: 59 single, 96 double
Bathrooms: 155 en suite
Credit Cards: Mastercard/Eurocard/ Visa/Barclaycard/American Express/ Switch/Delta/Diners

The Millennium Britannia

Grosvenor Square, London W1A 3AN
Tel: (0171) 629 9400
Fax: (0171) 629 7736
Bond Street
Located in the picturesque Grosvenor Square in Mayfair, offering traditional British hospitality with unobtrusive yet friendly service. Conveniently situated for the historic sites, London theatreland and prime shopping areas.
Bedrooms: 29 single, 200 double, 90 twin
Bathrooms: 319 en suite
Bed & Breakfast: single £169.00, double £179.00
Evening meal: 1830 (l.o. 2230)
Parking for: 210
Credit Cards: Mastercard/Visa/ Barclaycard/American Express/ Switch/Diners/Eurocheque

Mount Royal Hotel

Bryanston Street, Marble Arch, London W1A 4UR
Tel: (0171) 629 8040
Fax: (0171) 499 7792
E-mail: mtroyalhotel@clx.co.uk
Marble Arch
In the heart of London's busy West End, overlooking Oxford Street; close to shops, theatres and night clubs.
Bedrooms: 35 single, 153 double, 359 twin, 142 family
Bathrooms: 689 en suite
Evening meal: 1800 (l.o. 0100)
Credit Cards: Visa/Barclaycard/ American Express/Switch/ Delta/Diners

Palace Hotel

31 Great Cumberland Place, Marble Arch, London W1H 7LF
Tel: (0171) 262 5585
Fax: (0171) 706 2427
Marble Arch
A small, classical Georgian building located in the heart of London overlooking Great Cumberland Place.
Bedrooms: 13 double, 7 twin, 19 family
Bathrooms: 30 en suite
Bed & Breakfast: single £55.00-£70.00, double £70.00-£95.00
Parking for: 7
Credit Cards: Mastercard/Eurocard/ Visa/Barclaycard/American Express/ Switch/Delta/Diners/Eurocheque

The Park Lane Hotel

HIGHLY COMMENDED

Piccadilly, London W1Y 8BX
Tel: (0171) 499 6321
Fax: (0171) 499 1965
Hyde Park Corner/Green Park
Highly Commended hotel on Piccadilly overlooking Green Park towards Buckingham Palace, offering good service and modern facilities.
Bedrooms: 42 single, 100 double, 100 twin, 58 family
Bathrooms: 300 en suite
Evening meal: 1900 (l.o. 2300)
Parking for: 150
Credit Cards: Mastercard/Visa/ American Express/Switch/Diners/ Eurocheque

Piccadilly Thistle

39 Coventry Street, London W1V 7FH
Tel: (0171) 930 4033
Fax: (0171) 925 2586
⊖ Leicester Square
Just yards from Piccadilly Circus. Close to Regent Street, theatres and the National Gallery.
Bedrooms: 15 single, 27 double, 45 twin, 5 family
Bathrooms: 92 en suite
Bed only: single £150.00-£170.00, double £180.00-£190.00
Credit Cards: Mastercard/Eurocard/ Visa/Barclaycard/American Express/ Switch/Delta/Diners/Eurocheque

Radisson Edwardian Berkshire Hotel

350 Oxford Street, London W1N 0BY
Tel: (0171) 629 7474
Fax: (0171) 629 8156
⊖ Bond Street
Country-style hotel right in the centre of the famous West End shopping district.
Bedrooms: 24 single, 61 double, 62 twin
Bathrooms: 147 en suite
Bed only: single £230.00, double £255.00
Bed & Breakfast: single £245.00, double £275.00
Evening meal: 1800 (l.o. 2230)
Credit Cards: Mastercard/Eurocard/ Visa/Barclaycard/American Express/ Switch/Delta/Diners/Eurocheque

Radisson Edwardian Grafton Hotel

130 Tottenham Court Road, London W1P 9HP
Tel: (0171) 388 4131
Fax: (0171) 387 7394
⊖ Warren Street
Situated close to the West End. Edwardian decor and style with the atmosphere of an English country house.
Bedrooms: 80 single, 135 double, 80 twin, 29 family
Bathrooms: 323 en suite
Bed only: single £132.00-£203.00, double £132.00-£203.00
Evening meal: 1700 (l.o. 2200)
Credit Cards: Mastercard/Eurocard/ Visa/Barclaycard/American Express/ Switch/Delta/Diners/Eurocheque

Radisson Edwardian Savoy Court

19-25 Granville Place, London W1H 0EH
Tel: (0171) 408 0130
Fax: (0171) 493 2070
⊖ Marble Arch
In a quiet location just off Oxford Street at Marble Arch. The hotel provides traditional elegance at reasonable cost.
Bedrooms: 32 single, 37 double, 24 twin, 15 family
Bathrooms: 108 en suite
Bed only: single £106.00-£123.00, double £119.00-£126.00
Evening meal: (l.o. 2200)
Credit Cards: Mastercard/Eurocard/ Visa/Barclaycard/American Express/ Switch/Delta/Diners/Eurocheque

The Radisson SAS Portman Hotel

22 Portman Square, London W1H 9FL
Tel: (0171) 208 6000
Fax: (0171) 208 6001
E-mail: sales@lonza.rdsas.com
URL: www.radisson.com
⊖ Marble Arch
Modern hotel situated in the heart of London's West End with easy access to the business and entertainment centres. There are tennis courts in nearby Portman Square.
Evening meal: 1730 (l.o. 2300)
Bedrooms: 17 single, 156 double, 91 twin, 1 family
Bathrooms: 279 en suite
Credit Cards: Mastercard/Eurocard/ Visa/Barclaycard/American Express/ Switch/Delta/Diners

Rathbone Hotel

Rathbone Street, London W1P 2LB
Tel: (0171) 636 2001
Fax: (0171) 636 3882
⊖ Goodge Street
Located just off Oxford Street, this 72-bedroom hotel offers a wide range of amenities including air-conditioned rooms.
Bedrooms: 14 single, 48 double, 10 twin
Bathrooms: 72 en suite
Bed only: single £150.00-£160.00, double £180.00-£190.00
Bed & Breakfast: single £160.00-£170.00, double £200.00-£210.00
Credit Cards: Mastercard/Visa/ Barclaycard/American Express/ Switch/Delta/Diners

Regent Palace Hotel

Piccadilly Circus, London W1A 4BZ
Tel: (0171) 734 7000
Fax: (0171) 734 6435
⊖ Piccadilly Circus
Large hotel with a wide choice of restaurants, just behind Piccadilly Circus and Regent Street. Bathrooms are located along the corridors.
Bedrooms: 324 single, 213 double, 296 twin, 89 family
Bathrooms: 110 public
Bed only: single £59.00-£69.00, double £59.00-£69.00
Bed & Breakfast: single £65.95-£79.95, double £65.95-£79.95
Evening meal: 1715 (l.o. 2100)
Credit Cards: Mastercard/Eurocard/ Visa/Barclaycard/American Express/ Switch/Delta/Diners/Eurocheque

The Ritz Hotel

150 Piccadilly, London W1V 9DG
Tel: (0171) 493 8181
Fax: (0171) 493 2687
E-mail: enquire@theritzhotel.co.uk
URL: www.theritzhotel.co.uk
⊖ Green Park
A symbol of consummate hospitality since 1906, this international hotel is ideally situated for shopping, business and cultural activities.
Bedrooms: 17 single, 58 double, 55 twin
Bathrooms: 130 en suite
Bed only: single £293.75-£452.37, double £340.75-£452.37
Evening meal: 1830 (l.o. 2245)
Credit Cards: Mastercard/Eurocard/ Visa/Barclaycard/American Express/ Switch/Delta/Diners/Eurocheque

Saint Georges Hotel

♛♛♛♛ COMMENDED

Langham Place, Regent Street, London W1N 8QS
Tel: (0171) 580 0111
Fax: (0171) 436 7997
URL: www.forte-hotels.com
⊖ Oxford Circus
Modern hotel. Restaurant with panoramic views. Spacious rooms with bright decor and natural light.

Bedrooms: 3 single, 31 double, 52 twin
Bathrooms: 86 en suite
Bed only: single £160.00-£180.00, double £170.00-£190.00
Bed & Breakfast: single £173.50-£193.50, double £197.00-£217.00
Evening meal: 1900 (l.o. 2200)
Parking for: 2
Credit Cards: Mastercard/Eurocard/Visa/Barclaycard/American Express/Switch/Delta/Diners/Eurocheque

The Selfridge Hotel
(A Thistle Hotel)

Orchard Street, London W1H 0JS
Tel: (0171) 408 2080
Fax: (0171) 629 8849
Bond Street/Marble Arch
One of London's most central hotels in the heart of the West End, ideal for nightlife and with the shopping areas of Bond Street and Oxford Street nearby.
Bedrooms: 86 single, 62 double, 146 twin
Bathrooms: 294 en suite
Bed only: single £190.00-£210.00, double £210.00-£240.00
Evening meal: 1800 (l.o. 2300)
Credit Cards: Mastercard/Visa/Barclaycard/American Express/Switch/Delta/Diners/Eurocheque

Shaftesbury Hotel

65-73 Shaftesbury Avenue, London W1V 7AA
Tel: (0171) 434 4200
Fax: (0171) 437 1717
Piccadilly Circus
In the heart of the West End. Centrally located for London's visitor attractions, theatreland, nightlife and shops.
Bedrooms: 9 single, 22 double, 10 twin, 23 family
Bathrooms: 48 en suite
Bed & Breakfast: single £119.00-£139.00, double £129.00-£159.00
Credit Cards: Mastercard/Eurocard/Visa/Barclaycard/American Express/Switch/Delta/Diners/Eurocheque

Sherlock Holmes Hotel

108 Baker Street, London W1M 1LB
Tel: (0171) 486 6161
Fax: (0171) 486 0884
Baker Street
Well located for shopping in Oxford Street and Regent Street and convenient for major tourist attractions.
Bedrooms: 14 single, 58 double, 53 twin
Bathrooms: 125 en suite
Evening meal: 1900 (l.o. 2130)
Credit Cards: Mastercard/Eurocard/Visa/Barclaycard/American Express/Switch/Delta/Diners/Eurocheque

Wigmore Court Hotel
COMMENDED

23 Gloucester Place, Portman Square, London W1H 3PB
Tel: (0171) 935 0928
Fax: (0171) 487 4254
E-mail: info@wigmore-court-hotel.co.uk
URL: www.wigmore-court-hotel.co.uk
Baker Street
Small, clean, family-run bed and breakfast hotel with large en suite rooms. Three minutes' walk to Oxford Street and Marble Arch underground station. Competitively priced and ideal for families.
Bedrooms: 5 single, 7 double, 3 twin, 3 family
Bathrooms: 16 en suite, 1 public
Bed & Breakfast: single £55.00-£69.00, double £87.00-£97.00
Credit Cards: Mastercard/Visa/Barclaycard/Switch/Eurocheque

WC1/WC2 BLOOMSBURY/STRAND/LEICESTER SQUARE

Academy Hotel
COMMENDED

17-25 Gower Street, London WC1E 6HG
Tel: (0171) 631 4115
Fax: (0171) 636 3442
Goodge Street
Charming Georgian hotel in the heart of Bloomsbury.
Bedrooms: 13 single, 27 double, 8 twin
Bathrooms: 48 en suite, 1 public
Bed only: single £100.00-£115.00, double £125.00-£185.00
Evening meal: 1800 (l.o. 2300)
Credit Cards: Mastercard/Eurocard/Visa/Barclaycard/American Express/Switch/Delta/Diners/Eurocheque

Arran House Hotel
APPROVED

77 Gower Street, London WC1E 6HJ
Tel: (0171) 636 2186/(0171) 637 1140
Fax: (0171) 436 5328
Euston Square
A small, comfortable, family-run bed and breakfast hotel in central London, convenient for theatres, shopping and public transport.
Bedrooms: 6 single, 6 double, 4 twin, 12 family
Bathrooms: 5 en suite, 5 private, 4 private showers, 5 public
Bed & Breakfast: single £40.00-£50.00, double £50.00-£70.00
Parking for: 2
Credit Cards: Mastercard/Eurocard/Visa/Barclaycard/Switch/Delta/Eurocheque

Bedford/Cosmo House Hotel

27 Bloomsbury Square, London WC1A 2PJ
Tel: (0171) 636 4661/(0171) 636 0577
Fax: (0171) 636 0577
E-mail: cosmo.bedford.hotel@dial.pipex.com
URL: www.smoothhound.co.uk/hotels/cosmo.html
Holborn
A small, friendly hotel in the centre of London.
Bedrooms: 14 single, 4 double, 6 twin, 9 family
Bathrooms: 10 en suite, 8 public
Bed & Breakfast: single £30.00-£36.00, double £50.00-£56.00
Credit Cards: American Express/Diners/Eurocheque

Blooms Hotel
HIGHLY COMMENDED

7 Montague Street, London WC1B 5BP
Tel: (0171) 323 1717
Fax: (0171) 636 6498
Euston, Russell Square
Elegant 18th century town house, located in the quiet area of Bloomsbury and close to most major tourist attractions and shops.
Bedrooms: 5 single, 13 double, 9 twin
Bathrooms: 27 en suite
Bed & Breakfast: single £125.00, double £185.00-£200.00
Credit Cards: Mastercard/Eurocard/Visa/Barclaycard/American Express/Switch/Delta/Diners/Eurocheque

Bloomsbury Park Hotel

126 Southampton Row, London WC1B 5AD
Tel: (0171) 430 0434
Fax: (0171) 242 0665
⊖/⇌ Euston, ⊖ Russell Square
Midway between the West End and the City and close to Covent Garden and the British Museum, the hotel is convenient for Euston, St Pancras and King's Cross.
Bedrooms: 5 single, 44 double, 46 twin
Bathrooms: 95 en suite
Bed & Breakfast: single £116.00-£129.00, double £126.00-£136.00
Evening meal: 1800 (l.o. 2130)
Credit Cards: Mastercard/Visa/Barclaycard/American Express/Switch/Delta/Diners/Eurocheque

The Bonnington in Bloomsbury

COMMENDED

92 Southampton Row, London WC1B 4BH
Tel: (0171) 242 2828
Fax: (0171) 831 9170
E-mail: Sales@Bonnington-hotels.co.uk
⊖ Holborn/Russell Square
The Bonnington is situated between the City and West End and is close to train stations and on the bus routes to Heathrow.
Bedrooms: 109 single, 44 double, 45 twin, 17 family
Bathrooms: 215 en suite
Bed & Breakfast: single £82.00-£115.00, double £124.00-£145.00
Evening meal: 1730 (l.o. 2230)
Credit Cards: Mastercard/Eurocard/Visa/Barclaycard/American Express/Switch/Delta/Diners/Eurocheque

Charing Cross Hotel

Strand, London WC2N 5HX
Tel: (0171) 839 7282
Fax: (0171) 839 3933
⊖/⇌ Charing Cross
In the heart of London, close to theatreland and the art galleries, with easy access to airports, trains and buses. Grade II Listed building, totally refurbished in 1998.
Bedrooms: 113 double, 124 twin
Bathrooms: 237 en suite
Evening meal: 1730 (l.o. 2200)
Credit Cards: Mastercard/Visa/Barclaycard/American Express/Switch/Delta/Diners

Crescent Hotel

COMMENDED

49-50 Cartwright Gardens, London WC1H 9EL
Tel: (0171) 387 1515
Fax: (0171) 383 2054
⊖ Russell Square, ⊖/⇌ Euston
Comfortable Georgian town house, in a quiet crescent, with private gardens and tennis courts.
Bedrooms: 9 single, 2 double, 3 twin, 13 family
Bathrooms: 18 en suite, 3 private showers, 4 public
Bed & Breakfast: single £40.00-£65.00, double £75.00-£77.00
Credit Cards: Mastercard/Eurocard/Visa/Barclaycard/Delta/Eurocheque

Euro Hotel

APPLIED

53 Cartwright Gardens, London WC1H 9EL
Tel: (0171) 387 4321
Fax: (0171) 383 5044
E-mail: Reception@eurohotel.co.uk
URL: www.eurohotel.co.uk
⊖ Russell Square
Centrally located hotel close to the West End and British Museum.
Bedrooms: 8 single, 7 double, 10 twin, 9 family
Bathrooms: 9 en suite, 11 public
Bed & Breakfast: single £45.00-£47.00, double £60.00-£85.00
Credit Cards: Mastercard/Eurocard/Visa/Barclaycard/American Express/Switch/Delta/Eurocheque

Euston Plaza Hotel

17-18 Upper Woburn Place, London WC1H 0HT
Tel: (0171) 383 4105
Fax: (0171) 383 4106
⊖/⇌ Euston
Georgian building opposite Euston station and close to St Pancras. The hotel is of Swedish design with all modern amenities.
Bedrooms: 20 single, 50 double, 70 twin, 10 family
Bathrooms: 150 en suite
Evening meal: 1800 (l.o. 2200)
Credit Cards: Mastercard/Visa/Barclaycard/American Express/Switch/Diners/Eurocheque

Forte Posthouse Bloomsbury

COMMENDED

Coram Street, London WC1N 1HT
Tel: (0171) 837 1200
Fax: (0171) 837 5374
⊖/⇌ Euston, ⊖ Russell Square
Modern hotel. Ideally located for theatreland, shopping and the City.
Bedrooms: 135 single, 60 double, 59 twin, 30 family
Bathrooms: 284 en suite
Bed & Breakfast: single £75.00-£170.00, double £80.00-£175.00
Evening meal: 1800 (l.o. 2200)
Parking for: 201
Credit Cards: Mastercard/Eurocard/Visa/Barclaycard/American Express/Switch/Delta/Diners/Eurocheque

Garth Hotel

Listed APPROVED

69 Gower Street, London WC1E 6HJ
Tel: (0171) 636 5761
Fax: (0171) 637 4854
⊖/⇌ Euston, ⇌ St Pancras
Small, family-run hotel, convenient for tourist attractions.
Bedrooms: 3 single, 4 double, 5 twin, 5 family
Bathrooms: 2 en suite, 9 private showers, 3 public
Bed & Breakfast: single £30.00-£42.00, double £42.00-£64.00
Credit Cards: Mastercard/Eurocard/Visa/Barclaycard/American Express/Switch/Delta/Diners/Eurocheque

George Hotel

APPROVED

58-60 Cartwright Gardens, London WC1H 9EL
Tel: (0171) 387 8777
Fax: (0171) 387 8666
E-mail: ghotel@aol.com
URL: www.cityscan.co.uk/george
⊖ Russell Square
Traditional English bed and breakfast hotel in a quiet central location. Convenient for the West End and British Museum.
Bedrooms: 15 single, 4 double, 4 twin, 17 family
Bathrooms: 4 en suite, 4 private showers, 12 public

Bed & Breakfast: single £43.50-£48.50, double £59.50-£64.50
Credit Cards: Mastercard/Visa/Barclaycard/Switch/Delta/Eurocheque

Gower House Hotel

Listed APPROVED

57 Gower Street, London WC1E 6HJ
Tel: (0171) 636 4685
Fax: (0171) 636 4685
Goodge Street, Euston
Friendly bed and breakfast hotel within easy walking distance of the British Museum, shops, theatres and restaurants.
Bedrooms: 4 single, 2 double, 6 twin, 4 family
Bathrooms: 3 private, 3 public
Bed & Breakfast: single £38.00-£39.00, double £47.00-£49.00
Credit Cards: Mastercard/Eurocard/Visa/Barclaycard/Switch/Delta/Eurocheque

Holiday Inn London – King's Cross/Bloomsbury

1 King's Cross Road, London WC1X 9HX
Tel: (0171) 833 3900
Fax: (0171) 917 6163
King's Cross/Farringdon
Opened in April 1992, the building has a post-modern exterior and a traditional interior. Hotel features include: 405 bedrooms with air-conditioning, restaurant, cocktail bar, lounge and health club.
Bedrooms: 66 single, 176 double, 163 twin
Bathrooms: 405 en suite
Bed & Breakfast: single £190.00, double £200.00
Evening meal: 1800 (l.o. 2200)
Parking for: 12
Credit Cards: Mastercard/Eurocard/Visa/Barclaycard/American Express/Switch/Delta/Diners/Eurocheque

Hotel Russell

COMMENDED

Russell Square, London WC1B 5BE
Tel: (0171) 837 6470
Fax: (0171) 837 2857
Russell Square
Facing Russell Square and close to the British Museum. Underground station nearby offering a direct service to the West End and Heathrow. Prices are subject to change. In 1998 the hotel celebrated 100 years of operation.
Bedrooms: 107 single, 97 double, 103 twin, 22 family
Bathrooms: 329 en suite
Bed only: single £149.00-£169.00, double £189.00-£214.00
Evening meal: 1800 (l.o. 2230)
Credit Cards: Mastercard/Visa/Barclaycard/American Express/Switch/Delta/Diners/Eurocheque

Kingsley Hotel

Bloomsbury Way, London WC1A 2SD
Tel: (0171) 242 5881
Fax: (0171) 831 0225
Holborn, Euston
Edwardian hotel built in 1898 with original-style decor. Bar, carvery restaurant and full conference facilities.
Bedrooms: 8 single, 32 double, 79 twin, 19 family
Bathrooms: 138 en suite
Evening meal: 1730 (l.o. 2200)
Credit Cards: Mastercard/Eurocard/Visa/Barclaycard/American Express/Switch/Delta/Diners/Eurocheque

Le Meridien Waldorf

HIGHLY COMMENDED

Aldwych, London WC2B 4DD
Tel: (0171) 836 2400
Fax: (0171) 836 7244
Charing Cross/Waterloo
Winner of the Hotel of the Year (chain of five+ hotels) in the 1998 London Tourism Awards.
The Waldorf Meridien, located in London's theatreland, has 292 air-conditioned bedrooms, two restaurants, two bars and 14 conference suites.
Bedrooms: 110 single, 151 double, 31 twin
Bathrooms: 292 en suite
Bed only: single £255.00, double £295.00
Evening meal: 1800 (l.o. 2315)
Credit Cards: Mastercard/Visa/Barclaycard/American Express/Delta/Diners/Eurocheque

London Ryan Hotel

Gwynne Place, King's Cross Road, King's Cross, London WC1X 9QN
Tel: (0171) 278 2480
Fax: (0171) 837 3776
King's Cross
Modern hotel with parking facilities. Well situated for visiting the City and the West End.
Bedrooms: 30 single, 117 double, 46 twin, 18 family
Bathrooms: 211 en suite
Evening meal: 1800 (l.o. 2200)
Parking for: 26
Credit Cards: Mastercard/Eurocard/Visa/Barclaycard/American Express/Switch/Delta/Diners/Eurocheque

The Montague

APPLIED

15 Montague Street, Bloomsbury, London WC1B 5BJ
Tel: (0171) 637 1001
Fax: (0171) 637 2516
Euston, Russell Square
Georgian-style, traditional town house hotel. Centrally but quietly located within walking distance of Covent Garden, Oxford Street and theatres. Opposite the British Museum. Close to the City.
Bedrooms: 26 single, 35 double, 9 twin, 6 family
Bathrooms: 76 en suite
Bed only: single £155.00-£191.00, double £185.00-£240.00
Evening meal: 1730 (l.o. 2200)
Credit Cards: Mastercard/Eurocard/Visa/Barclaycard/American Express/Diners

Radisson Edwardian Hampshire Hotel

HIGHLY COMMENDED

31-36 Leicester Square, London WC2H 7LH
Tel: (0171) 839 9399
Fax: (0171) 930 8122
Leicester Square
Country house-style hotel in the heart of theatreland. Within walking distance of the main shopping areas and tourist attractions.
Bedrooms: 18 single, 77 double, 27 twin, 2 family
Bathrooms: 124 en suite
Bed only: single £220.00-£315.00, double £220.00-£315.00
Evening meal: 1800 (l.o. 2300)
Credit Cards: Mastercard/Eurocard/Visa/Barclaycard/American Express/Switch/Delta/Diners/Eurocheque

Radisson Edwardian Kenilworth

Great Russell Street, London WC1B 3LB
Tel: (0171) 637 3477
Fax: (0171) 631 3133
⊖ Tottenham Court Road
Thoroughly English hotel near to theatreland, Oxford Street shops and the City.
Bedrooms: 54 single, 82 double, 42 twin, 7 family
Bathrooms: 185 en suite
Bed only: single £109.00-£160.00, double £140.00-£193.00
Evening meal: 1800 (l.o. 2200)
Credit Cards: Mastercard/Eurocard/Barclaycard/American Express/Switch/Delta/Diners/Eurocheque

Radisson Edwardian Marlborough

Bloomsbury Street, London WC1B 3QD
Tel: (0171) 636 5601
Fax: (0171) 636 0532
⊖ Tottenham Court Road
Near the British Museum and in the heart of Bloomsbury, London's literary centre.
Bedrooms: 15 single, 99 double, 56 twin
Bathrooms: 170 en suite
Bed only: single £142.00-£205.00, double £163.00-£225.00
Evening meal: 1750 (l.o. 2200)
Credit Cards: Mastercard/Eurocard/Visa/Barclaycard/American Express/Switch/Delta/Diners/Eurocheque

Radisson Edwardian Mountbatten

20 Monmouth Street, Seven Dials, Covent Garden, London WC2H 9HD
Tel: (0171) 836 4300
Fax: (0171) 240 3540
⊖ Covent Garden
Delightful English country house-style hotel, including memorabilia from Lord Mountbatten's family home. Convenient for the West End and theatreland.
Bedrooms: 23 single, 57 double, 47 twin
Bathrooms: 127 en suite
Bed only: single £171.00-£242.00, double £184.00-£256.00
Evening meal: 1800 (l.o. 2300)
Credit Cards: Mastercard/Eurocard/Visa/Barclaycard/American Express/Switch/Delta/Diners/Eurocheque

Radisson Edwardian Pastoria Hotel

3-6 St Martin's Street, Leicester Square, London WC2H 7HL
Tel: (0171) 930 8641
Fax: (0171) 925 0551
⊖ Leicester Square
The hotel is located at the centre of many top attractions, including the West End and theatreland. Decorated in a charming Edwardian style.
Bedrooms: 10 single, 18 double, 30 twin
Bathrooms: 58 en suite
Bed only: single £135.00-£180.00, double £156.00-£220.00
Evening meal: (l.o. 2200)
Credit Cards: Mastercard/Eurocard/Visa/Barclaycard/American Express/Switch/Delta/Diners/Eurocheque

Repton Hotel

APPLIED

31-32 Bedford Place, London WC1 5JH
Tel: (0171) 436 4922
Fax: (0171) 636 7045
E-mail: repton@lhghotels.demon.co.uk
⊖ Holborn
Georgian building of historical interest in a quiet street. Ideal location close to British Museum, Oxford Street and theatreland. Comfortable and good value for money.
Bedrooms: 9 single, 8 double, 6 twin, 7 family
Bathrooms: 30 en suite, 1 public
Credit Cards: Mastercard/Visa/Barclaycard/Switch/Delta/Diners/Eurocheque

Royal Adelphi Hotel

Listed APPROVED

21 Villiers Street, London WC2N 6ND
Tel: (0171) 930 8764
Fax: (0171) 930 8735
⊖/⇌ Charing Cross, ⊖ Embankment
Two minutes from Trafalgar Square and Covent Garden and close to theatreland.
Bedrooms: 20 single, 12 double, 13 twin, 2 family
Bathrooms: 34 en suite, 4 public
Bed & Breakfast: single £45.00-£63.00, double £63.00-£80.00
Evening meal: 1800 (l.o. 2300)
Credit Cards: Mastercard/Eurocard/Visa/Barclaycard/American Express/Switch/Delta/Diners/Eurocheque

Royal Scot Hotel

100 King's Cross Road, London WC1X 9DT
Tel: (0171) 278 2434
Fax: (0171) 833 0798
⊖/⇌ King's Cross
Centrally located hotel, a few minutes' walk from King's Cross station and Thameslink.
Bedrooms: 29 single, 32 double, 261 twin, 29 family
Bathrooms: 351 en suite
Bed only: single £100.00-£115.00, double £110.00-£140.00
Bed & Breakfast: single £110.00-£125.00, double £130.00-£160.00
Evening meal: 1800 (l.o. 2145)
Parking for: 35
Credit Cards: Mastercard/Eurocard/Visa/Barclaycard/American Express/Switch/Delta/Diners/Eurocheque

Royal Trafalgar Thistle Hotel

Whitcomb Street, London WC2H 7HG
Tel: (0171) 930 4477
Fax: (0171) 925 2149
⊖ Leicester Square
Located between Trafalgar Square and Leicester Square ideal for theatreland, shopping, sightseeing and business.
Bedrooms: 36 single, 24 double, 48 twin
Bathrooms: 108 en suite
Bed & Breakfast: single £105.00-£140.00, double £140.00-£180.00
Evening meal: 1700 (l.o. 2330)
Credit Cards: Mastercard/Eurocard/Visa/Barclaycard/American Express/Switch/Delta/Diners/Eurocheque

St Athan's Hotel

Listed APPROVED

20 Tavistock Place, Russell Square, London WC1H 9RE
Tel: (0171) 837 9140/(0171) 837 9627
Fax: (0171) 833 8352
⊖ Russell Square
Small, family-run hotel.
Bedrooms: 14 single, 13 double, 15 twin, 6 family
Bathrooms: 8 en suite 12 public
Bed & Breakfast: single £30.00-£40.00, double £40.00-£50.00
Credit Cards: Mastercard/Eurocard/Visa/Barclaycard/American Express/Diners/Eurocheque

St Giles Hotel

Bedford Avenue, London WC1B 3AS
Tel: (0171) 300 3000/
(0171) 300 3030
Fax: (0171) 300 3003
Tottenham Court Road
Situated at the junction of Oxford Street and Tottenham Court Road. Close to the British Museum. Underground car park (NCP).
Bedrooms: 214 single, 256 double, 228 twin, 13 family
Bathrooms: 711 en suite
Bed only: single £79.00-£94.00, double £104.00-£124.00
Evening meal: 1700 (l.o. 2300)
Parking for: 140
Credit Cards: Mastercard/Eurocard/Visa/Barclaycard/American Express/Switch/Delta/Diners

The Savoy

The Strand, London WC2R 0EU
Tel: (0171) 836 4343
Fax: (0171) 240 6040
E-mail: info@the-savoy.co.uk
URL: www.savoy-group.co.uk
Charing Cross
Midway between the City and the West End, in the heart of theatreland, and with excellent views of the Thames.
Bedrooms: 55 single, 100 twin, 52 family
Bathrooms: 207 en suite
Evening meal: 1800 (l.o. 2400)
Parking for: 58
Credit Cards: Mastercard/Eurocard/Visa/Barclaycard/American Express/Switch/Delta/Diners

Strand Palace Hotel — Commended

Strand, London WC2R 0JJ
Tel: (0171) 836 8080
Fax: (0171) 836 2077
Charing Cross
Situated in the heart of theatreland, adjacent to Covent Garden. A perfect base for leisure and business travellers. Prices quoted are for 1998 and are subject to change.
Bedrooms: 380 single, 135 double, 254 twin, 14 family
Bathrooms: 783 en suite
Bed only: single £174.00, double £196.00
Evening meal: 1730 (l.o. 2330)
Credit Cards: Mastercard/Eurocard/Visa/Barclaycard/American Express/Switch/Diners/Eurocheque

W2 Paddington/Bayswater

Abbey Court & Westpoint Hotel — Listed Approved

170-174 Sussex Gardens, London W2 1TP
Tel: (0171) 402 0281/(0171) 402 0704
Fax: (0171) 224 9114/
(0171) 262 2055
E-mail: info@AbbeyCourt.com
URL: www.AbbeyCourt.com
Paddington, Lancaster Gate
Budget accommodation in central London, with easy access to London's tourist attractions and shopping areas. Within walking distance of Hyde Park. Car parking available.
Bedrooms: 26 single, 39 double, 23 twin, 32 family
Bathrooms: 88 en suite, 9 private showers, 10 public
Bed & Breakfast: single £32.00-£45.00, double £48.00-£64.00
Parking for: 35
Credit Cards: Mastercard/Visa/American Express/Switch

Admiral Hotel — Listed Approved

143 Sussex Gardens, Hyde Park, London W2 2RY
Tel: (0171) 723 7309
Fax: (0171) 723 8731
E-mail: frank@admiral143.demon.co.uk
URL: www.admiral143.demon.co.uk
Paddington, Lancaster Gate
A bed and breakfast with 19 en suite bedrooms, five minutes from Hyde Park and Paddington station. Clean and comfortable accommodation at economic prices.
Bedrooms: 2 single, 2 double, 6 twin, 9 family
Bathrooms: 19 en suite, 1 public
Bed only: single £35.00-£40.00, double £58.00-£62.00
Bed & Breakfast: single £38.00-£45.00, double £64.00-£68.00
Parking for: 1
Credit Cards: Mastercard/Eurocard/Visa/Barclaycard/Switch/Delta/Eurocheque

Albro House Hotel — Approved

155 Sussex Gardens, London W2 2RY
Tel: (0171) 724 2931/(0171) 706 8153
Fax: (0171) 262 2278
Paddington
Pleasant hotel near Hyde Park. All rooms with private facilities, radio, telephone, TV, tea making facilities and a hairdryer. Central location, ideal for shopping and sightseeing.
Bedrooms: 2 single, 6 double, 6 twin, 4 family
Bathrooms: 16 en suite, 1 public
Bed & Breakfast: single £38.00-£56.00, double £54.00-£78.00
Parking for: 1
Credit Cards: Mastercard/Eurocard/Visa/Barclaycard/Diners/Eurocheque

Allandale Hotel — Listed Approved

3 Devonshire Terrace, Lancaster Gate, London W2 3DN
Tel: (0171) 723 8311/(0171) 723 7807
Fax: (0171) 723 8311
Lancaster Gate
Small, family-run hotel, close to the West End and many of London's attractions.
Bedrooms: 2 single, 8 double, 5 twin, 5 family
Bathrooms: 18 en suite, 1 public
Bed & Breakfast: single £40.00-£45.00, double £55.00-£60.00
Credit Cards: Mastercard/Eurocard/Visa/Barclaycard/American Express/Delta/Diners/Eurocheque

Balmoral House Hotel

156 Sussex Gardens, London W2 1UD
Tel: (0171) 723 7445
Fax: (0171) 402 0118
Paddington
One of the few original and traditionally family-run bed and breakfast hotels in the Hyde Park area. (Payment by credit card is subject to a five per cent surcharge.)
Bedrooms: 4 single, 9 double, 7 twin, 10 family
Bathrooms: 24 en suite, 4 private showers, 5 public
Bed & Breakfast: single £40.00-£45.00, double £60.00-£65.00
Parking for: 3
Credit Cards: Mastercard/Eurocard/Visa/Barclaycard/Eurocheque

NORFOLK COURT & St. David's Hotel

16 Norfolk Square, near Hyde Park, London W2 1RS

Stay in central London, yet in a quiet Norfolk Square Garden. One minute from Paddington Station, ten minutes' from Oxford Street and Hyde Park. Members of the Hotels and Caterers Association and London Tourist Board. Famous for their cooked English Breakfast.

Single room basic £35.00 Single room with facilities £50.00
Double room basic £54.00 Double room with facilities £64.00
Triple room basic from £20.00 per person
Triple room with facilities from £25.00 per person

En-suite rooms available. Plus new telephone system with automatic wake up call and message and direct line in all rooms. Recommended by Frommer's and Fodor's Travel Guide Books. Personally managed by George.

Telephone: 0171-723 4963, 0171-402 9061 0171-723 3856 Fax: 0171-402 9061

MIDLAND HOTEL

2/5 St Chad's Street, King's Cross, London WC1H 8BD

Tel: 0171 837 1940 Fax: 0171 278 5033

- *Ideal for the young and budget conscious*
- *Centrally located – 3 minutes' walking distance from King's Cross underground station*
- *Rooms with ensuite facilities*
- *Colour TV Lounge with satellite channels*
- *Close to tourist attractions*
- *Friendly staff*
- *Games and Common Room*

Group discounts and special rates upon request.

ROYAL ADELPHI HOTEL

21 VILLIERS STREET
LONDON WC2N 6ND
TEL: 0171 930 8764 FAX: 0171 930 8735

All major credit cards accepted **English Tourist Board Listed and Approved**

This small and friendly hotel is a popular choice with tourists. Very centrally located in a prime position between Charing Cross and Embankment underground stations. Walking distance to Covent Garden, River Thames, Trafalgar Square, Piccadilly, Leicester Square, theatreland, the galleries and museums. All rooms with colour TV/Radio, telephone, hairdryer, tea/coffee facilities. Most rooms with private bathroom. Prices from £45.00 per night.

Hyde Park Rooms Hotel

Welcome to London
Nice Central Location
Car Parking Available

Tel: 0171 723 0225
0171 723 0965

137 Sussex Gardens, Hyde Park, W2 2RX

Singles from £26
Doubles from £38
Family Rooms from £50

RUDDIMANS HOTEL

...a warm and friendly atmosphere in the heart of London...

All rooms equipped with satellite TV, telephone, central heating and lounge for your relaxation. Outstanding English & Continental buffet breakfast included in the price of your stay.

160 - 162 Sussex Gardens
London W2 1UD
United Kingdom
Tel: 0171 723 1026
Fax: 0171 262 2983
www.characom.com/ruddhotel.co.uk

Rose Court Hotel

APPROVED

TEL: 0171-723-5128 FAX: 0171-723-1855
1 TALBOT SQUARE LONDON W2 1TR
ENGLAND

Easy to reach, close to Paddington Station and Lancaster Gate Underground. To ensure your stay is comfortable all our rooms have ensuite facilities, TV, telephone and central heating. Rates are from just £45 single and £60 double and this even includes VAT and full English breakfast. We accept all major credit cards.

LONDON

eurohotel

51-53 Cartwright Gardens, London WC1H 9EL
Tel: +44 (0) 171 387 4321
Fax: +44 (0) 171 383 5044

Visit our web site before you visit us. Meet the staff, view photos of our hotel and be surprised by our excellent prices and perfect location.

Web: www.eurohotel.co.uk

Where everybody is welcome

Barry House Hotel
APPROVED

12 Sussex Place, London W2 2TP
Tel: (0171) 723 7340/
(0171) 723 0994
Fax: (0171) 723 9775
E-mail: bh-hotel@liaison.demon.co.uk
URL: www.hotel.uk.com/barryhouse
⊖/⇌ Paddington, ⊖ Lancaster Gate
Friendly, family-run bed and breakfast close to Paddington station and Hyde Park. En suite rooms with TV, telephone and tea and coffee making facilities.
Bedrooms: 4 single, 4 double, 7 twin, 3 family
Bathrooms: 14 en suite, 1 private shower, 2 public
Bed & Breakfast: single £30.00-£52.00, double £64.00-£75.00
Credit Cards: Mastercard/Eurocard/Visa/Barclaycard/American Express/Switch/Delta/Diners/Eurocheque

Bayswater Inn

8-16 Princes Square, London W2 4NT
Tel: (0171) 727 8621
Fax: (0171) 727 3346
⊖ Bayswater/Queensway
In a quiet residential square in close proximity to Portobello Road market, Oxford Street, Marble Arch and many tourist attractions.
Bedrooms: 22 single, 35 double, 79 twin, 55 family
Bathrooms: 191 en suite
Bed & Breakfast: single £50.00-£75.00, double £60.00-£90.00
Evening meal: 1800 (l.o. 0100)
Credit Cards: Mastercard/Eurocard/Barclaycard/American Express/Switch/Delta/Diners/Eurocheque

Beverley House Hotel
COMMENDED

142 Sussex Gardens, London W2 1UB
Tel: (0171) 723 3380
Fax: (0171) 262 0324
⊖/⇌ Paddington, ⊖ Lancaster Gate
A completely refurbished hotel, close to Paddington and Lancaster Gate stations and within walking distance of Hyde Park and Oxford Street.
Bedrooms: 6 single, 5 double, 6 twin, 6 family
Bathrooms: 23 en suite
Bed & Breakfast: single £43.00-£58.00, double £52.00-£78.00
Parking for: 2
Credit Cards: Mastercard/Eurocard/Visa/Barclaycard/American Express/Switch/Delta/Diners/Eurocheque

The Blakemore Hotel

30 Leinster Gardens, London W2 3AN
Tel: (0171) 262 4591
Fax: (0171) 724 1472
E-mail: blake@star.u-net.com
⊖/⇌ Paddington, ⊖ Bayswater
The hotel is situated close to Hyde Park and Oxford Street and has a bar, coffee lounge, restaurant and three conference rooms.
Bedrooms: 58 single, 27 double, 59 twin, 19 family
Bathrooms: 163 en suite
Bed only: single £82.50, double £132.00
Evening meal: 1730 (l.o. 2130)
Credit Cards: Mastercard/Eurocard/Visa/Barclaycard/American Express/Diners/Eurocheque

Blue Bells Hotel
APPLIED

14 Pembridge Square, London W2 4EH
Tel: (0171) 727 6666/
(0171) 727 6677
Fax: (0171) 727 6677
⊖ Notting Hill Gate/Bayswater,
⊖/⇌ Paddington
Blue Bells Hotel is a detached property in Pembridge Square, situated just north of Notting Hill Gate. Five minutes' walk from Notting Hill Gate underground station and half a mile from Paddington underground and train station.
Bedrooms: 8 single, 2 double, 3 twin, 12 family
Bathrooms: 10 en suite, 2 private, 10 public
Bed only: single £35.00, double £40.00-£60.00
Credit Cards: Mastercard/Visa/Barclaycard

Cardiff Hotel

5-9 Norfolk Square, London W2 1RU
Tel: (0171) 723 9068/(0171) 723 3513
Fax: (0171) 402 2342
⊖/⇌ Paddington
Friendly, family-run hotel situated on a beautiful garden square, with easy access to tourist attractions and shopping. Underground and bus links to all of London. Close to Paddington station and Heathrow Express link.
Bedrooms: 18 single, 14 double, 11 twin, 15 family
Bathrooms: 47 en suite, 9 private showers, 1 public
Bed & Breakfast: single £40.00-£52.00, double £57.00-£75.00
Credit Cards: Mastercard/Eurocard/Visa/Barclaycard/Switch/Delta/Eurocheque

Caring Hotel

24 Craven Hill Gardens, London W2 3EA
Tel: (0171) 262 8708
Fax: (0171) 262 8590
⊖ Queensway, ⊖/⇌ Paddington
Small bed and breakfast hotel within easy access of Marble Arch and the West End. Close to Paddington underground station.
Bedrooms: 11 double, 7 twin, 8 family
Bathrooms: 13 private, 7 private showers, 4 public
Bed & Breakfast: single £38.00-£44.00, double £44.00-£65.00
Credit Cards: Mastercard/Eurocard/Visa/Barclaycard/American Express/Switch/Delta/Eurocheque

Castleton Hotel
Listed APPROVED

164-166 Sussex Gardens, London W2 1UD
Tel: (0171) 706 4666
Fax: (0171) 706 2288
⊖/⇌ Paddington
Small, friendly bed and breakfast near Paddington station. All rooms are en suite and have TV and telephone. A bar and restaurant are available.
Bedrooms: 3 single, 10 double, 12 twin, 6 family
Bathrooms: 31 en suite
Bed & Breakfast: single £40.00-£55.00, double £60.00-£65.00
Evening meal: 1700 (l.o. 2400)
Parking for: 8
Credit Cards: Mastercard/Eurocard/Visa/Barclaycard/Switch/Delta/Diners/Eurocheque

Good Value Accommodation
in Central London

Central Reservations Telephone 0171 402 0202

Abbey Court and Westpoint Hotel

Central London hotel - two minute walk to Paddington and Lancaster Gate Stations. This hotel has long been a popular choice amongst tourists due to its pleasant central location, with easy access to London's major tourist attractions, museums, theatres, Oxford Street and Piccadilly Circus. Choice of rooms with en suite bathrooms, colour TV and radio/intercom.

200m from Paddington station for connection to Heathrow Express

Car Park - Bed and Breakfast

RATES	LOW SEASON	HIGH SEASON
Singles	from £30.00	from £46.00
Doubles *pp*	from £26.00	from £31.00
Triples *pp*	from £24.00	from £26.00
Family Room *pp*	from £19.00	from £22.00

Abbey Court and Westpoint Hotel
170-174 Sussex Gardens
Hyde Park London W2 1TP

***Tel* 0171 402 0704**
***Fax* 0171 262 2055**
***http//www.*westpointhotel.com**
***e-mail* info@westpointhotel.com**

***Tel* 0171 402 0281**
***Fax* 0171 224 9114**
***http//www.*abbeycourt.com**
***e-mail* info@abbeycourt.com**

Sass House Hotel

Central London hotel located within two minutes walk from Hyde Park. Most rooms with private showers/toilets. All rooms have colour TV and radio. Easy access to all tourist attractions – within 5 minutes walking distance of Lancaster Gate and Paddington underground/mainline stations and Heathrow Express.

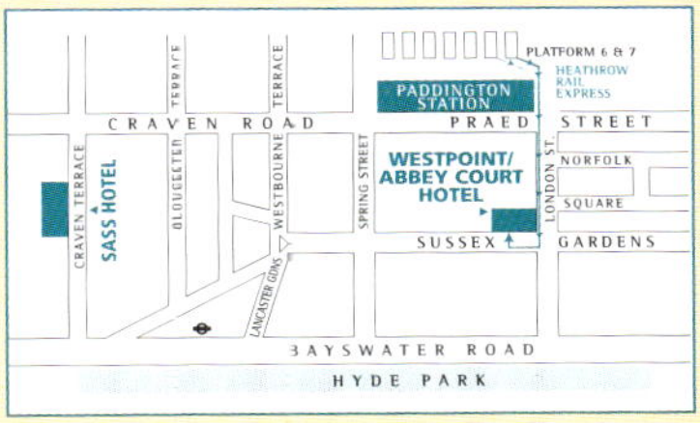

RATES	LOW SEASON	HIGH SEASON
Twin *pp*	from £23.00	from £28.00
Doubles *pp*	from £19.00	from £24.00
Triples *pp*	from £20.00	from £26.00

Sass House Hotel
11 Craven Terrace,
Hyde Park,
London W2 3QT

***Tel* 0171 262 2325**
***Fax* 0171 262 0889**
***http//www.*sasshotel.com**
***e-mail* info@sasshotel.com**

Central Park Hotel

Commended

49 Queensborough Terrace, London W2 3SS
Tel: (0171) 229 2424
Fax: (0171) 229 2904
⊖ Queensway/Bayswater
Modern hotel in a central, yet quiet location, close to many attractions and well served by public transport.
Bedrooms: 39 single, 33 double, 134 twin, 45 family
Bathrooms: 251 en suite
Bed & Breakfast: single £105.00-£115.00, double £115.00-£130.00
Evening meal: 1745 (l.o. 2045)
Parking for: 22
Credit Cards: Mastercard/Visa/Barclaycard/American Express/Switch/Delta/Diners

Charles Dickens Hotel

66 Lancaster Gate, Bayswater Road, London W2 3NZ
Tel: (0171) 262 5090
Fax: (0171) 723 1244
⊖ Lancaster Gate
Set in a Georgian terrace and close to Kensington Gardens, the Charles Dickens is convenient for theatres and museums.
Bedrooms: 13 single, 62 double, 100 twin, 13 family
Bathrooms: 185 en suite
Bed only: single £98.00-£112.00, double £113.00-£129.00
Bed & Breakfast: single £107.20-£121.20, double £122.20-£138.20
Evening meal: 1800 (l.o. 2145)
Credit Cards: Mastercard/Visa/Barclaycard/American Express/Switch/Delta/Diners/Eurocheque

Classic Hotel

92 Sussex Gardens, Hyde Park, London W2 1UH
Tel: (0171) 706 7776
Fax: (0171) 706 8136
E-mail: classichotel@compuserve.com
⊖/⇌ Paddington
Listed Grade II building. Exclusive front garden with trees on either side.
Bedrooms: 2 single, 3 double, 6 twin, 2 family
Bathrooms: 13 en suite
Bed only: single £40.00-£45.00, double £55.00-£60.00
Bed & Breakfast: single £45.00-£52.00, double £60.00-£70.00
Parking for: 2
Credit Cards: Mastercard/Eurocard/Visa/Barclaycard/American Express/Delta/Diners/Eurocheque

Commodore Hotel

50 Lancaster Gate, Hyde Park, London W2 3NA
Tel: (0171) 402 5291
Fax: (0171) 262 1088
⊖ Lancaster Gate
In a quiet Victorian square opposite Hyde Park.
Bedrooms: 9 single, 21 double, 34 twin, 26 family
Bathrooms: 90 en suite
Bed & Breakfast: single £95.00, double £109.00
Evening meal: 1800 (l.o. 2300)
Credit Cards: Mastercard/Eurocard/Visa/Barclaycard/American Express/Delta/Diners/Eurocheque

Cordova House Hotel

14-16 Craven Hill, London W2 3DU
Tel: (0171) 723 1065/(0171) 262 0111
Fax: (0171) 262 7772
⊖/⇌ Paddington, ⊖ Lancaster Gate
Most of London's many colourful attractions are within easy reach, including the famous department stores and London's bustling nightlife.
Bedrooms: 4 single, 6 double, 39 twin, 10 family
Bathrooms: 59 en suite
Bed & Breakfast: single £75.00, double £100.00
Credit Cards: Mastercard/Visa/Barclaycard/American Express/Diners/Eurocheque

The Delmere Hotel

Commended

128-130 Sussex Gardens, Hyde Park, London W2 1UB
Tel: (0171) 706 3344
Fax: (0171) 262 1863
E-mail: 100255.3347@compuserve.com
⊖/⇌ Paddington
A quality, Victorian town house close to Marble Arch and Hyde Park. La Perla Restaurant at the Delmere is also open in the evenings to non-residents.
Bedrooms: 10 single, 13 double, 12 twin, 3 family
Bathrooms: 38 en suite
Bed & Breakfast: single £66.00-£78.00, double £83.00-£98.00
Evening meal: 1800 (l.o. 2200)
Parking for: 2
Credit Cards: Mastercard/Eurocard/Visa/Barclaycard/American Express/Switch/Delta/Diners/Eurocheque

Duke of Leinster

Listed Approved

34 Queen's Gardens, London W2 3AA
Tel: (0171) 258 0079/(0171) 258 1839
Fax: (0171) 262 0741
E-mail: DukeofLeinsterHotel@Go-fax.com
⊖ Queensway/Bayswater
Ideally situated near Hyde Park and Marble Arch and near to rail and underground stations.
Bedrooms: 8 single, 13 double, 13 twin, 7 family
Bathrooms: 41 en suite
Bed & Breakfast: single £54.00, double £74.00
Credit Cards: Mastercard/Eurocard/Visa/Barclaycard/American Express/Switch/Delta/Diners

Dylan Hotel

Listed Approved

14 Devonshire Terrace, Lancaster Gate, London W2 3DW
Tel: (0171) 723 3280
Fax: (0171) 402 2443
⊖/⇌ Paddington, ⊖ Lancaster Gate
Small hotel in central London. Near Hyde Park and Kensington Gardens.
Bedrooms: 4 single, 4 double, 7 twin, 3 family
Bathrooms: 7 en suite, 4 private showers, 3 public
Bed & Breakfast: single £35.00-£48.00, double £55.00-£68.00
Credit Cards: Barclaycard/American Express/Diners/Eurocheque

Europa House Hotel

Listed Approved

151 Sussex Gardens, London W2 2RY
Tel: (0171) 723 7343/(0171) 402 1923
Fax: (0171) 224 9331
E-mail: europahouse@enterprise.net
⊖/⇌ Paddington, ⊖ Lancaster Gate
Small, family-run hotel convenient for Hyde Park, the Heathrow Airbus stop and the Paddington rail link to Heathrow.
Bedrooms: 3 single, 3 double, 6 twin, 6 family

For a friendly atmosphere, stay at…

Springfield Hotel

- Ideally situated just minutes from Paddington Station, Hyde Park and Marble Arch.
- All the comforts you require. All rooms with ensuite, colour satellite TV, direct dial telephone, tea making facilities and full central heating.
- Generous English breakfast and VAT included in price.

Rates from just £45-£50 single and £55-£60 double. Family rooms from £70 per night.

To book now contact: 154 Sussex Gardens, Hyde Park, London W2
Tel: 0171-723-9898 Fax: 0171-723-0874

Access MasterCard VISA Eurocard English Tourist Board LONDON MEMBER

THE KINGSWAY HOTEL

COMMENDED

Situated in a beautifully landscaped garden square, in the heart of London, 2 mins' walk from Paddington Station. Hyde Park and Marble Arch also within walking distance. Completely refurbished to a high standard, rooms have TV, direct-dial telephone, tea/coffee making facilities and hairdryer; most with full en-suite bathrooms, and ironing facilities.

Single £38 - £56 Double £54-£76

incl. of 17½% VAT, service charge and English Breakfast

27 Norfolk Square, Hyde Park, London W2 1RX
Tel: 0171 723 5569/7784 Fax: 0171 723 7317
E-mail: kingsway.hotel@btinternet.com
Web: http://www.btinternet.com/~kingsway hotel/index.html

GOWER HOTEL

129 Sussex Gardens
London W2 2RX
0171 262 2262 Fax: 0171 262 2006

Small family-run hotel, centrally located close to Paddington Station, excellent for sightseeing and shopping, Hyde Park, Madame Tussaud's, Oxford Street plus many more attractions close by. All rooms are en-suite, with radio, TV (video & Satellite), direct-dial telephone and tea & coffee facilities. Single rooms £44. Double/Twin £60. Triple £22-£28. Family Room £20-£24. Prices per person & include full English breakfast and VAT.
Credit cards welcome.

BARRY HOUSE HOTEL

12, Sussex Place, Hyde Park, London W2 2TP

Friendly family-run B&B
Comfortable en-suite rooms
Convenient Central Location
English Breakfast included
Call now!

RAC Listed

APPROVED

0171 723 7340 / 0171 723 0994

Fax: 0171 723 9775 www.hotel.uk.com

Whenever you think of London, think of

Prince William Hotel

The Friendly Efficient hotel of London

minutes to Hyde Park, Oxford Street, Paddington & Heathrow Express. Tube and Bus to the West End, Entertainment and Shopping. Most rooms with private facilities, all with direct dial telephone, free Sky TV & radio, and complimentary tea & coffee making facilities. 24 hour reception, lounge, hair dryers and ironing facilities. Sight seeing and theatre tickets available on request.

Single rooms from £39, Double rooms from £59
All inclusive of service, VAT and continental breakfast
42-44 Gloucester Terrace, London W2 3DA
Tel - 0171 724 7414 or Fax - 0171 706 2411

Location, Friendliness and Value

EUROPA HOUSE HOTEL

COMFORTABLE
CONVENIENT
CENTRAL...

yet very economical

For details of our warm family welcome contact:

151 Sussex Gardens, Hyde Park, London W2

Tel: 0171 723 7343/402 1923
Fax: 0171 224 9331

English Tourist Board Listed
Member of the London Tourist Board
email: europahouse@enterprise.net

Bathrooms: 18 en suite, 1 public
Bed & Breakfast: single £45.00, double £65.00
Parking for: 1
Credit Cards: Visa/Barclaycard/American Express/Switch/Delta/Diners/Eurocheque

Garden Court Hotel

COMMENDED

30-31 Kensington Gardens Square, London W2 4BG
Tel: (0171) 229 2553
Fax: (0171) 727 2749
⊖/⇌ Paddington
Friendly, family-owned hotel, in a quiet Victorian garden square in central London. Convenient for all transport facilities.
Bedrooms: 11 single, 7 double, 6 twin, 8 family
Bathrooms: 16 en suite, 1 private shower, 5 public
Bed & Breakfast: single £34.00-£48.00, double £50.00-£76.00
Credit Cards: Eurocard/Visa/Barclaycard/Eurocheque

Gower Hotel

Listed APPROVED

129 Sussex Gardens, Hyde Park, London W2 2RX
Tel: (0171) 262 2262
Fax: (0171) 262 2006
⊖/⇌ Paddington
Family-run hotel, convenient for Hyde Park and Oxford Street.
Bedrooms: 5 single, 3 double, 2 twin, 10 family
Bathrooms: 18 en suite, 1 public
Bed & Breakfast: single £44.00-£48.00, double £60.00-£68.00
Parking for: 1
Credit Cards: Mastercard/Eurocard/Visa/Barclaycard/Switch/Delta/Eurocheque

Henry VIII Hotel

19 Leinster Gardens, London W2 3AN
Tel: (0171) 262 0117
Fax: (0171) 706 0472
E-mail: hotels@vienna-group.co.uk
URL: www.vienna-group.co.uk
⊖ Bayswater, ⊖/⇌ Paddington
The hotel is close to Hyde Park. Banqueting facilities are available for up to 100 people.
Bedrooms: 30 single, 13 double, 57 twin, 7 family
Bathrooms: 107 en suite
Bed & Breakfast: single £99.00, double £120.00
Evening meal: 1800 (l.o. 2200)
Credit Cards: Mastercard/Visa/Barclaycard/American Express/Switch/Diners/Eurocheque

Hospitality Inn Bayswater

104 Bayswater Road, London W2 3HL
Tel: (0171) 262 4461
Fax: (0171) 706 4560
⊖/⇌ Paddington, ⊖ Bayswater
Modern hotel overlooking Kensington Gardens and Hyde Park. Close to shops and tourist attractions. Free car parking available.
Bedrooms: 48 single, 46 double, 62 twin, 9 family
Bathrooms: 165 en suite
Bed only: single £105.00-£120.00, double £130.00-£145.00
Evening meal: 1800 (l.o. 2215)
Parking for: 80
Credit Cards: Mastercard/Eurocard/Visa/Barclaycard/American Express/Switch/Delta/Diners/Eurocheque

Hotel Slavia

2 Pembridge Square, London W2 4EW
Tel: (0171) 727 1316/(0171) 229 0803
Fax: (0171) 229 0803
⊖ Notting Hill Gate
Family-run hotel in a quiet garden square, 150 yards from Bayswater Road and public transport. Close to Portobello market.
Bedrooms: 4 single, 6 double, 13 twin, 8 family
Bathrooms: 31 en suite
Bed & Breakfast: single £40.00-£47.00, double £47.00-£65.00
Parking for: 1
Credit Cards: Mastercard/Eurocard/Visa/Barclaycard/American Express/Diners/Eurocheque

Hyde Park House

Listed

48 St Petersburgh Place, Queensway, London W2 4LD
Tel: (0171) 229 9652/(0171) 229 1687
⊖ Bayswater/Queensway
Near Hyde Park and Queensway and convenient for restaurants and wine bars.
Bedrooms: 4 single, 3 double, 2 twin, 3 family
Bathrooms: 1 private, 4 public
Bed & Breakfast: single £26.00-£28.00, double £38.00-£40.00
Credit Cards: Eurocheque

Hyde Park Rooms Hotel

Listed

137 Sussex Gardens, Hyde Park, London W2 2RX
Tel: (0171) 723 0225/(0171) 723 0965
⊖/⇌ Paddington, ⊖ Lancaster Gate
Small, family-run, centrally located hotel. Within walking distance of Hyde Park and Paddington station. Car parking available.
Bedrooms: 5 single, 6 double, 2 twin, 1 family
Bathrooms: 7 en suite, 2 private, 2 public
Parking for: 3
Credit Cards: Mastercard/Eurocard/Visa/Barclaycard/American Express/Diners/Eurocheque

Jarvis London Embassy Hotel

150 Bayswater Road, London W2 4RT
Tel: (0171) 229 1212
Fax: (0171) 229 2623
E-mail: londonembassy@jarvis.co.uk
⊖ Queensway
Overlooking Kensington Palace Gardens, a few minutes from Oxford Street and the West End.
Bedrooms: 37 single, 71 double, 105 twin
Bathrooms: 213 en suite
Bed only: single £120.00-£130.00, double £140.00-£150.00
Evening meal: 1730 (l.o. 2215)
Parking for: 34
Credit Cards: Mastercard/Eurocard/Visa/Barclaycard/American Express/Switch/Delta/Diners/Eurocheque

Kings Arms Hotel

APPROVED

254 Edgware Road, Paddington, London W2 1DS
Tel: (0171) 262 8441
Fax: (0171) 258 0556
E-mail: kingsarmshotel@compuserve.com
⊖ Edgware Road, ⊖/⇌ Paddington
Victorian public house hotel in London's West End, within walking distance of Oxford Street and conveniently located for all public transport.

A Country House in the Capital

THE BYRON HOTEL

36-38 Queensborough Terrace, London W2 3SH
Tel: +44 (0)171 243 0987 Fax: +44 (0)171 792 1957
e-mail: byron@capitalhotels.co.uk
http://www.capitalhotels.co.uk/

The Byron Hotel is ideally situated for visitors to central London. It provides modern standards of comfort in traditional surroundings which recapture some of the charm and elegance of Victorian England.

- Individually decorated rooms
- Full air conditioning
- 24-hour service
- TV, video and satellite
- All rooms with trouser press and hairdryer
- Excellent transport links

Room rates from £40 per person inclusive of breakfast and VAT

CLASSIC HOTEL, 92 SUSSEX GARDENS, HYDE PARK, LONDON W2 1UH.

Quality traditional London B & B hotel.

• All bedrooms with en-suite shower & toilet, central heating, direct-dial telephone, remote control colour T.V.s and drinks fridge.

• Travel/taxi/theatre bookings, 24 hour fax, e-mail messages, bureau-de-change, safe keeping of valuables and left luggage facilities for short and long terms.

• Within 5 minutes' walk of Paddington main line station and the newly opened London-Heathrow Express link. Hyde Park & West End are within easy reach of the Hotel. Restaurants, shops and banks are all nearby.

Train:	Paddington rail and tube station (District, Circle, Hammersmith & City Lines). New Heathrow Express Link
Air Bus:	A2 from Paddington to Heathrow Airport.
Buses:	7, 15, 27, 36, 12, 16, 23, 6, 98. at the doorstep Guests car parking available

Tariff:	Single from £45	Twin from £65
	Double from £60	Triple from £70

Tel: 0171 706 7776 Fax: 0171 706 8136
E-mail: classichotel@compuserve.com

HOLIDAY APARTMENTS

CRAVEN GARDENS Lodge

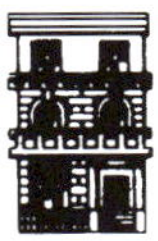

Seconds from Hyde Park, minutes from Oxford Street. Fully equipped apartments inc. TV and telephone. Private bathrooms and kitchens. Maid Service.

Studios from GBP350.00 per week
1 Bedroom Flats from GBP450.00 per week
2 Bedroom Flats from GBP800.00 per week
Tube: Queensway & Lancaster Gate

Contact: Lero Properties
24 Leinster Terrace, London W2 3ET
Tel: 0171 402 7768/0393, Fax: 0171 262 7179

Linden House

6 Sussex Place, Hyde Park, London W2 2TP
Tel: 0171 723 9853 Fax: 0171 724 1454

The friendly, family-run hotel in Central London.
Ideally situated for visiting West End theatres, sights and popular shopping stores. Good value prices inclusive of full English breakfast
All rooms en-suite

Top Quality Budget Accommodation

LEISURE INN

40 / 41 Leinster Gardens,
Bayswater, London W2 3AN
Tel: 0171 262 0757 Fax: 0171 252 1248

- Open 24 hours
- Colour TV Lounge with satellite Television
- Many rooms with private facilities
- All rooms with TV and telephone
- Situated in one of the finest streets in London
- Chambermaids service rooms daily
- Friendly staff

Group discounts and special rates on request

Bedrooms: 2 single, 2 double, 7 twin, 2 family
Bathrooms: 10 en suite, 2 public
Bed only: single £39.00-£59.00, double £65.00-£75.00
Bed & Breakfast: single £45.00-£65.00, double £75.00-£85.00
Evening meal: 1700 (l.o. 2200)
Credit Cards: Mastercard/Eurocard/Visa/Barclaycard/American Express/Switch/Delta/Eurocheque

Kingsway Hotel
COMMENDED

27 Norfolk Square, Hyde Park, London W2 1RX
Tel: (0171) 723 5569/(0171) 723 7784
Fax: (0171) 723 7317
E-mail: Kingsway.hotel@btinternet.com
URL: www.btinternet.com/~Kingsway.hotel/index.html
⊖/⇌ Paddington
Owner-managed hotel situated in a quiet garden square close to Hyde Park and Paddington station.
Bedrooms: 9 single, 7 double, 7 twin, 6 family
Bathrooms: 29 en suite, 2 public
Bed & Breakfast: single £40.00-£56.00, double £52.00-£76.00
Credit Cards: Mastercard/Eurocard/Visa/Barclaycard/American Express/Switch/Delta/Diners/Eurocheque

Lancaster Court Hotel
Listed APPROVED

202-204 Sussex Gardens, Hyde Park, London W2 3UA
Tel: (0171) 402 8438/0958 626225
Fax: (0171) 706 3794
E-mail: 100705.1225@compuserve.com
URL: www.lancaster-court-hotel.co.uk
⊖/⇌ Paddington, ⊖ Lancaster Gate
Centrally located. Close to tourist attractions. Two minutes' walk from Hyde Park. Near A2 Airbus stop, Lancaster Gate and Paddington stations. Conference facilities. Luggage room. Parking facilities available at £12 per car per day.
Bedrooms: 13 single, 10 double, 7 twin, 12 family
Bathrooms: 24 en suite, 14 private showers, 2 public
Bed & Breakfast: single £30.00-£48.00, double £58.00-£72.00
Parking for: 10
Credit Cards: Mastercard/Eurocard/Visa/Barclaycard/American Express/Switch/Delta/Diners/Eurocheque

Linden House Hotel
Listed APPROVED

4-6 Sussex Place, London W2 2TP
Tel: (0171) 723 9853/(0171) 262 0804
Fax: (0171) 724 1454
⊖/⇌ Paddington
Regency-style building close to Hyde Park, with a friendly, family atmosphere.
Bedrooms: 6 single, 7 double, 9 twin, 10 family
Bathrooms: 32 en suite, 2 public
Bed & Breakfast: single £38.50-£50.50, double £40.00-£75.50
Credit Cards: Mastercard/Eurocard/Visa/Barclaycard/American Express/Switch/Delta/Eurocheque

London Guards Hotel
COMMENDED

36-37 Lancaster Gate, London W2 3NA
Tel: (0171) 402 1101
Fax: (0171) 262 2551
⊖ Lancaster Gate
Refurbished completely in April 1997. Air-conditioned throughout. All rooms are en suite with security boxes and fridges; daily servicing. Reception open 24 hours. Coffee shop and bar.
Bedrooms: 2 single, 14 double, 11 twin, 13 family
Bathrooms: 40 en suite
Bed & Breakfast: single £95.00-£125.00, double £115.00-£140.00
Evening meal: 1900 (l.o. 2100)
Credit Cards: Mastercard/Barclaycard/American Express/Switch/Diners

Manor Court Hotel
Listed

7 Clanricarde Gardens, London W2 4JJ
Tel: (0171) 727 5407/(0171) 792 3361
Fax: (0171) 229 2875
⊖ Notting Hill Gate
Bed and breakfast hotel run by management.
Bedrooms: 5 single, 5 double, 4 twin, 6 family
Bathrooms: 6 en suite, 3 private, 7 private showers, 4 public
Bed & Breakfast: single £30.00-£40.00, double £45.00-£55.00
Credit Cards: Mastercard/Eurocard/Visa/Barclaycard/American Express/Diners

Mitre House Hotel
COMMENDED

178-184 Sussex Gardens, Hyde Park, London W2 1TU
Tel: (0171) 723 8040/(0171) 402 5695
Fax: (0171) 402 0990
E-mail: reservations@mitrehousehotel.com
URL: www.mitrehousehotel.com
⊖/⇌ Paddington, ⊖ Lancaster Gate
A family-run hotel with en suite facilities. Convenient for shops and sights. Free parking. Junior and family suites available.
Bedrooms: 9 single, 18 double, 26 twin, 17 family
Bathrooms: 70 en suite, 3 public
Bed & Breakfast: single £55.00-£70.00, double £70.00-£80.00
Parking for: 20
Credit Cards: Mastercard/Eurocard/Visa/Barclaycard/American Express/Diners/Eurocheque

Mornington Hotel

12 Lancaster Gate, London W2 3LG
Tel: (0171) 262 7361
Fax: (0171) 706 1028
URL: www.mornington.se
⊖ Lancaster Gate
Hotel situated in a quiet residential street opposite Hyde Park. Victorian exterior with cosy and comfortable interior.
Bedrooms: 25 single, 12 double, 25 twin, 6 family
Bathrooms: 66 en suite
Bed & Breakfast: single £104.00, double £121.00-£147.00
Credit Cards: Mastercard/Eurocard/Visa/Barclaycard/American Express/Switch/Delta/Diners/Eurocheque

Nayland Hotel
COMMENDED

132-134 Sussex Gardens, London W2 1UB
Tel: (0171) 723 4615
Fax: (0171) 402 3292
⊖/⇌ Paddington, ⊖ Lancaster Gate
Close to Paddington and Lancaster Gate stations. Madame Tussaud's and Buckingham Palace very near. Walking distance to Hyde Park and Oxford Street.
Bedrooms: 11 single, 8 double, 17 twin, 5 family
Bathrooms: 41 en suite
Bed & Breakfast: single £49.00-£64.00, double £56.00-£84.00
Parking for: 5

Credit Cards: Mastercard/Eurocard/ Visa/Barclaycard/American Express/ Switch/Delta/Diners/Eurocheque

The New Linden Hotel

58-60 Leinster Square, London W2 4PS
Tel: (0171) 221 4321
Fax: (0171) 727 3156
E-mail: hotels@vienna-group.co.uk
URL: www.vienna-group.co.uk
Bayswater

Small, friendly and comfortable hotel situated in the heart of Bayswater.

Bedrooms: 5 single, 10 double, 34 twin, 3 family
Bathrooms: 52 en suite
Bed & Breakfast: single £95.00, double £119.00
Credit Cards: Mastercard/Eurocard/ Visa/Barclaycard/American Express/ Switch/Delta/Diners/Eurocheque

Norfolk Plaza Hotel

29-33 Norfolk Square, London W2 1RX
Tel: (0171) 723 0792
Fax: (0171) 224 8770
E-mail: reservations@norfolkplazahotel.co.uk
URL: www.norfolkplazahotel.co.uk.
/ Paddington

Edwardian Grade II Listed building located in a quiet garden square. One minute's walk from Paddington station.

Bedrooms: 1 single, 8 double, 50 twin, 28 family
Bathrooms: 87 en suite
Bed & Breakfast: single £88.00-£98.00, double £108.00-£118.00
Credit Cards: Mastercard/Visa/ American Express/Diners/Eurocheque

Norfolk Towers Hotel

34 Norfolk Place, London W2 1QW
Tel: (0171) 262 3123
Fax: (0171) 224 8687
E-mail: blake@star.u_net.com
/ Paddington

The hotel is situated close to Hyde Park and Oxford Street, with a bar and restaurant.

Bedrooms: 14 single, 22 double, 46 twin, 3 family
Bathrooms: 84 en suite, 1 private
Bed only: single £80.00, double £120.00
Evening meal: 1730 (l.o. 2130)
Credit Cards: Mastercard/Eurocard/ Visa/Barclaycard/American Express/ Diners/Eurocheque

Olympic House Hotel

Approved

138-140 Sussex Gardens, London W2 1UB
Tel: (0171) 723 5935
Fax: (0171) 224 8144
/ Paddington

Small, centrally located, privately run hotel.

Bedrooms: 11 single, 1 double, 4 twin, 20 family
Bathrooms: 30 en suite, 3 private showers, 2 public
Bed & Breakfast: single £40.00-£55.00, double £54.00-£68.00
Parking for: 4
Credit Cards: Mastercard/Eurocard/ Visa/Barclaycard/American Express/ Diners/Eurocheque

Oxford Hotel

Listed Approved

13-14 Craven Terrace, Paddington, London W2 3QD
Tel: (0171) 402 6860/0800 318798
Fax: (0171) 262 7574
Queensway, / Paddington

Located in a quiet one-way street, close to Hyde Park and near Lancaster Gate underground station, bus routes and the Airbus stop for Heathrow. All rooms are fitted with a microwave and fridge.

Bedrooms: 1 double, 7 twin, 9 family
Bathrooms: 17 en suite, 1 public
Credit Cards: Mastercard/Eurocard/ Visa/Barclaycard/American Express/ Diners/Eurocheque

Park Lodge Hotel

Approved

73 Queensborough Terrace, Bayswater, London W2 3SU
Tel: (0171) 229 6424
Fax: (0171) 221 4772
Bayswater/Queensway

Situated in Bayswater.

Bedrooms: 11 single, 10 double, 6 twin, 2 family
Bathrooms: 29 en suite
Bed & Breakfast: single £60.00-£70.00, double £75.00-£85.00
Credit Cards: Mastercard/Visa/ Barclaycard/American Express/ Switch/Delta/Diners/Eurocheque

Parkwood Hotel

Approved

4 Stanhope Place, London W2 2HB
Tel: (0171) 402 2241
Fax: (0171) 402 1574
Marble Arch

Small town house hotel with friendly atmosphere, in a quiet area close to Marble Arch and Hyde Park.

Bedrooms: 5 single, 2 double, 7 twin, 4 family
Bathrooms: 12 en suite, 2 public
Bed & Breakfast: single £49.50-£69.50, double £64.50-£87.50
Credit Cards: Mastercard/Eurocard/ Barclaycard/Switch/Delta/ Eurocheque

The Pavilion Holiday Villa Hotel

Listed Commended

37 Leinster Gardens, London W2 3AR
Tel: (0171) 258 0269
Fax: (0171) 723 7295
E-mail: phv@rebel.net.uk
Bayswater, / Paddington

Friendly hotel situated within easy walking distance of Hyde Park and the West End. With six conference rooms.

Bedrooms: 15 single, 32 double, 41 twin, 9 family
Bathrooms: 97 en suite
Evening meal: 1800 (l.o. 2130)
Credit Cards: Mastercard/Visa/ Barclaycard/American Express/ Switch/Delta/Diners/Eurocheque

Phoenix Hotel

1-8 Kensington Gardens Square, Queensway, London W2 4BH
Tel: (0171) 229 2494
Fax: (0171) 727 1419
E-mail: phoenixhotel@dial.pipex.com
URL: www.bestwestern.com/ best.html
Bayswater, / Paddington

Centrally located hotel, close to many amenities and situated within walking distance of Hyde Park and Oxford Street.

Bedrooms: 42 single, 17 double, 52 twin, 14 family
Bathrooms: 125 en suite
Bed & Breakfast: single £69.00-£79.00, double £85.00-£110.00

Credit Cards: Mastercard/Eurocard/Visa/Barclaycard/American Express/Switch/Delta/Diners/Eurocheque

Prince William Hotel
Listed APPROVED

42-44 Gloucester Terrace, London W2 3DA
Tel: (0171) 724 7414
Fax: (0171) 706 2411
Paddington, Lancaster Gate
Friendly, clean, town house hotel close to Hyde Park and Oxford Street. Secretarial and fax services available.
Bedrooms: 23 single, 6 double, 12 twin, 2 family
Bathrooms: 34 en suite, 6 private showers, 2 public
Bed & Breakfast: single £35.00-£59.00, double £49.00-£75.00
Evening meal: 1730 (l.o. 2230)
Credit Cards: Mastercard/Eurocard/Visa/Barclaycard/American Express/Switch/Delta/Diners/Eurocheque

Rhodes House Hotel
COMMENDED

195 Sussex Gardens, London W2 2RJ
Tel: (0171) 262 5617/(0171) 262 0537
Fax: (0171) 723 4054
E-mail: chris@rhodeshotel.co.uk
URL: www.rhodeshotel.co.uk
Paddington, Lancaster Gate
Family-run hotel offering a high standard of accommodation to an international clientele. Families and small groups specially catered for.
Bedrooms: 3 single, 3 double, 4 twin, 8 family
Bathrooms: 15 en suite, 1 public
Bed & Breakfast: single £40.00-£60.00, double £60.00-£80.00
Credit Cards: Visa/Switch/Delta/Eurocheque

Rose Court Hotel
APPROVED

1-3 Talbot Square, London W2 1TR
Tel: (0171) 723 5128/(0171) 723 8671
Fax: (0171) 723 1855
E-mail: rosehotel@aol.com
URL: www.yell.co.uk/sites/rosecourthotellondon
Paddington, Lancaster Gate
Privately run Victorian town house in a quiet garden square. Close to Paddington and the West End.
Bedrooms: 7 single, 11 double, 16 twin, 8 family
Bathrooms: 41 en suite, 1 public
Bed & Breakfast: single £40.00-£60.00, double £50.00-£75.00
Evening meal: 1800 (l.o. 2100)
Credit Cards: Mastercard/Eurocard/Visa/Barclaycard/American Express/Switch/Delta/Diners/Eurocheque

Royal Lancaster Hotel
HIGHLY COMMENDED

Lancaster Terrace, London W2 2TY
Tel: (0171) 262 6737
Fax: (0171) 724 3191
URL: www.royallancaster.co.uk
Lancaster Gate
Winner of the Independent Hotel of the Year in the 1998 London Tourism Awards.
Overlooking Hyde Park and within walking distance of Marble Arch and Oxford Street. The hotel has three conference suites, three restaurants, a lounge bar, car parking and a business centre.
Bedrooms: 5 single, 216 double, 172 twin, 25 family
Bathrooms: 418 en suite
Evening meal: 1830 (l.o. 2230)
Parking for: 100
Credit Cards: Mastercard/Eurocard/Visa/Barclaycard/American Express/Switch/Delta/Diners/Eurocheque

Royal Norfolk Hotel

25 London Street, London W2 1HH
Tel: (0171) 402 5221/(0171) 723 3386
Fax: (0171) 723 3505
E-mail: 106165.1413@compuserve.com
URL: www.hotel.uk.comm/royalnorfolk
Paddington
Offering immediate access to Paddington station and within walking distance of Oxford Street and Hyde Park.
Bedrooms: 14 single, 14 double, 28 twin, 3 family
Bathrooms: 59 en suite, 4 public
Credit Cards: Mastercard/Eurocard/Visa/Barclaycard/American Express/Diners/Eurocheque

Royal Park Hotel
APPROVED

2-5 Westbourne Terrace, London W2 3UL
Tel: (0171) 402 6187
Fax: (0171) 224 9426
Paddington
Built in 1854, this family-run hotel is well placed for the West End.
Bedrooms: 8 single, 10 double, 35 twin, 10 family
Bathrooms: 63 en suite
Bed & Breakfast: single £45.00-£64.00, double £62.00-£85.00
Evening meal: 1800 (l.o. 2200)
Parking for: 15
Credit Cards: Mastercard/Eurocard/Visa/Barclaycard/American Express/Switch/Eurocheque

Ruddimans Hotel
Listed APPROVED

160-162 Sussex Gardens, London W2 1UD
Tel: (0171) 723 1026
Fax: (0171) 262 2983
E-mail: ruddimans@characom.com
URL: www.characom.com/ruddhotel.co.uk
Paddington
Nineteenth century, Victorian, town house bed and breakfast near Hyde Park. London's main attractions, shopping areas and airports are all easily accessible via Paddington station. (Credit card payments subject to an eight per cent surcharge.)
Bedrooms: 8 single, 13 double, 6 twin, 14 family
Bathrooms: 33 en suite, 2 public
Bed & Breakfast: single £30.00-£40.00, double £48.00-£58.00
Parking for: 4
Credit Cards: Mastercard/Eurocard/Visa/American Express/Switch/Eurocheque

St David's and Norfolk Court Hotel
Listed APPROVED

16 Norfolk Square, Hyde Park, London W2 1RS
Tel: (0171) 723 3856/(0171) 723 4963
Fax: (0171) 402 9061
Paddington
Small, friendly hotel in front of a quiet garden square.
Bedrooms: 16 single, 16 double, 6 twin, 32 family
Bathrooms: 26 en suite, 16 public
Bed & Breakfast: single £35.00-£45.00, double £50.00-£60.00
Credit Cards: Mastercard/Eurocard/Visa/American Express/Switch/Diners/Eurocheque

Sass Hotel

Listed Approved

10-11 Craven Terrace, London W2 3QD
Tel: (0171) 262 2325
Fax: (0171) 262 0889
E-mail: Info@SassHotel.com
URL: www.SassHotel.com
Paddington, Lancaster Gate
Budget accommodation in central London. Easy access to London's tourist attractions and shopping. Walking distance to Hyde Park and underground stations. Car parking available.
Bedrooms: 8 double, 7 twin, 8 family
Bathrooms: 23 en suite, 1 public
Bed & Breakfast: single £25.00-£36.00, double £40.00-£50.00
Credit Cards: Mastercard/Visa/Barclaycard/American Express/Switch/Eurocheque

Springfield Hotel

Listed Approved

154 Sussex Gardens, London W2 1UD
Tel: (0171) 723 9898
Fax: (0171) 723 0874
Paddington
Small, family-run hotel close to Hyde Park and Marble Arch.
Bedrooms: 2 single, 6 double, 6 twin, 6 family
Bathrooms: 20 en suite, 3 public
Bed & Breakfast: single £35.00-£45.00, double £55.00-£65.00
Parking for: 2
Credit Cards: Mastercard/Eurocard/Visa/Barclaycard/Switch/Delta/Eurocheque

Stakis Hyde Park

129 Bayswater Road, Hyde Park, London W2 4RJ
Tel: (0171) 221 2217
Fax: (0171) 229 0557
Queensway/Bayswater
Traditional British hotel offering a warm welcome to both business and holiday travellers.
Bedrooms: 25 single, 51 double, 52 twin, 8 family
Bathrooms: 132 en suite
Bed only: single £125.00, double £155.00
Evening meal: 1900 (l.o. 2200)
Credit Cards: Mastercard/Eurocard/Visa/Barclaycard/American Express/Switch/Delta/Diners/Eurocheque

Stakis London Metropole Hotel

Edgware Road, London W2 1JU
Tel: (0171) 402 4141
Fax: (0171) 724 8866
Edgware Road
Modern hotel close to West End theatres and shops. Banqueting for up to 1,325 people.
Bedrooms: 5 single, 337 double, 372 twin, 28 family
Bathrooms: 742 en suite, 4 public
Bed & Breakfast: single £185.00-£210.00, double £210.00-£225.00
Evening meal: 1800 (l.o. 2300)
Parking for: 80
Credit Cards: Mastercard/Eurocard/Visa/Barclaycard/American Express/Switch/Delta/Diners/Eurocheque

Wedgewood Hotel

49-51 Leinster Square, London W2 4PU
Tel: (0171) 229 8990
Fax: (0171) 792 8927
Bayswater
Set in the heart of Bayswater, the Wedgewood Hotel welcomes visitors to London with its own special blend of elegance and comfort.
Bedrooms: 6 single, 13 double, 30 twin, 11 family
Bathrooms: 60 en suite
Bed & Breakfast: single £53.00-£58.00, double £65.00-£75.00
Evening meal: 1800 (l.o. 0100)
Credit Cards: Mastercard/Eurocard/Barclaycard/American Express/Diners/Eurocheque

Westland Hotel

Commended

154 Bayswater Road, London W2 4HP
Tel: (0171) 229 9191
Fax: (0171) 727 1054
Notting Hill Gate
Small, friendly hotel, well located for West End shopping, touring or relaxing in a beautiful park.
Bedrooms: 2 single, 6 double, 19 twin, 4 family
Bathrooms: 31 en suite
Bed & Breakfast: double £104.00-£120.00
Evening meal: 1830 (l.o. 2230)
Parking for: 9
Credit Cards: Mastercard/Eurocard/Visa/Barclaycard/American Express/Switch/Diners/Eurocheque

Westminster

16 Leinster Square, London W2 4PR
Tel: (0171) 221 9131
Fax: (0171) 221 4073
E-mail: hotels@vienna-group.co.uk
URL: www.vienna-group.co.uk
Bayswater, Paddington
Victorian hotel. Central London location close to Hyde Park. Convenient for major shopping areas, museums and places of interest.
Bedrooms: 30 single, 27 double, 51 twin, 8 family
Bathrooms: 116 en suite
Bed & Breakfast: single £105.00, double £130.00
Evening meal: 1800 (l.o. 2200)
Credit Cards: Mastercard/Eurocard/Visa/Barclaycard/American Express/Switch/Diners/Eurocheque

Whiteleaf Hotel

Approved

66-68 Inverness Terrace, London W2 3LB
Tel: (0171) 727 0681/(0171) 727 0682
Fax: (0171) 792 2808
Queensway/Bayswater
Small, privately owned hotel in a Listed building. Within a short walk of Kensington Gardens and Hyde Park.
Bedrooms: 4 single, 9 double, 6 twin, 9 family
Bathrooms: 24 en suite, 1 public
Bed & Breakfast: single £45.00-£60.00, double £55.00-£85.00
Evening meal: 1700 (l.o. 2130)
Credit Cards: Eurocard/Visa/Barclaycard/American Express/Switch/Delta/Diners/Eurocheque

Whites

(A Thistle Country House Hotel)

90-92 Lancaster Gate, London W2 3NR
Tel: (0171) 262 2711
Fax: (0171) 262 2147
Paddington
One of London's traditional hotels, overlooking Kensington Gardens and Hyde Park. Easy access to the City and the West End.
Bedrooms: 17 single, 21 double, 16 twin

Bathrooms: 54 en suite
Bed only: single £175.00-£195.00, double £230.00-£285.00
Evening meal: 1830 (l.o. 2230)
Parking for: 25
Credit Cards: Mastercard/Eurocard/Visa/Barclaycard/American Express/Switch/Delta/Diners/Eurocheque

SW3/5/7 Chelsea/Earl's Court/South Kensington

Abcone Hotel
APPLIED

10 Ashburn Gardens, London SW7 4DG
Tel: (0171) 460 3400
Fax: (0171) 460 3444
E-mail: aliuk@compuserve.com.
⊖ Gloucester Road
Convenient for High Street Kensington, Olympia and Earl's Court exhibition centres. Also close to Harrods, the Natural History and Victoria and Albert museums.
Bedrooms: 17 single, 15 double, 3 twin
Bathrooms: 28 en suite, 4 public
Evening meal: 1900 (l.o. 2230)
Credit Cards: Mastercard/Eurocard/Visa/Barclaycard/American Express/Switch/Delta/Diners/Eurocheque

Amsterdam Hotel
Listed COMMENDED

7 Trebovir Road, London SW5 9LS
Tel: (0171) 370 5084
Fax: (0171) 244 7608
URL: www.cityscan.co.uk
⊖ Earl's Court
Modern, comfortable, attractively furnished rooms, all with bathroom, hairdryer, colour TV and telephone.
Bedrooms: 6 single, 6 double, 4 twin, 4 family
Bathrooms: 20 en suite, 1 public
Bed & Breakfast: single £65.00-£75.00, double £78.00-£88.00
Credit Cards: Mastercard/Visa/Barclaycard/American Express/Switch/Eurocheque

The Basil Street Hotel
HIGHLY COMMENDED

Basil Street, Knightsbridge, London SW3 1AH
Tel: (0171) 581 3311
Fax: (0171) 581 3693
E-mail: TheBasil@aol.com
URL: www.absite.com/basil
⊖ Knightsbridge
An English country house-style hotel in the centre of London, a short distance from Harrods.
Bedrooms: 42 single, 20 double, 25 twin, 4 family
Bathrooms: 89 en suite, 6 public
Bed only: single £141.00-£148.00, double £210.33-£220.00
Bed & Breakfast: single £150.50-£157.50, double £230.00-£239.00
Evening meal: 1830 (l.o. 2200)
Parking for: 2
Credit Cards: Mastercard/Eurocard/Visa/Barclaycard/American Express/Switch/Delta/Diners/Eurocheque

Beaver Hotel
APPROVED

57-59 Philbeach Gardens, London SW5 9ED
Tel: (0171) 373 4553
Fax: (0171) 373 4555
⊖ Earl's Court
In a quiet, tree-lined crescent of Victorian terraced houses, close to Earl's Court Exhibition Centre and ten minutes from the West End.
Bedrooms: 17 single, 9 double, 7 twin, 5 family
Bathrooms: 26 en suite, 3 public
Bed & Breakfast: single £35.00-£55.00, double £78.00
Parking for: 23
Credit Cards: Mastercard/Eurocard/Visa/Barclaycard/American Express/Delta/Diners/Eurocheque

Blair House Hotel
APPROVED

34 Draycott Place, London SW3 2SA
Tel: (0171) 581 2323/ (0171) 225 0771
Fax: (0171) 823 7752
⊖/⇄ Victoria, ⊖ Sloane Square
In a quiet street close to Harrods and the South Kensington museums.
Bedrooms: 1 single, 4 double, 6 twin
Bathrooms: 11 en suite, 1 public
Bed & Breakfast: single £85.00-£87.50, double £105.00-£117.50
Credit Cards: Mastercard/Eurocard/Visa/Barclaycard/American Express/Switch/Delta/Diners/Eurocheque

The Burns Hotel
COMMENDED

18-26 Barkston Gardens, Kensington, London SW5 0EN
Tel: (0171) 373 3151
Fax: (0171) 370 4090
E-mail: hotels@vienna-group.co.uk
⊖ Earl's Court
Attractive Victorian building situated in a quiet residential square in Kensington, within walking distance of Earl's Court underground station.
Bedrooms: 38 single, 14 double, 43 twin, 10 family
Bathrooms: 105 en suite
Bed only: single £110.00, double £135.00
Evening meal: 1830 (l.o. 2130)
Credit Cards: Mastercard/Visa/Barclaycard/American Express/Switch/Delta/Diners/Eurocheque

Cranley Gardens Hotel

8 Cranley Gardens, London SW7 3DB
Tel: (0171) 373 3232
Fax: (0171) 373 7944
⊖ Gloucester Road
Located in the heart of Chelsea and Kensington and close to the museums and exhibition centres.
Bedrooms: 12 single, 19 double, 41 twin, 13 family
Bathrooms: 85 en suite
Bed & Breakfast: single £75.00-£85.00, double £99.00-£105.00
Credit Cards: Mastercard/Eurocard/Visa/Barclaycard/American Express/Switch/Delta/Diners/Eurocheque

Derby Hotel
COMMENDED

155-157 Cromwell Road, London SW5 0TQ
Tel: (0171) 465 5150
Fax: (0171) 465 0465
⊖ Earl's Court/Gloucester Road
Newly refurbished, centrally situated hotel en route to Heathrow, Olympia and Earl's Court. Within five minutes' walk of bus routes and underground station.
Bedrooms: 4 single, 15 double, 5 twin
Bathrooms: 25 en suite
Credit Cards: Mastercard/Eurocard/Visa/Barclaycard/American Express/Switch/Delta/Diners/Eurocheque

Eden Plaza Hotel

68-69 Queensgate, London SW7 5JJ
Tel: (0171) 370 6111
Fax: (0171) 370 0932
⊖ South Kensington
Centrally located in Kensington, the hotel is within easy reach of the airport, London's museums, exhibition centres and the West End.
Bedrooms: 13 single, 28 double, 15 twin, 6 family
Bathrooms: 62 en suite
Bed only: single £63.00, double £73.00
Bed & Breakfast: single £68.00, double £83.00
Credit Cards: Mastercard/Eurocard/Visa/Barclaycard/American Express/Delta/Diners/Eurocheque

Enterprise Hotel

15-25 Hogarth Road, London SW5 0QJ
Tel: (0171) 373 4502/(0171) 373 4503
Fax: (0171) 373 5115
E-mail: ehotel@aol.com
⊖ Earl's Court
Conveniently located for the West End and Knightsbridge. Kensington High Street shops and museums are also nearby.
Bedrooms: 11 single, 15 double, 42 twin, 20 family
Bathrooms: 88 en suite, 12 public
Bed & Breakfast: single £45.00-£70.00, double £80.00-£99.00
Evening meal: 1800 (l.o. 2230)
Credit Cards: Mastercard/Eurocard/Visa/Barclaycard/American Express/Switch/Delta/Diners/Eurocheque

Five Sumner Place Hotel

Listed HIGHLY COMMENDED

5 Sumner Place, South Kensington, London SW7 3EE
Tel: (0171) 584 7586
Fax: (0171) 823 9962
E-mail: no.5@dial.pipex.com
URL: dspace.dial.pipex.com/no.5
⊖ South Kensington
This family-owned hotel offers excellent service and personal attention. All rooms are luxuriously appointed.
Bedrooms: 3 single, 5 double, 5 twin
Bathrooms: 13 en suite, 1 public
Bed & Breakfast: single £90.00-£141.00, double £120.00-£141.00
Credit Cards: Mastercard/Eurocard/Visa/Barclaycard/American Express

Forum Hotel London

♛♛♛♛♛ COMMENDED

97 Cromwell Road, London SW7 4DN
Tel: (0171) 370 5757
Fax: (0171) 373 1448
E-mail: forumlondon@interconti.com
URL: www.interconti.com
⊖ Gloucester Road
All 910 rooms are en suite with colour TV, telephone and tea and coffee making facilities. The hotel has three restaurants, two bars, fitness room, business centre and car park.
Bedrooms: 448 double, 448 twin, 36 family
Bathrooms: 932 en suite
Bed only: single £150.00-£170.00, double £170.00-£190.00
Bed & Breakfast: single £160.00-£180.00, double £190.00-£210.00
Evening meal: 1730 (l.o. 2330)
Parking for: 80
Credit Cards: Mastercard/Eurocard/Visa/Barclaycard/American Express/Switch/Delta/Diners/Eurocheque

Half Moon Hotel

Listed APPROVED

10 Earl's Court Square, London SW5 9DP
Tel: (0171) 373 9956
Fax: (0171) 373 8456
⊖ Earl's Court
In a central position two minutes' walk from the underground station and with easy access to the M4 and Heathrow.
Bedrooms: 10 single, 8 twin, 9 family
Bathrooms: 9 en suite, 2 private showers, 5 public
Bed & Breakfast: single £35.00-£45.00, double £55.00-£65.00
Credit Cards: Mastercard/Eurocard/Visa/Barclaycard/Delta/Eurocheque

Harrington Hall

5-25 Harrington Gardens, London SW7 4JW
Tel: (0171) 396 9696
Fax: (0171) 396 9090
E-mail: 101752.2030@compuserve.com
URL: www.harringtonhall.co.uk
⊖ Gloucester Road
All 200 bedrooms are spacious and fully air-conditioned with trouser press, mini-bar and tea and coffee tray. Satellite TV and personalised telephones.
Bedrooms: 100 double, 94 twin, 6 family
Bathrooms: 200 en suite
Bed only: single £150.00, double £165.00
Bed & Breakfast: single £164.00, double £188.00
Evening meal: 1730 (l.o. 2230)
Credit Cards: Mastercard/Barclaycard/American Express/Diners/Eurocheque

Henley House Hotel

♛♛ COMMENDED

30 Barkston Gardens, Earl's Court, London SW5 0EN
Tel: (0171) 370 4111
Fax: (0171) 370 0026
E-mail: henleyhse@aol.com
⊖ Earl's Court
Overlooking a garden square, the hotel is now a member of the prestigious European consortium 'Inter-Europe Hotels'.
Bedrooms: 5 single, 8 double, 5 twin, 2 family
Bathrooms: 20 en suite
Bed & Breakfast: single £70.00-£76.00, double £90.00-£103.00
Credit Cards: Mastercard/Eurocard/Barclaycard/American Express/Delta/Diners/Eurocheque

Hotel 167

167 Old Brompton Road, London SW5 0AN
Tel: (0171) 373 0672/(0171) 373 3221
Fax: (0171) 373 3360
⊖ South Kensington
Each room has an individual style.
Bedrooms: 2 single, 9 double, 6 twin, 1 family
Bathrooms: 18 en suite, 2 public
Bed & Breakfast: single £72.50-£85.50, double £90.00-£99.00
Credit Cards: Mastercard/Eurocard/Barclaycard/American Express/Switch/Delta/Diners/Eurocheque

Hotel Europe

131-137 Cromwell Road, London SW7 4DU
Tel: (0171) 370 2336
Fax: (0171) 244 6985

Merlyn Court Hotel

The Merlyn Court Hotel is a family run English Tourist Board assessed bed and breakfast hotel, situated in a quiet Edwardian Square in Kensington.
Comfortable, good value accommodation and friendly, multilingual staff, have ensured the regular return of our guests - tourist and business alike.
Most bedrooms have private facilities and some are large enough to accommodate three or four people.

Airport: Heathrow - forty minutes Gatwick - one hour
Underground: Earl's Court - very central
2 Barkston Gardens, London SW5 0EN
Tel: 0171 370 1640 Fax: 0171 370 4986

English Tourist Board APPROVED
Listed

LONDON HOTEL

BEST RATES!

WINDSOR HOUSE HOTEL, 12 PENYWERN RD, LONDON SW5 9ST
Tel: +44 (0)171 373 9087 Fax: +44 (0)171 385 2417

3/4/5 ROOMS: £14-£26 pppn
TWINS: £18-£28 pppn
SINGLES: £26-£46 pppn

INCLUDES BIG BREAKFAST
USE OF KITCHEN. GARDEN
CENTRAL LONDON!

HOTEL OLIVER

198 Cromwell Rd, Earl's Court,
London SW5 0SN
Tel: 0171 3706881 Fax: 0171 370 6556

£5 DISCOUNT WITH THIS ADVERTISEMENT

50 bedrooms with bath/shower, colour TV/Radio, direct-dial telephone, lift, tea & coffee facilities, hairdryers. Earl's Court underground 2 mins' walk. Harrods, museums, shopping centre close by. A1 airbus from Heathrow stops outside hotel. Major credit cards accepted.
HOLIDAY APARTMENTS.

OLIVER PLAZA HOTEL

33 TREBOVIR ROAD, EARL'S COURT,
LONDON SW5 9NF
TEL: 0171 373 7183 FAX: 0171 244 6021
e-mail: oliverplaza@capitalhotels.co.uk
http://www.capitalhotels.co.uk/

- Recently fully refurbished.
- All rooms en-suite with colour TV. and direct-dial telephone.
- Private car park.
- Excellent transport links.
- Near all the major museums and shopping facilities.

ROOM RATES FROM £25 PER PERSON
INCLUSIVE OF BREAKFAST AND VAT

The Enterprise Hotel

LONDON

15-25 Hogarth Road, London SW5 0QJ
Telephone: 0171 373 4502 (6 lines) Fax: 0171 373 5115
E-mail: ehotel@aol.com

EARLS COURT

Fully Licensed
Business & Tourist Class hotel with superb cosy bar and restaurant
Comfortable 100-bedroom hotel.
A minute's walk from Earl's Court Station. All rooms with colour TV and direct-dial phone and en-suite facilities

EXCELLENT VALUE FOR MONEY
TO SUIT YOUR BUDGET

E-mail: hoteleuropelondon@compuserve.com
⊖ Gloucester Road
Close to Natural History, Science and V & A museums. Also close to West End, theatreland and shopping districts.
Bedrooms: 18 single, 6 double, 29 twin, 37 family
Bathrooms: 78 en suite, 5 public
Bed & Breakfast: single £40.00-£45.00, double £50.00-£60.00
Evening meal: 1800 (l.o. 2000)
Credit Cards: Mastercard/Eurocard/Visa/Barclaycard/American Express/Switch/Delta/Diners/Eurocheque

Hotel Number Sixteen

HIGHLY COMMENDED

16 Sumner Place, London SW7 3EG
Tel: (0171) 589 5232
Fax: (0171) 584 8615
E-mail: reservations@numbersixteenhotel.co.uk
URL: www.numbersixteenhotel.co.uk
⊖ South Kensington
A comfortable town house with atmosphere, in four adjoining Victorian houses in an attractive street with award-winning gardens.
Bedrooms: 9 single, 23 double, 4 family
Bathrooms: 32 en suite, 2 private, 1 private shower
Bed & Breakfast: single £90.00-£125.00, double £160.00-£200.00
Credit Cards: Mastercard/Visa/Barclaycard/American Express/Switch/Delta/Diners/Eurocheque

Hotel Oliver

APPROVED

198 Cromwell Road, London SW5 0SN
Tel: (0171) 370 6881
Fax: (0171) 370 6556
⊖ Earl's Court
Hotel with 48 bedrooms, all en suite. All rooms have colour TV, radio, hairdryer and telephone. Lift to all floors. Situated close to Harrods, the South Kensington museums and shops. All major credit cards are accepted.
Bedrooms: 20 single, 11 double, 11 twin, 6 family
Bathrooms: 48 en suite
Bed & Breakfast: single £45.00-£55.00, double £60.00-£75.00
Credit Cards: Mastercard/Eurocard/Visa/Barclaycard/American Express/Switch/Diners/Eurocheque

The Jarvis Embassy House

COMMENDED

31-33 Queen's Gate, London SW7 5JA
Tel: (0171) 584 7222
Fax: (0171) 589 3910
⊖ Gloucester Road
The hotel is ideally situated for the Royal Albert Hall, the South Kensington museums, Hyde Park, Harrods and Earl's Court.
Bedrooms: 7 single, 22 double, 22 twin, 18 family
Bathrooms: 69 en suite
Bed only: single £115.00, double £136.00
Bed & Breakfast: single £128.00, double £159.00
Evening meal: 1730 (l.o. 2130)
Credit Cards: Mastercard/Eurocard/Visa/Barclaycard/American Express/Switch/Delta/Diners/Eurocheque

K & K Hotel George

1-15 Templeton Place, Earl's Court, London SW5 9NB
Tel: (0171) 370 1092
Fax: (0171) 370 2285
E-mail: hotelgeorge@kkhotels.co.uk
URL: www.kkhotels.com
⊖ Earl's Court
Hotel with garden and private car park. Easy access to Heathrow and the attractions of Kensington and Knightsbridge.
Bedrooms: 7 single, 24 double, 86 twin, 37 family
Bathrooms: 154 en suite
Bed & Breakfast: single £130.00, double £165.00
Evening meal: 1800 (l.o. 2200)
Parking for: 36
Credit Cards: Mastercard/Eurocard/Visa/Barclaycard/American Express/Switch/Delta/Diners/Eurocheque

Kensington Court Hotel

33-35 Nevern Place, Earl's Court, London SW5 9NP
Tel: (0171) 370 5151
Fax: (0171) 370 3499
⊖ Earl's Court
Purpose-built hotel with private car park. Centrally situated for both the underground and exhibition centres. All rooms with en suite facilities.
Bedrooms: 10 single, 5 double, 5 twin, 15 family
Bathrooms: 35 en suite
Bed & Breakfast: single £65.00, double £85.00
Evening meal: 1900 (l.o. 2100)
Parking for: 10
Credit Cards: Visa/American Express/Delta

Kensington Plaza Hotel

61 Gloucester Road, London SW7 4PE
Tel: (0171) 584 8100
Fax: (0171) 823 9175
⊖ Gloucester Road
A recently refurbished Victorian building close to the underground, Harrods, Hyde Park and the museums. The hotel has a Mongolian barbecue restaurant.
Bedrooms: 28 single, 20 double, 39 twin, 3 family
Bathrooms: 90 en suite
Bed only: single £65.00-£90.00, double £80.00-£110.00
Bed & Breakfast: single £70.00-£95.00, double £90.00-£120.00
Evening meal: 1800 (l.o. 2300)
Credit Cards: Mastercard/Eurocard/Visa/Barclaycard/American Express/Switch/Delta/Diners/Eurocheque

London Town Hotel

COMMENDED

15 Penywern Road, Earl's Court, London SW5 9TT
Tel: (0171) 370 4356/(0171) 229 6666
Fax: (0171) 370 7923
E-mail: town@lth-hotels.com
⊖ Earl's Court
Situated within two minutes' walk of Earl's Court underground with direct connections to Heathrow, Victoria and Piccadilly Circus. All rooms with colour TV and telephone.
Bedrooms: 9 single, 4 double, 13 twin, 6 family
Bathrooms: 32 en suite
Parking for: 4
Credit Cards: Mastercard/Eurocard/Visa/Barclaycard/American Express/Switch/Delta/Diners/Eurocheque

CRANLEY GARDENS
HOTEL

8 CRANLEY GARDENS, SOUTH KENSINGTON, LONDON SW7 3DB

Cranley Gardens Hotel is situated in the fashionable Kensington and Chelsea area of London, and overlooks a private garden square.

The hotel has 85 bedrooms, all with private bath/shower, WC, colour TV with teletext, radio, direct dial telephone and hair dryer. A lounge bar/coffee-shop is also available.

Gloucester Road and South Kensington tube stations (direct link to Heathrow) are within walking distance. Olympia and Earl's Court are easily accessible.

TEL: 0171-373 3232 FAX: 0171-373 7944

Welcome to

HOTEL EUROPE

South Kensington

131-137 Cromwell Rd, South Kensington London SW7 1DU

The hotel for the budget traveller

Comfortable and friendly hotel with 100 rooms, restaurant, bar and TV lounge. **Very moderate prices.** Centrally located: museums, shopping districts of Knightsbridge and Chelsea, Hyde Park and Royal Albert Hall in walking distance. Underground station - Gloucester Road (Piccadilly/Circle/District lines) and bus stop close to hotel.

Tel: 0171 370-2336
Fax: 0171 244 6985
Email: hoteleuropelondon@compuserve.com

RASOOL COURT HOTEL

19-21 Penywern Road, Earl's Court, London SW5 9TT
Tel: 0171 373 8900 Fax: 0171 244 6835
E-mail: rasool@rasool.demon.co.uk

Central location near Earl's Court tube station, 10 mins. from West End. All rooms with direct-dialling telephones, colour TVs and Sky channels.

Singles from £32.00
Doubles from £44.00
Triples from £59.00

NUMBER SIXTEEN

16 Sumner Place,
London SW7 3EG
Tel: 0171 589 5232
Fax: 0171 584 8615
E-mail: reservations@numbersixteenhotel.com.uk

Relax by the open fire, read a book in the conservatory or stroll in our pretty, secluded walled garden. Rest assured that you will be provided with every comfort in our Victorian Town House hotel in the heart of South Kensington. Discreet service for the discerning visitor.

Lord Jim Hotel
Listed APPROVED

23-25 Penywern Road, London SW5 9TT
Tel: (0171) 370 6071/0956 238277
Fax: (0171) 373 8919
Earl's Court
An attractive, well-appointed and moderately priced hotel. Located centrally for easy access to museums, the City and Earl's Court and Olympia exhibition halls.
Bedrooms: 8 single, 6 double, 5 twin, 16 family
Bathrooms: 11 en suite, 3 private showers, 6 public
Bed & Breakfast: single £22.00-£52.00, double £35.00-£59.00
Credit Cards: Mastercard/Eurocard/Visa/Barclaycard/American Express/Delta/Diners/Eurocheque

Manor Hotel
Listed APPROVED

23 Nevern Place, London SW5 9NR
Tel: (0171) 370 6018
Fax: (0171) 244 6610
Earl's Court
Centrally located hotel offering a pleasant atmosphere. Car parking available. Convenient for Heathrow.
Bedrooms: 6 single, 11 double, 10 family
Bathrooms: 9 en suite, 5 public
Bed & Breakfast: single £45.00-£55.00, double £60.00-£80.00
Parking for: 4
Credit Cards: Mastercard/Eurocard/Visa/Barclaycard/Delta

Mayflower Hotel
APPLIED

26-28 Trebovir Road, London SW5 9NJ
Tel: (0171) 370 0991
Fax: (0171) 370 0994
E-mail: mayfhotel@aol.com
Earl's Court
Clean, bright, family-run, centrally located hotel with easy access to transport, major tourist attractions and exhibition centres. Open all year.
Bedrooms: 6 single, 18 double, 15 twin, 9 family
Bathrooms: 46 en suite
Bed & Breakfast: single £55.00-£65.00, double £69.00-£89.00
Credit Cards: Mastercard/Eurocard/Visa/Barclaycard/American Express/Switch/Delta/Eurocheque

Merlyn Court Hotel
Listed APPROVED

2 Barkston Gardens, London SW5 0EN
Tel: (0171) 370 1640
Fax: (0171) 370 4986
Earl's Court
A good-value, well-established, family-run hotel in a quiet garden square in Kensington. Close to Earl's Court and Olympia exhibition centres, with direct underground link to Heathrow and West End.
Bedrooms: 4 single, 4 double, 4 twin, 5 family
Bathrooms: 11 en suite, 1 private shower, 6 public
Bed & Breakfast: single £28.00-£50.00, double £40.00-£65.00
Credit Cards: Mastercard/Eurocard/Eurocheque

The Millennium Bailey's London

140 Gloucester Road, London SW7 4QH
Tel: (0171) 373 6000
Fax: (0171) 370 3760
E-mail: baileys@mill-cop.com
URL: www.mill-cop.com
Gloucester Road
Traditional Victorian property, built and opened as a hotel in 1876. Close to Knightsbridge, Kensington Palace and Gardens, the South Kensington museums, the Royal Albert Hall and Earl's Court and Olympia exhibition centres.
Bedrooms: 36 single, 121 double, 44 twin, 1 family
Bathrooms: 202 en suite
Evening meal: 1830 (l.o. 2230)
Parking for: 75
Credit Cards: Mastercard/Eurocard/Visa/Barclaycard/American Express/Switch/Delta/Diners/Eurocheque

The Millennium Gloucester Hotel
HIGHLY COMMENDED

4-18 Harrington Gardens, London SW7 4LH
Tel: (0171) 373 6030
Fax: (0171) 373 0409
URL: www.mill-cop.com
Gloucester Road
Newly refurbished, luxury hotel, situated in Kensington and Chelsea, with direct link to Heathrow and Gatwick airports and the City. Elegant stores of Knightsbridge and Kensington only minutes away.
Bedrooms: 11 single, 318 double, 259 twin, 13 family
Bathrooms: 601 en suite
Bed only: single £215.00, double £250.00
Evening meal: 1800 (l.o. 2245)
Parking for: 100
Credit Cards: Mastercard/Eurocard/Visa/Barclaycard/American Express/Switch/Delta/Diners/Eurocheque

Montana Hotel
APPROVED

67-69 Gloucester Road, London SW7 4PG
Tel: (0171) 584 7654
Fax: (0171) 581 3109
Gloucester Road
Centrally located hotel. Convenient for Knightsbridge, Kensington and Earl's Court Exhibition Centre. Gloucester Road underground opposite gives direct link to Heathrow and West End.
Bedrooms: 14 single, 5 double, 21 twin, 15 family
Bathrooms: 45 en suite, 6 public
Bed & Breakfast: single £25.00-£50.00, double £50.00-£70.00
Evening meal: 1800 (l.o. 2330)
Credit Cards: Mastercard/Eurocard/Visa/Barclaycard/American Express/Diners/Eurocheque

Mowbray Court Hotel
Listed APPROVED

28-32 Penywern Road, Earl's Court, London SW5 9SU
Tel: (0171) 370 2316/(0171) 370 3690
Fax: (0171) 370 5693
Earl's Court
Tourist-class hotel near Earl's Court Exhibition Centre.
Bedrooms: 30 single, 15 double, 15 twin, 28 family
Bathrooms: 72 en suite, 8 public
Bed & Breakfast: single £45.00-£55.00, double £65.00
Credit Cards: Mastercard/Eurocard/Visa/Barclaycard/American Express/Switch/Delta/Diners/Eurocheque

Nevern Hotel

29-31 Nevern Place, London SW5 9NP
Tel: (0171) 244 8366/(0171) 370 4827
Fax: (0171) 370 1541
Earl's Court

Small hotel located in a quiet residential area. Convenient for Earl's Court and Olympia, also within easy reach of the West End.
Bedrooms: 4 single, 6 double, 9 twin, 16 family
Bathrooms: 19 en suite, 7 public
Bed & Breakfast: single £30.00-£50.00, double £40.00-£74.00
Credit Cards: Mastercard/Visa/Barclaycard/American Express/Eurocheque

The OKi Kensington
COMMENDED

25 Courtfield Gardens, London SW5 0PG
Tel: (0171) 565 2222
Fax: (0171) 565 2223
⊖ Earl's Court
Within walking distance of Earl's Court and Olympia exhibition centres, the South Kensington museums and the Knightsbridge shopping area.
Bedrooms: 6 single, 27 double, 8 twin
Bathrooms: 41 en suite
Bed & Breakfast: single £110.00, double £110.00
Parking for: 2
Credit Cards: Mastercard/Visa/Barclaycard/American Express/Switch/Delta/Diners/Eurocheque

Oliver Plaza Hotel
Listed APPROVED

33 Trebovir Road, Earl's Court, London SW5 9NF
Tel: (0171) 373 7183
Fax: (0171) 244 6021
⊖ Earl's Court
A small hotel with the emphasis on efficiency of service and comfort for guests.
Bedrooms: 3 single, 13 double, 8 twin, 8 family
Bathrooms: 32 en suite
Bed & Breakfast: single £50.00, double £59.00
Parking for: 7
Credit Cards: Visa/Barclaycard/American Express/Diners/Eurocheque

Park Consul
HIGHLY COMMENDED

35 Ixworth Place, Chelsea, London SW3 3QX
Tel: (0171) 225 7500
Fax: (0171) 225 7555
E-mail: park-con@dircon.co.uk
URL: consul-hotels.com/pcberlin.
⊖ South Kensington
Affordably luxurious, 46-room, brand-new, air-conditioned English town house hotel, close to Harrods, the Kensington museums and fashionable Chelsea.
Bedrooms: 4 single, 22 double, 20 twin
Bathrooms: 46 en suite
Bed only: single £140.00-£160.00, double £180.00-£202.00
Bed & Breakfast: single £155.00-£175.00, double £210.00-£235.00
Evening meal: 1800 (l.o. 2200)
Credit Cards: Mastercard/Eurocard/Visa/Barclaycard/American Express/Switch/Delta/Diners

Penn Court Hotel
Listed APPROVED

54-56 Cromwell Road, London SW7 5DA
Tel: (0171) 584 3499/(0171) 584 9657
Fax: (0171) 584 3466
⊖ Gloucester Road
Budget accommodation near South Kensington museums.
Bedrooms: 12 single, 10 double, 5 twin, 12 family
Bathrooms: 2 en suite, 21 public
Bed & Breakfast: single £50.00, double £65.00
Credit Cards: Visa/Barclaycard

Radisson Edwardian Vanderbilt Hotel

68-86 Cromwell Road, London SW7 5BT
Tel: (0171) 589 2424
Fax: (0171) 225 2293
⊖ Gloucester Road
The hotel is located a short walk from Harrods and is easily recognisable by its classical Victorian facade. Country house-style hotel.
Bedrooms: 81 single, 56 double, 86 twin
Bathrooms: 223 en suite
Bed only: single £105.00-£149.00, double £116.00-£160.00
Evening meal: 1700 (l.o. 2200)
Credit Cards: Mastercard/Eurocard/Visa/Barclaycard/American Express/Switch/Delta/Diners/Eurocheque

Rasool Court Hotel
Listed APPROVED

19-21 Penywern Road, Earl's Court, London SW5 9TT
Tel: (0171) 373 8900/(0171) 373 4893
Fax: (0171) 244 6835
E-mail: younis@rasool.demon.co.uk
⊖ Earl's Court
Situated near Earl's Court underground station, 20 minutes from the West End and Heathrow by train.
Bedrooms: 27 single, 15 double, 7 twin, 8 family
Bathrooms: 20 en suite, 25 private showers, 4 public
Bed & Breakfast: single £32.00-£38.00, double £44.00-£49.00
Credit Cards: Mastercard/Eurocard/Visa/Barclaycard/American Express/Switch/Delta/Diners/Eurocheque

Regency Hotel

100 Queen's Gate, South Kensington, London SW7 5AG
Tel: (0171) 370 4595
Fax: (0171) 370 5555
E-mail: regency.london@dial.pipex.com
⊖ South Kensington
The privately owned Regency Hotel offers traditional personal service, with easy access to all of London's major attractions and amenities.
Bedrooms: 25 single, 58 double, 115 twin
Bathrooms: 198 en suite
Bed & Breakfast: single £185.65, double £200.93
Evening meal: 1730 (l.o. 2215)
Credit Cards: Mastercard/Eurocard/Visa/Barclaycard/American Express/Switch/Diners/Eurocheque

Rushmore Hotel
APPLIED

11 Trebovir Road, London SW5 9LS
Tel: (0171) 370 3839/(0171) 370 6505
Fax: (0171) 370 0274
⊖ Earl's Court
Small, family-run hotel with individually themed rooms. Situated in the centre of Earl's Court, within one minute's walk from the local underground station. Conservatory and lounge recently added.
Bedrooms: 4 single, 7 double, 6 twin, 5 family
Bathrooms: 22 en suite
Bed & Breakfast: single £63.00-£73.00, double £84.00-£90.00
Credit Cards: Mastercard/Visa/Barclaycard/American Express/Switch/Eurocheque

Stuart Hotel

110-112 Cromwell Road, London SW7 4ES
Tel: (0171) 373 1004/0973 220173
Fax: (0171) 370 2548
⊖ Gloucester Road
Convenient for the Royal Albert Hall, South Kensington museums and the West End. Direct link to Heathrow. Two minutes' walk to the underground station.
Bedrooms: 17 single, 12 double, 18 twin, 10 family
Bathrooms: 53 en suite, 3 public
Bed & Breakfast: single £53.00, double £69.00
Parking for: 1
Credit Cards: Mastercard/Eurocard/ Visa/Barclaycard/American Express/ Switch

Swallow International Hotel

COMMENDED

Cromwell Road, London SW5 0TH
Tel: (0171) 973 1000
Fax: (0171) 244 8194
⊖ Gloucester Road
Modern hotel, near the museums and Earl's Court and Olympia exhibition centres. Within walking distance of fashionable Knightsbridge and Kensington's parks and museums. The hotel also has a leisure club.
Bedrooms: 28 single, 131 double, 226 twin, 36 family
Bathrooms: 421 en suite
Bed only: single £140.00-£160.00, double £160.00-£175.00
Evening meal: 1800 (l.o. 2345)
Parking for: 70
Credit Cards: Barclaycard/American Express/Switch/Delta/Diners/ Eurocheque

Swiss House Hotel

Listed COMMENDED

171 Old Brompton Road, London SW5 0AN
Tel: (0171) 373 2769/(0171) 373 9383
Fax: (0171) 373 4983
E-mail: recep@swiss-hh.demon.co.uk
URL: www.webscape.co.uk/ swiss_house
⊖ South Kensington
Comfortable, conveniently situated hotel near London museums, shopping and exhibition centres. Room service from 1200-2100.
Bedrooms: 5 single, 5 double, 2 twin, 4 family
Bathrooms: 15 en suite, 1 private shower, 1 public
Bed & Breakfast: single £44.00-£61.00, double £77.50-£85.00
Credit Cards: Mastercard/Eurocard/ Visa/Barclaycard/American Express/ Switch/Delta/Diners/Eurocheque

Town House Hotel

APPLIED

44-48 West Cromwell Road, London SW5 9QL
Tel: (0171) 373 4546
Fax: (0171) 373 8142
⊖ Earl's Court
Close to Kensington, Knightsbridge and Chelsea shopping centres. Ideal for Earl's Court and Olympia exhibition halls. Twenty minutes from Heathrow.
Bedrooms: 13 single, 7 double, 18 twin, 8 family
Bathrooms: 27 en suite, 19 private showers, 2 public
Bed & Breakfast: single £40.00-£55.00, double £60.00-£75.00
Credit Cards: Mastercard/Eurocard/ Visa/Barclaycard/American Express/ Switch/Delta/Diners/Eurocheque

Uptown Reservations

50 Christchurch Street, Chelsea, London SW3 4AR
Tel: (0171) 351 3445
Fax: (0171) 351 9383
E-mail: uptown@dial.pipex.com
URL: fenet.co.uk/uptown
⊖ Sloane Square
Grade II Listed building in Chelsea, with an upmarket friendly family. Also 70 other properties near Knightsbridge, South Kensington and Holland Park underground stations.
Bedrooms: 35 single, 35 double, 35 twin, 4 family
Bathrooms: 109 private
Bed & Breakfast: single £65.00, double £85.00
Credit Cards: Mastercard/Eurocard/ Visa/Barclaycard/American Express/ Switch/Delta

Westbury Hotel

Listed COMMENDED

22-24 Collingham Place, London SW5 0PZ
Tel: (0171) 373 0666
Fax: (0171) 835 0338
⊖ Earl's Court
The Westbury Hotel has 40 rooms of which 35 are en suite. All rooms have TV, telephone and radio.
Bedrooms: 17 single, 4 double, 7 twin, 12 family
Bathrooms: 35 en suite, 5 private showers, 5 public
Bed & Breakfast: single £45.00-£65.00, double £65.00-£85.00
Credit Cards: Mastercard/Eurocard/ Visa/Barclaycard/American Express/ Switch/Delta

Windsor House

Listed APPROVED

12 Penywern Road, London SW5 9ST
Tel: (0171) 373 9087
Fax: (0171) 385 2417
⊖ Earl's Court
Budget-priced bed and breakfast establishment in Earl's Court. Easily reached from airports and the motorway. The West End is minutes away by underground.
Bedrooms: 2 single, 4 double, 4 twin, 8 family
Bathrooms: 10 en suite, 7 private showers, 6 public
Bed only: single £28.00-£44.00, double £36.00-£56.00
Credit Cards: Eurocheque

York House Hotel

APPROVED

27-28 Philbeach Gardens, London SW5 9EA
Tel: (0171) 373 7519/(0171) 373 7579
Fax: (0171) 370 4641
⊖ Earl's Court
Bed and breakfast hotel, located close to Earl's Court station, served by Piccadilly Line, with direct links to Heathrow and West End.
Bedrooms: 16 single, 3 double, 3 twin, 5 family
Bathrooms: 1 en suite, 6 public
Bed & Breakfast: single £31.00-£32.00, double £49.00-£70.00
Credit Cards: Mastercard/Eurocard/ Visa/Barclaycard/American Express/ Delta/Diners/Eurocheque

EC1/2/3/4
City of London

The Barbican Hotel

Central Street, Clerkenwell, London EC1V 8DS
Tel: (0171) 251 1565
Fax: (0171) 253 1005
E-mail: barbican_hotel@cix.compulink.co.uk
Old Street/King's Cross
A modern hotel within easy walking distance of the Barbican Centre and the historic City of London. The hotel has conference rooms, a restaurant and bars.
Bedrooms: 76 single, 79 double, 268 twin, 44 family
Bathrooms: 467 en suite
Bed only: single £125.00, double £140.00
Bed & Breakfast: single £135.00, double £160.00
Evening meal: 1800 (l.o. 2230)
Parking for: 12
Credit Cards: Mastercard/Eurocard/Visa/Barclaycard/American Express/Switch/Delta/Diners/Eurocheque

W8/11/14
Kensington/Notting Hill Gate/Holland Park

Avonmore Hotel
Commended

66 Avonmore Road, Kensington, London W14 8RS
Tel: (0171) 603 3121/(0171) 603 4296
Fax: (0171) 603 4035
West Kensington
Privately owned, with a friendly atmosphere. Three minutes' walk from Olympia Exhibition Centre, ten minutes from Earl's Court Exhibition Centre and five minutes from West Kensington underground station.
Bedrooms: 1 single, 2 double, 3 twin, 3 family
Bathrooms: 7 en suite, 1 public
Bed & Breakfast: single £54.00-£78.00, double £78.00-£88.00
Credit Cards: Mastercard/Eurocard/Visa/Barclaycard/American Express/Switch/Eurocheque

B & B Flatlets

72 Holland Park Avenue, London W11 3QZ
Tel: (0171) 229 9233
Fax: (0171) 221 1077
E-mail: HoteLondon@aol.com
Holland Park
Small, family-run guesthouse in a pleasant central location. One minute from Holland Park underground station, buses and Airbus direct from Heathrow. All rooms have cable TV and cooking facilities. English breakfast served in bedrooms.
Bedrooms: 3 twin, 3 family
Bathrooms: 1 en suite, 2 public
Bed & Breakfast: single £25.00-£30.00, double £43.00-£55.00
Credit Cards: Mastercard/Eurocard/Visa/Barclaycard/American Express/Switch/Delta/Eurocheque

The Copthorne Tara
Highly Commended

Scarsdale Place, Kensington, London W8 5SR
Tel: (0171) 937 7211
Fax: (0171) 937 7100
High Street Kensington
Modern hotel near Earl's Court and Olympia exhibition centres and with easy access to the M4, Heathrow, Knightsbridge and the West End. Full meeting and business facilities available.
Bedrooms: 48 single, 317 double, 459 twin, 1 family
Bathrooms: 825 en suite
Bed only: single £165.00-£190.00, double £180.00-£205.00
Bed & Breakfast: single £189.00-£203.00, double £223.00-£231.00
Evening meal: 1730 (l.o. 2230)
Parking for: 88
Credit Cards: Mastercard/Eurocard/Barclaycard/American Express/Diners/Eurocheque

Forte Posthouse Kensington
Commended

Wright's Lane, London W8 5SP
Tel: (0171) 937 8170
Fax: (0171) 937 8289
High Street Kensington
Large, modern hotel close to Kensington High Street and Kensington Gardens. Easy access to the West End.
Bedrooms: 189 single, 96 double, 259 twin, 6 family
Bathrooms: 544 en suite, 6 private showers
Bed & Breakfast: single £142.00, double £166.00
Evening meal: 1730 (l.o. 2230)
Parking for: 70
Credit Cards: Mastercard/Visa/Barclaycard/American Express/Diners/Eurocheque

Hilton National London Olympia

380 Kensington High Street, London W14 8NL
Tel: (0171) 603 3333
Fax: (0171) 603 4846
E-mail: sales_olympia@hilton.com
URL: www.hilton.com
Kensington (Olympia)
Convenient for Kensington High Street and the West End. Close to Olympia.
Bedrooms: 69 single, 165 double, 130 twin, 40 family
Bathrooms: 404 en suite
Bed only: single £160.00-£200.00, double £170.00-£210.00
Evening meal: 1700 (l.o. 2230)
Parking for: 50
Credit Cards: Mastercard/Eurocard/Visa/Barclaycard/American Express/Switch/Delta/Diners/Eurocheque

Holland Court Hotel
Listed Commended

31-33 Holland Road, Kensington, London W14 8HJ
Tel: (0171) 371 1133
Fax: (0171) 602 9114
Kensington (Olympia)
Warm and friendly hotel close to Olympia and Earl's Court exhibition centres. Convenient for shops in Kensington High Street and Hammersmith.
Bedrooms: 4 single, 10 double, 6 twin, 2 family
Bathrooms: 22 en suite
Bed & Breakfast: single £75.00-£80.00, double £90.00-£95.00
Credit Cards: Mastercard/Eurocard/Visa/Barclaycard/American Express/Switch/Delta/Diners/Eurocheque

Hotel Atlas-Apollo
Commended

18-30 Lexham Gardens, London W8 5JE
Tel: (0171) 835 1155
Fax: (0171) 370 4853
Earl's Court
Friendly, well-established hotel situated close to Knightsbridge, Kensington High Street and Earl's Court and Olympia exhibition centres.

Bedrooms: 28 single, 7 double, 44 twin, 14 family
Bathrooms: 93 en suite
Bed & Breakfast: single £70.00-£75.00, double £85.00-£90.00
Credit Cards: Mastercard/Eurocard/Visa/Barclaycard/American Express/Switch/Delta/Diners/Eurocheque

Janus Hotel

26 Hazlitt Road, London W14 0JY
Tel: (0171) 603 6915/(0171) 603 3119
Fax: (0171) 370 1541
⊖ West Kensington
Homely hotel, quietly but centrally situated within easy reach of the West End.
Bedrooms: 5 single, 3 double, 3 twin, 6 family
Bathrooms: 5 private showers, 4 public
Bed & Breakfast: single £28.00, double £39.00
Credit Cards: Eurocheque

Kensington Palace Thistle Hotel

De Vere Gardens, London W8 5AF
Tel: (0171) 937 8121
Fax: (0171) 937 2816
⊖ High Street Kensington
Large hotel overlooking Kensington Gardens. Close to the shopping areas of Knightsbridge and the West End.
Bedrooms: 64 single, 84 double, 143 twin, 7 family
Bathrooms: 298 en suite
Bed only: single £115.00-£150.00, double £128.00-£210.00
Bed & Breakfast: single £129.00-£164.00, double £156.00-£238.00
Evening meal: 1700 (l.o. 2330)
Credit Cards: Mastercard/Eurocard/Visa/Barclaycard/American Express/Switch/Delta/Diners/Eurocheque

Kensington Park Thistle Hotel

16-32 De Vere Gardens, London W8 5AG
Tel: (0171) 937 8080
Fax: (0171) 937 7616
⊖ High Street Kensington
Located in Kensington, the hotel offers guests luxury and comfort within easy reach of the city centre.
Bedrooms: 80 single, 122 double, 145 twin, 5 family
Bathrooms: 352 en suite
Bed only: single £145.00-£170.00, double £170.00-£220.00
Bed & Breakfast: single £169.00-£189.00, double £191.00-£248.00
Evening meal: 1800 (l.o. 2300)
Credit Cards: Mastercard/Eurocard/Visa/Barclaycard/American Express/Switch/Delta/Diners/Eurocheque

London Kensington Hilton

Commended

179-199 Holland Park Avenue, London W11 4UL
Tel: (0171) 603 3355
Fax: (0171) 602 9397
URL: www.hilton.com
⊖ Holland Park
Modern hotel with easy access to exhibition centres, Holland Park and the West End. Express bus link to Heathrow.
Bedrooms: 19 single, 319 double, 265 twin
Bathrooms: 603 en suite
Bed & Breakfast: single £126.00-£215.00, double £138.00-£215.00
Evening meal: 1730 (l.o. 2230)
Parking for: 100
Credit Cards: Eurocard/Visa/Barclaycard/American Express/Switch/Delta/Diners/Eurocheque

London Lodge Hotel

Commended

134-136 Lexham Gardens, London W8 6JE
Tel: (0171) 244 8444
Fax: (0171) 373 6661
E-mail: London_Lodge_Hotel@compuserve.com
⊖ Earl's Court
A newly refurbished town house hotel. All rooms are en suite with satellite TV, mini bar, hairdryer, trouser press and direct dial telephone. Close to public transport and convenient for Kensington museums and Earl's Court.
Bedrooms: 7 single, 8 double, 12 twin, 1 family
Bathrooms: 28 en suite
Bed only: single £65.00-£120.00, double £75.00-£140.00
Bed & Breakfast: single £70.00-£130.00, double £85.00-£155.00
Evening meal: 1800 (l.o. 2230)
Credit Cards: Mastercard/Visa/American Express/Switch/Delta/Diners/Eurocheque

Royal Garden Hotel

Kensington High Street, London W8 4PT
Tel: (0171) 937 8000
Fax: (0171) 361 1991
E-mail: guest@royalgdn.co.uk
⊖ High Street Kensington
Recently refurbished 400-bedroom hotel with two restaurants, health and fitness facilities, extensive conference and banqueting facilities and car parking. Excellent location overlooking Hyde Park and Kensington Gardens.
Bedrooms: 123 single, 144 double, 87 twin, 41 family
Bathrooms: 392 en suite, 3 private
Bed only: single £200.00-£260.00, double £260.00-£300.00
Bed & Breakfast: single £220.00-£280.00, double £300.00-£350.00
Evening meal: 1730 (l.o. 2330)
Parking for: 160
Credit Cards: Mastercard/Eurocard/Visa/Barclaycard/American Express/Switch/Delta/Diners/Eurocheque

W3/4/5/6/7/12 Acton/Chiswick/Ealing/Hammersmith

Acton Park Hotel

Approved

116 The Vale, Acton, London W3 7JT
Tel: (0181) 743 9417
Fax: (0181) 743 9417
⇌ Acton Central
Small, family-run hotel, overlooking parkland, between Heathrow and the West End. Parking available.
Bedrooms: 7 single, 4 double, 8 twin, 2 family
Bathrooms: 21 en suite
Bed & Breakfast: single £48.00-£60.00, double £59.00-£73.00
Evening meal: 1800 (l.o. 2200)
Parking for: 15
Credit Cards: Mastercard/Barclaycard/American Express/Switch/Delta/Diners/Eurocheque

Boston Manor Hotel

Approved

146-152 Boston Road, Hanwell, London W7 2HJ
Tel: (0181) 566 1534
Fax: (0181) 567 9510

E-mail: bmh@boston-manor-htl.demon.co.uk
URL: www.boston-manor-htl.demon.co.uk
⊖ Boston Manor
Family-run hotel located close to Heathrow, with easy access to central London. Large car park and restaurant. Luxury suites available.
Bedrooms: 6 single, 17 double, 3 twin, 5 family
Bathrooms: 26 en suite, 4 private, 1 private shower, 4 public
Bed & Breakfast: single £40.00-£45.00, double £50.00-£55.00
Evening meal: 1800 (l.o. 2330)
Parking for: 20
Credit Cards: Mastercard/Eurocard/Visa/Barclaycard/American Express/Switch/Delta/Diners/Eurocheque

Chiswick Hotel
♛♛♛♛ COMMENDED

73 High Road, London W4 2LS
Tel: (0181) 994 1712
Fax: (0181) 742 2585
E-mail: Chishot@clara.net
⊖ Turnham Green
Large, carefully converted Victorian house, retaining many original features and with a friendly personal atmosphere. Located between Heathrow and central London.
Bedrooms: 28 single, 11 double, 7 twin, 7 family
Bathrooms: 53 en suite, 2 public
Bed & Breakfast: single £80.00-£90.00, double £102.00-£115.00
Evening meal: 1800 (l.o. 2100)
Parking for: 20
Credit Cards: Mastercard/Eurocard/Visa/Barclaycard/American Express/Switch/Delta/Diners/Eurocheque

Creffield Lodge
Listed APPROVED

2-4 Creffield Road, Ealing, London W5 3HN
Tel: (0181) 993 2284
Fax: (0181) 992 7082
⊖ Ealing Common
Victorian-style property, located in a quiet residential road, adjacent to the Jarvis International Hotel.
Bedrooms: 12 single, 5 double, 3 twin, 4 family
Bathrooms: 14 en suite, 4 public
Bed only: single £42.00-£90.00, double £85.00-£95.00
Bed & Breakfast: single £52.00-£100.00, double £105.00-£115.00
Evening meal: 1830 (l.o. 2230)
Parking for: 20
Credit Cards: Mastercard/Eurocard/Visa/Barclaycard/American Express/Switch/Delta/Diners/Eurocheque

Foubert's Hotel
♛ APPROVED

162-166 Chiswick High Road, London W4 1PR
Tel: (0181) 994 5202/(0181) 995 6743
⊖ Turnham Green
Family-run hotel close to Heathrow Airport and central London. Fully licensed restaurant and candlelit wine cellars. Live music and dancing at weekends.
Bedrooms: 15 single, 9 double, 4 twin, 3 family
Bathrooms: 16 en suite, 15 private, 4 public
Bed & Breakfast: single £33.00-£38.00, double £55.00-£60.00
Evening meal: (l.o. 2300)
Credit Cards: Mastercard/Visa/Barclaycard/Eurocheque

Holiday Inn London Ealing

Western Avenue, Hanger Lane, London W5 1HG
Tel: (0181) 233 3200
Fax: (0181) 233 3201
⊖ Hanger Lane
This modern hotel offers an ideal base for exploring the heart of London. Located close to Wembley Stadium and with easy access to the M1 and M4. The hotel has 138 bedrooms, seven conference rooms, a restaurant and bar.
Bedrooms: 64 double, 74 twin
Bathrooms: 138 en suite
Bed & Breakfast: single £133.00-£163.00, double £146.00-£176.00
Evening meal: 1830 (l.o. 2230)
Parking for: 95
Credit Cards: Mastercard/Visa/Barclaycard/American Express/Diners

Jarvis International, Ealing
♛♛♛♛ HIGHLY COMMENDED

Ealing Common, London W5 3HN
Tel: (0181) 992 5399
Fax: (0181) 992 7082
⊖ Ealing Common
Modern, purpose-built five-storey building close to Ealing town centre and within easy reach of central London.
Bedrooms: 95 double, 55 twin
Bathrooms: 150 en suite
Bed only: single £115.00-£125.00, double £130.00-£145.00
Bed & Breakfast: single £125.00-£135.00, double £150.00-£165.00
Evening meal: 1830 (l.o. 2230)
Parking for: 150
Credit Cards: Mastercard/Eurocard/Visa/Barclaycard/American Express/Switch/Delta/Diners/Eurocheque

Kenton House Hotel

5 Hillcrest Road, Ealing, London W5 2JL
Tel: (0181) 997 8436
Fax: (0181) 998 0037
⊖/⇌ Ealing Broadway
Family-run hotel in a quiet location opposite a park. Convenient for access to central London.
Bedrooms: 30 single, 9 double, 2 twin, 18 family
Bathrooms: 59 en suite
Evening meal: 1830 (l.o. 2200)
Parking for: 27
Credit Cards: Mastercard/Visa/Barclaycard/American Express/Switch/Delta/Diners/Eurocheque

Lime Grove Hotel
Listed COMMENDED

32 Lime Grove, London W12 8EA
Tel: (0181) 743 5243
Fax: (0181) 740 0364
⊖ Goldhawk Road
Bed and breakfast hotel. Fifteen-bedroom town house, plus recently refurbished annex providing a further 12 bedrooms.
Bedrooms: 3 single, 8 double, 3 twin
Bathrooms: 14 en suite, 1 public
Bed & Breakfast: single £40.00-£55.00, double £65.00-£80.00
Parking for: 4
Credit Cards: Mastercard/Eurocard/Visa/Barclaycard/American Express/Switch/Delta/Diners/Eurocheque

Novotel London Hammersmith
♛♛♛♛ COMMENDED

1 Shortlands, Hammersmith, London W6 8DR
Tel: (0181) 741 1555/(0181) 237 7437
Fax: (0181) 741 2120
⊖ Hammersmith

A modern, international hotel with easy access to Heathrow and central London; conference and exhibition facilities and car park. All rooms have en suite bathrooms, satellite TV and tea and coffee facilities.
Bedrooms: 126 double, 450 twin, 64 family
Bathrooms: 640 en suite
Bed & Breakfast: single £142.00, double £165.00
Evening meal: 1700 (l.o. 2355)
Parking for: 250
Credit Cards: Mastercard/Eurocard/Visa/Barclaycard/American Express/Switch/Delta/Diners/Eurocheque

St Peters Hotel
Listed COMMENDED

407-411 Goldhawk Road, London W6 0SA
Tel: (0181) 741 4239
Fax: (0181) 748 3845
Stamford Brook
A small, well-appointed establishment where customer care is a priority. Within easy reach of Heathrow and central London. Good value for money.
Bedrooms: 5 single, 5 double, 8 twin
Bathrooms: 12 en suite, 1 public
Credit Cards: Mastercard/Eurocard/Visa/Barclaycard/American Express/Switch/Delta/Eurocheque

Wellmeadow Lodge Hotel
HIGHLY COMMENDED

24 Wellmeadow Road, London W7 2AL
Tel: (0181) 567 7294
Fax: (0181) 566 3468
Boston Manor
Delightful establishment providing high standards at fair prices.
Bedrooms: 3 single, 4 double, 3 twin
Bathrooms: 10 en suite
Bed & Breakfast: single £70.00-£120.00, double £86.00-£128.00
Evening meal: 1800 (l.o. 1900)
Credit Cards: Mastercard/Eurocard/Visa/Barclaycard/American Express/Switch/Delta/Eurocheque

NORTH WEST LONDON

Americana Hotel
Listed APPROVED

172 Gloucester Place, Regent's Park, London NW1 6DS
Tel: (0171) 723 1452
Fax: (0171) 723 4641
E-mail: manager@americanahotel.demon.co.uk
Baker Street
Quiet hotel with friendly staff, ideally situated for shopping in central London. Near to Baker Street underground and Madame Tussaud's.
Bedrooms: 1 single, 14 double, 10 twin
Bathrooms: 25 en suite
Bed & Breakfast: single £75.00, double £100.00
Credit Cards: Mastercard/Eurocard/Visa/Barclaycard/American Express/Switch/Delta/Eurocheque

Anchor-Nova Hotel
Listed COMMENDED

10 West Heath Drive, Golders Green, London NW11 7QH
Tel: (0181) 458 8764
Fax: (0181) 455 3204
E-mail: raab@dircon.co.uk
Golders Green
A small, well-furnished hotel with many amenities. Situated close to the underground. Free parking available.
Bedrooms: 2 single, 5 double, 4 twin
Bathrooms: 8 en suite, 1 public
Bed & Breakfast: single £32.00-£48.00, double £43.00-£57.00
Parking for: 4
Credit Cards: Mastercard/Eurocard/Visa/Barclaycard/American Express/Switch/Delta/Eurocheque

Charlotte Guest House & Restaurant
Listed APPROVED

221 West End Lane, West Hampstead, London NW6 1XJ
Tel: (0171) 794 6476
Fax: (0171) 431 3584
West Hampstead
Close to public transport and only 12 minutes from Piccadilly. Free London Travelcard for a visit of a week or more.
Bedrooms: 12 single, 12 double, 12 twin
Bathrooms: 18 en suite, 6 public
Bed & Breakfast: single £30.00-£40.00, double £46.00-£50.00
Evening meal: 1800 (l.o. 2200)
Credit Cards: Eurocheque

Croft Court Hotel

44 Ravenscroft Avenue, London NW11 8AY
Tel: (0181) 458 3331
Fax: (0181) 455 9175
Golders Green/Brent Cross
Within 20 minutes of central London and close to the M1, M4, Brent Cross shopping centre and Wembley complex. Good service and personal attention.
Bedrooms: 3 single, 2 double, 14 twin
Bathrooms: 19 en suite
Evening meal: 1800 (l.o. 2200)
Parking for: 3
Credit Cards: Mastercard/Barclaycard/Switch/Delta/Eurocheque

Dawson House Hotel
COMMENDED

72 Canfield Gardens, London NW6 3ED
Tel: (0171) 624 0079/(0171) 624 6525
Fax: (0171) 644 6321
E-mail: dawsonhtl@aol.com
Finchley Road
Convenient for West End shops and theatres.
Bedrooms: 6 single, 5 double, 1 twin, 3 family
Bathrooms: 15 en suite, 2 public
Bed & Breakfast: single £45.00-£55.00, double £65.00-£70.00
Credit Cards: Mastercard/Eurocard/Visa/Barclaycard/American Express/Switch/Delta/Eurocheque

Dillons Hotel
Listed APPROVED

21 Belsize Park, Hampstead, London NW3 4DU
Tel: (0171) 794 3360
Fax: (0171) 431 7900
Swiss Cottage
Small private guesthouse, close to central London and with excellent transport facilities.
Bedrooms: 2 single, 3 double, 4 twin, 4 family
Bathrooms: 7 en suite, 3 public
Bed & Breakfast: single £27.00-£35.00, double £39.00-£47.00
Credit Cards: Mastercard/Eurocard/Visa/Barclaycard/Switch/Delta/Eurocheque

Hendon Hall Hotel

Ashley Lane, off Parson Street, Hendon, London NW4 1HF
Tel: (0181) 203 3341
Fax: (0181) 203 9709
Hendon Central

Elegant, 18th century Georgian mansion set in its own grounds. Underwent major bedroom refurbishment in 1996 and 1997.
Bedrooms: 1 single, 36 double, 21 twin
Bathrooms: 58 en suite
Bed only: single £125.00-£215.00, double £155.00-£250.00
Bed & Breakfast: single £137.50-£227.50, double £180.00-£275.00
Evening meal: 1900 (l.o. 2200)
Parking for: 70
Credit Cards: Mastercard/Eurocard/Visa/Barclaycard/American Express/Switch/Delta/Diners/Eurocheque

Hotel Ibis Euston

3 Cardington Street, Euston, London NW1 2LW
Tel: (0171) 388 7777
Fax: (0171) 388 0001
Euston
Situated near Euston station.
Bedrooms: 240 double, 60 twin
Bathrooms: 300 en suite
Bed only: single £56.00, double £56.00
Bed & Breakfast: single £61.75, double £67.50
Evening meal: 1800 (l.o. 2230)
Parking for: 100
Credit Cards: Eurocard/Visa/American Express/Switch/Delta/Diners/Eurocheque

The Kennedy Hotel

43 Cardington Street, London NW1 2LP
Tel: (0171) 387 4400
Fax: (0171) 387 5122
Euston
Modern air-conditioned hotel with easy access to the West End. Weekend rates available. Adjacent to Euston station.
Bedrooms: 60 single, 67 double, 172 twin, 61 family
Bathrooms: 360 en suite
Bed only: single £106.00-£127.00, double £121.00-£154.00
Bed & Breakfast: single £114.95-£116.95, double £138.90-£142.90
Evening meal: 1730 (l.o. 2230)
Parking for: 20
Credit Cards: Mastercard/Eurocard/Visa/Barclaycard/American Express/Switch/Delta/Diners/Eurocheque

The Landmark, London

De Luxe

222 Marylebone Road, London NW1 6JQ
Tel: (0171) 631 8000
Fax: (0171) 631 8080
E-mail: corporate@landmark.btinternet.com
URL: **www.landmarklondon.co.uk**
Baker Street, Marylebone
Originally built in 1899 as the Great Central Hotel. Offers extensive conference facilities.
Bedrooms: 28 single, 190 double, 81 twin
Bathrooms: 299 en suite
Bed only: single £311.00, double £311.00
Evening meal: 1900 (l.o. 2230)
Parking for: 80
Credit Cards: Mastercard/Eurocard/Visa/Barclaycard/American Express/Switch/Delta/Diners/Eurocheque

The Langorf Hotel

Commended

20 Frognal, Hampstead, London NW3 6AG
Tel: (0171) 794 4483
Fax: (0171) 435 9055
Finchley Road, Finchley Road & Frognal
Edwardian residence three minutes' walk from the underground. Bedrooms with full facilities and friendly atmosphere.
Bedrooms: 1 single, 18 double, 8 twin, 4 family
Bathrooms: 31 en suite
Bed & Breakfast: single £73.00-£80.00, double £90.00-£99.00
Credit Cards: Mastercard/Visa/Barclaycard/American Express/Switch/Delta/Diners/Eurocheque

London Euston Travel Inn Capital

141 Euston Road, London NW1 2AU
Tel: (0171) 554 3400/(01582) 414341
Fax: (0171) 554 3419
URL: **www.travelinn.co.uk**
King's Cross/Euston
Bedrooms: 100 double, 120 twin
Bathrooms: 220 en suite
Bed only: single £55.00, double £55.00
Evening meal: 1700 (l.o. 2300)
Parking for: 50
Credit Cards: Mastercard/Eurocard/Visa/Barclaycard/American Express/Switch/Delta/Diners

London Regent's Park Hilton

Commended

18 Lodge Road, St John's Wood, London NW8 7JT
Tel: (0171) 722 7722
Fax: (0171) 483 2408
Saint John's Wood
Overlooking Lords Cricket Ground and adjacent to Regent's Park. Near West End.
Bedrooms: 224 double, 149 twin, 4 family
Bathrooms: 377 en suite
Bed only: single £180.00, double £200.00
Bed & Breakfast: single £195.50, double £231.00
Evening meal: 1830 (l.o. 2230)
Parking for: 80
Credit Cards: Mastercard/Eurocard/Visa/Barclaycard/American Express/Switch/Delta/Diners

Regents Plaza Hotel & Suites

Plaza Parade, Maida Vale, London NW6 5RP
Tel: (0171) 543 6000
Fax: (0171) 543 2100
E-mail: regentsplaza.sales@btinternet.com
Maida Vale
Luxury hotel located ten minutes from Marble Arch, Regent's Park and Lords Cricket Ground. The hotel has two restaurants, bar, health and leisure club, large pool, business centre, landscape gardens and private parking.
Bedrooms: 96 double, 40 twin, 48 family
Bathrooms: 184 en suite
Bed & Breakfast: single £189.00, double £200.00
Evening meal: 1800 (l.o. 2300)
Parking for: 141
Credit Cards: Mastercard/Eurocard/Visa/Barclaycard/American Express/Switch/Delta/Diners/Eurocheque

Stakis Harewood London Hotel

Harewood Row, Marylebone, London NW1 6SE
Tel: (0171) 262 2707
Fax: (0171) 262 2975
Marylebone

Located centrally for the West End and City. Five minutes' walk to Madame Tussaud's and Baker Street. Two stops on the underground to Paddington station and the Heathrow Express.
Bedrooms: 22 single, 25 double, 45 twin
Bathrooms: 92 en suite
Bed only: single £60.00-£100.00, double £74.00-£140.00
Bed & Breakfast: single £64.00-£144.00, double £82.00-£160.00
Evening meal: 1800 (l.o. 2100)
Credit Cards: Mastercard/Visa/Barclaycard/American Express/Switch/Diners/Eurocheque

Welcome Lodge/Welcome Break

Scratchwood Service Area, M1 Motorway, London NW7 3HB
Tel: (0181) 906 0611
Fax: (0181) 906 3654
Mill Hill Broadway
Lodge with 101 bedrooms, situated between junctions 2 and 4 on the M1 just outside London.
Bedrooms: 41 double, 48 twin, 12 family
Bathrooms: 101 en suite
Bed & Breakfast: single £55.00, double £55.00
Evening meal: 1800 (l.o. 2200)
Parking for: 100
Credit Cards: Mastercard/Visa/Barclaycard/American Express/Switch/Delta/Diners/Eurocheque

The White House — Commended

Albany Street, Regent's Park, London NW1 3UP
Tel: (0171) 387 1200
Fax: (0171) 388 0091
Great Portland Street
The White House is close to London Zoo and Madame Tussaud's and about ten minutes' walk from Oxford Circus.
Bedrooms: 53 single, 216 double, 239 twin, 53 family
Bathrooms: 561 en suite
Bed only: single £156.00-£193.00, double £165.00-£205.00
Bed & Breakfast: single £168.00-£205.00, double £189.00-£229.00
Evening meal: 1830 (l.o. 2230)
Parking for: 7

Credit Cards: Mastercard/Eurocard/Visa/Barclaycard/American Express/Switch/Delta/Diners/Eurocheque

North London

Costello Palace Hotel — Listed Approved

374 Seven Sisters Road, Finsbury Park, London N4 2PG
Tel: (0181) 802 6551
Fax: (0181) 802 9461
Manor House
Overlooking Finsbury Park, with its own car park and fully licensed bar. All rooms are en suite with tea and coffee making facilities, Sky TV and 24-hour reception.
Bedrooms: 3 single, 17 double, 20 twin, 4 family
Bathrooms: 44 en suite, 1 public
Bed & Breakfast: single £40.00-£45.00, double £55.00-£65.00
Parking for: 35
Credit Cards: Mastercard/Eurocard/Visa/Barclaycard/Switch/Delta/Diners

Five Kings Guest House — Approved

59 Anson Road, Tufnell Park, London N7 0AR
Tel: (0171) 607 3996/(0171) 607 6466
Kentish Town, Tufnell Park
Privately run guesthouse situated in a quiet residential area. Fifteen minutes from central London. Parking with no restrictions available in Anson Road.
Bedrooms: 6 single, 3 double, 3 twin, 4 family
Bathrooms: 9 en suite, 2 private showers, 3 public
Bed & Breakfast: single £22.00-£28.00, double £32.00-£40.00
Credit Cards: Mastercard/Eurocard/Visa/Barclaycard/Eurocheque

Highfield Lodge Hotel — Applied

2 Dalmeny Road, London N7 0HH
Tel: (0171) 607 8889
Fax: (0171) 607 6821
Tufnell Park
Friendly, family-run business providing a comfortable bed and a traditional breakfast. Ideal for business people or tourists.
Bedrooms: 9 single, 4 double, 4 twin, 2 family
Bathrooms: 19 en suite, 2 public

Bed & Breakfast: single £30.00-£34.00, double £45.00-£50.00
Credit Cards: Mastercard/Eurocard/Visa/Barclaycard/Switch/Delta/Eurocheque

Kandara Guest House — Listed Commended

68 Ockendon Road, London N1 3NW
Tel: (0171) 226 5721/(0171) 226 3379
Fax: (0171) 226 3379
Angel, Highbury & Islington
Small, family-run guesthouse close to the West End and public transport. Free street parking.
Bedrooms: 4 single, 2 double, 2 twin, 2 family
Bathrooms: 3 public
Bed & Breakfast: single £33.00-£36.00, double £44.00-£48.00
Credit Cards: Mastercard/Eurocard/Visa/Barclaycard

New Pembury Hotel — Approved

328 Seven Sisters Road, Finsbury Park, London N4 2AP
Tel: (0181) 800 5310
Fax: (0181) 809 6362
Finsbury Park
Newly renovated modern rooms. All rooms are en suite and have satellite TV. Within 15 minutes of central London. Competitive prices. Friendly and welcoming.
Bedrooms: 22 single, 15 double, 16 twin, 6 family
Bathrooms: 59 en suite, 4 public
Bed & Breakfast: single £43.00-£48.00, double £65.00-£70.00
Evening meal: 1800 (l.o. 2200)
Parking for: 30
Credit Cards: Mastercard/Visa/Barclaycard/American Express/Switch/Delta/Eurocheque

Spring Park Hotel — Approved

400 Seven Sisters Road, London N4 2LX
Tel: (0181) 800 6030
Fax: (0181) 802 5652
Manor House, Finsbury Park
Direct link (Piccadilly line) to the West End and Heathrow. Overlooking Finsbury Park.
Bedrooms: 10 single, 19 double, 20 twin, 1 family

Bathrooms: 36 en suite, 7 public
Bed only: single £25.00-£40.00, double £40.00-£55.00
Bed & Breakfast: single £30.00-£50.00, double £45.00-£65.00
Evening meal: 1800 (l.o. 2300)
Parking for: 70
Credit Cards: Mastercard/Eurocard/Visa/Barclaycard/American Express/Switch/Delta/Eurocheque

Stakis London Islington

53 Upper Street, London N1 0UY
Tel: (0171) 354 7700/(0171) 354 7777
Fax: (0171) 354 7711
Angel
Brand-new hotel located next to the Business Design Centre in Islington.
Bedrooms: 3 single, 148 double, 26 twin, 6 family
Bathrooms: 183 en suite
Bed only: single £149.00, double £169.00
Bed & Breakfast: single £157.00, double £188.00
Evening meal: 1800 (l.o. 2230)
Credit Cards: Mastercard/Eurocard/Visa/Barclaycard/American Express/Switch/Delta/Diners

White Lodge Hotel

APPROVED

1 Church Lane, Hornsey, London N8 7BU
Tel: (0181) 348 9765
Fax: (0181) 340 7851
Hornsey, Turnpike Lane
Small, friendly family hotel offering personal service and easy access to all transport facilities.
Bedrooms: 7 single, 3 double, 3 twin, 3 family
Bathrooms: 8 en suite, 3 public
Bed & Breakfast: single £28.00-£30.00, double £38.00-£46.00
Evening meal: 1800 (l.o. 1900)
Credit Cards: Mastercard/Eurocard/Visa/Barclaycard/Eurocheque

South West London

Barclay Court Private Hotel

APPROVED

12-14 Hafer Road, London SW11 1HF
Tel: (0171) 228 5272
Fax: (0171) 924 5431
Clapham Junction
Family-run establishment on the A3, with direct connections to Gatwick and Victoria station from nearby Clapham Junction.
Bedrooms: 6 single, 3 double, 3 twin, 2 family
Bathrooms: 1 en suite, 9 private showers, 3 public
Bed & Breakfast: single £35.00-£38.00, double £46.00-£50.00
Credit Cards: Mastercard/Eurocard/Visa/Barclaycard/American Express/Switch/Diners

The Brewers Inn

COMMENDED

147 East Hill, Wandsworth, London SW18 2QB
Tel: (0181) 874 4128
Fax: (0181) 877 1953
Wandsworth Town
The Brewers Inn has 16 en suite bedrooms, a large bar, restaurant and car park.
Bedrooms: 4 single, 9 double, 3 twin
Bathrooms: 16 en suite
Bed & Breakfast: single £65.00-£85.00, double £70.00-£90.00
Evening meal: 1800 (l.o. 2200)
Parking for: 10
Credit Cards: Mastercard/Eurocard/Visa/Barclaycard/American Express/Switch/Delta/Diners/Eurocheque

Cannizaro House

(A Thistle Country House Hotel)

Westside, Wimbledon Common, London SW19 4UE
Tel: (0181) 879 1464
Fax: (0181) 879 7338
/ Wimbledon
A historic Georgian mansion set in the gardens of Cannizaro Park on the edge of Wimbledon Common. Meeting and conference facilities for up to 100 people available.
Bedrooms: 31 double, 15 twin
Bathrooms: 46 en suite
Evening meal: 1900 (l.o. 2230)
Parking for: 90
Credit Cards: Mastercard/Eurocard/Visa/Barclaycard/American Express/Switch/Delta/Diners/Eurocheque

Chelsea Village Hotel

Stamford Bridge, Fulham Road, London SW6 1HS
Tel: (0171) 565 1400
Fax: (0171) 565 1450
Fulham Broadway
Purpose-built, 160-bedroom hotel with four themed restaurants and bars. Fully integrated business centre. Modem and fax link available from all bedrooms.
Bedrooms: 84 double, 52 twin, 14 family
Bathrooms: 150 en suite
Bed only: single £135.00-£145.00, double £155.00-£165.00
Evening meal: 1700 (l.o. 2330)
Parking for: 500
Credit Cards: Mastercard/American Express/Switch/Eurocheque

Conrad International, London

Chelsea Harbour, London SW10 0XG
Tel: (0171) 823 3000
Fax: (0171) 351 6525
Earl's Court
Located on the Thames in the attractive surroundings of Chelsea Harbour.
Bedrooms: 132 double, 28 twin
Bathrooms: 160 en suite
Bed & Breakfast: single £193.00, double £215.35
Evening meal: 1800 (l.o. 2230)
Parking for: 2000
Credit Cards: Mastercard/Visa/Barclaycard/American Express/Switch/Diners/Eurocheque

Grosvenor Arms

Listed APPROVED

204 Garratt Lane, Wandsworth, London SW18 4ED
Tel: (0181) 874 2709
Earlsfield
Well-maintained pub over 100 years old, on three floors with a large garden.
Bedrooms: 3 twin, 1 family
Bathrooms: 2 public
Bed & Breakfast: single £30.00-£35.00, double £40.00-£48.00
Evening meal: 1830 (l.o. 1930)
Credit Cards: Mastercard/Eurocard/Visa/Barclaycard

Lavender Guest House

Listed APPROVED

18 Lavender Sweep, London SW11 1HA
Tel: (0171) 585 2767/(0171) 223 1973
Fax: (0171) 224 6274

Clapham Junction
Detached Victorian building with a mature, well-stocked garden for guests' use.
Bedrooms: 1 single, 2 double, 4 twin, 2 family
Bathrooms: 5 en suite, 1 private shower, 2 public
Bed & Breakfast: single £45.00, double £55.00
Credit Cards: Eurocheque

The Paragon Hotel

47 Lillie Road, London SW6 1UD
Tel: (0171) 385 1255
Fax: (0171) 381 4450
West Brompton
Modern hotel with two restaurants, bar and parking facilities.
Bedrooms: 102 double, 379 twin, 20 family
Bathrooms: 501 en suite
Bed only: single £105.00, double £115.00
Evening meal: 1800 (l.o. 2230)
Parking for: 130
Credit Cards: Mastercard/Barclaycard/American Express/Diners/Eurocheque

Travel Inn Capital Putney Bridge

3-5 Putney Bridge Approach, London SW6 3JD
Tel: (0171) 471 8300
Fax: (0171) 471 8315
URL: www.Travelinn.co.uk
Putney Bridge
Budget accommodation situated on the north bank of the Thames, ideal for access to Earl's Court, Olympia and Wimbledon.
Bedrooms: 2 single, 96 double, 56 twin
Bathrooms: 154 en suite
Bed only: single £55.00, double £55.00
Evening meal: 1700 (l.o. 2230)
Parking for: 32
Credit Cards: Mastercard/Visa/Barclaycard/American Express/Switch/Delta/Diners

Trochee Hotel

Approved

21 Malcolm Road, Wimbledon, London SW19 4AS
Tel: (0181) 946 1579/(0181) 946 3924
Fax: (0181) 785 4058
Wimbledon
Small bed and breakfast hotel located in a quiet residential area.
Bedrooms: 9 single, 2 double, 5 twin, 1 family
Bathrooms: 3 public
Bed & Breakfast: single £39.00-£44.00, double £54.00-£57.00
Parking for: 3
Credit Cards: Mastercard/Eurocard/Visa/Barclaycard/American Express/Eurocheque

Trochee Hotel Annexe

Approved

52 Ridgway Place, Wimbledon, London SW19 4SW
Tel: (0181) 946 9425/(0181) 946 9400
Fax: (0181) 785 4058
Wimbledon
Small hotel located in a quiet residential area.
Bedrooms: 4 single, 2 double, 6 twin, 4 family
Bathrooms: 9 en suite, 3 public
Bed & Breakfast: single £52.00-£55.00, double £64.00-£67.00
Parking for: 6
Credit Cards: Mastercard/Eurocard/Visa/Barclaycard/American Express/Eurocheque

Windmill on the Common

Highly Commended

Southside, Clapham Common, London SW4 9DE
Tel: (0181) 673 4578
Fax: (0181) 675 1486
Clapham Common
Well-appointed bedrooms overlooking the Common. Restaurant offering à la carte food and a traditional busy Young's pub serving bar food.
Bedrooms: 20 double, 9 twin
Bathrooms: 29 en suite
Bed & Breakfast: single £92.00, double £102.00
Evening meal: 1900 (l.o. 2200)
Parking for: 30
Credit Cards: Mastercard/Eurocard/Visa/Barclaycard/American Express/Switch/Delta/Diners/Eurocheque

East London

Forest View Hotel

Approved

227 Romford Road, Forest Gate, London E7 9HL
Tel: (0181) 534 4844
Fax: (0181) 534 8959
Forest Gate, Stratford
Fully equipped hotel catering for both business and tourist customers. Most rooms are en suite with tea and coffee making facilities, TV, radio and telephone. Close to London Docklands.
Bedrooms: 8 single, 5 double, 2 twin, 5 family
Bathrooms: 3 en suite, 4 private, 3 public
Bed & Breakfast: single £38.00, double £55.25-£66.25
Evening meal: 1830 (l.o. 2100)
Parking for: 15
Credit Cards: Mastercard/Eurocard/Visa/Barclaycard/Switch/Delta/Eurocheque

Grangewood Lodge Hotel

Listed Approved

104 Clova Road, Forest Gate, London E7 9AF
Tel: (0181) 534 0637/(0181) 503 0941
Fax: (0181) 257 0392
Stratford, Forest Gate
Comfortable, budget accommodation in a quiet road, with pleasant garden. Good access to central London, Docklands and M11.
Bedrooms: 10 single, 1 double, 5 twin, 2 family
Bathrooms: 1 private shower, 3 public
Bed & Breakfast: single £18.00-£20.00, double £30.00-£36.00
Parking for: 2
Credit Cards: Mastercard/Visa/Barclaycard/Switch

Sleeping Beauty Motel

Approved

543 Lea Bridge Road, Leyton, London E10 7EB
Tel: (0181) 556 8080
Fax: (0181) 556 8080
Walthamstow Central
Motel on four floors. New wing open from May 1998, built on two and three floors. Car and coach park.
Bedrooms: 17 double, 68 twin
Bathrooms: 85 en suite

Bed & Breakfast: single £45.00-£50.00, double £50.00-£55.00
Parking for: 79
Credit Cards: Mastercard/Eurocard/Visa/Barclaycard/American Express/Switch/Delta/Diners/Eurocheque

The Tower Thistle Hotel

St Katharine's Way, London E1 9LD
Tel: (0171) 481 2575
Fax: (0171) 488 4106
Fenchurch Street, Tower Hill
Next to Tower Bridge and the Tower of London and overlooking St Katharine Docks. Close to the City and the West End. Ideally located for both business and pleasure.
Bedrooms: 96 single, 189 double, 475 twin, 42 family
Bathrooms: 780 en suite
Bed only: single £165.00-£195.00, double £185.00-£240.00
Bed & Breakfast: single £178.50-£208.50, double £221.00-£267.00
Evening meal: 1730 (l.o. 2230)
Parking for: 116
Credit Cards: Mastercard/Visa/Barclaycard/American Express/Switch/Delta/Diners

South East London

Bedknobs
Listed COMMENDED

58 Glengarry Road, East Dulwich, London SE22 8QD
Tel: (0181) 299 2004
Fax: (0181) 693 5611
North Dulwich/East Dulwich
Carefully restored, Victorian, family-run house offering many home comforts, excellent service and a warm welcome.
Bedrooms: 2 double, 1 twin
Bathrooms: 2 public
Bed & Breakfast: single £25.00-£40.00, double £45.00-£65.00
Credit Cards: Mastercard/Eurocard/Visa/Barclaycard/Switch/Delta/Eurocheque

Benvenuti
Listed HIGHLY COMMENDED

217 Court Road, Eltham, London SE9 4TG
Tel: (0181) 857 4855
Fax: (0181) 256 5635
Mottingham
Family-run bed and breakfast. Four minutes' walk from train station. Central London is 25 minutes by train. Convenient for the M25, M20, A20, A2 and M2. No smoking establishment.
Bedrooms: 1 double, 1 twin, 1 family
Bathrooms: 1 public
Bed & Breakfast: single £25.00-£30.00, double £45.00-£60.00
Parking for: 4

Clarendon Hotel
APPROVED

8-16 Montpelier Row, Blackheath, London SE3 0RW
Tel: (0181) 318 4321
Fax: (0181) 318 4378
Blackheath
Facing the heath and 22 minutes by train from central London. Ten minutes' walk from Greenwich, five minutes' walk from Greenwich Royal Park. Two-hundred-and-fifty-year-old Listed building.
Bedrooms: 44 single, 54 double, 69 twin, 26 family
Bathrooms: 160 en suite, 4 private, 14 public
Bed only: single £55.00-£90.00, double £72.00-£150.00
Bed & Breakfast: single £60.00-£90.00, double £80.00-£150.00
Evening meal: 1830 (l.o. 2145)
Parking for: 80
Credit Cards: Mastercard/Visa/Barclaycard/American Express/Switch/Diners/Eurocheque

Glenthurston Holiday Apartments
APPLIED

27 Canadian Avenue, London SE6 3AU
Tel: (0181) 265 5872
Fax: (0181) 265 5872
Catford Bridge
Large Victorian house. Use of heated indoor pool, sauna and steam room.
Bedrooms: 1 family
Bathrooms: 1 public
Parking for: 4

Highfield House
Listed HIGHLY COMMENDED

12 Dowanhill Road, London SE6 1HJ
Tel: (0181) 698 8038
Fax: (0181) 698 8039
Hither Green
Winner of the Bed and Breakfast of the Year in the 1998 London Tourism Awards.
Highfield House is a beautifully refurbished Victorian house situated in a quiet residential area. Convenient for access to central London and Channel routes.
Bedrooms: 2 double, 1 twin
Bathrooms: 1 en suite, 1 public
Bed & Breakfast: single £40.00, double £45.00-£60.00
Evening meal: (l.o. 2100)
Parking for: 1
Credit Cards: Mastercard/Eurocard/Visa/Barclaycard/Switch/Delta/Eurocheque

Holiday Inn Nelson Dock
COMMENDED

265 Rotherhithe Street, London SE16 1EJ
Tel: (0171) 231 1001
Fax: (0171) 231 0599
Rotherhithe
A tasteful mixture of old and new, this riverside hotel is situated on Nelson Dock, which dates back to the 18th century.
Bedrooms: 41 single, 191 double, 116 twin, 20 family
Bathrooms: 344 en suite
Bed only: single £115.00-£157.00, double £137.00-£157.00
Bed & Breakfast: single £126.50-£170.50, double £161.00-£182.00
Evening meal: 1830 (l.o. 2300)
Parking for: 150
Credit Cards: Mastercard/Visa/Barclaycard/American Express/Switch/Delta/Diners/Eurocheque

London Bridge Hotel

8-18 London Bridge Street, London SE1 9SG
Tel: (0171) 855 2200
Fax: (0171) 855 2233
E-mail: enquiries@London-bridge-hotel.co.uk
London Bridge
Privately owned hotel situated opposite London Bridge station. Redevelopment of a 1915 building with health club, wine bar and restaurant operated by Simply Nico.
Bedrooms: 3 single, 44 double, 72 twin
Bathrooms: 119 en suite

Bed only: single £154.00-£181.50, double £170.50-£192.50
Bed & Breakfast: single £162.75-£166.05, double £187.99-£216.59
Credit Cards: Mastercard/Visa/Barclaycard/American Express/Diners

London County Hall Travel Inn Capital

Belvedere Road, London SE1 7PB
Tel: (0171) 902 1600
Fax: (0171) 902 1619
Waterloo
Situated in the magnificent County Hall, overlooking the River Thames opposite the Houses of Parliament.
Bedrooms: 201 double, 112 family
Bathrooms: 313 en suite
Bed only: single £55.00, double £55.00
Evening meal: 1800 (l.o. 2230)
Credit Cards: Mastercard/Eurocard/Visa/Barclaycard/American Express/Switch/Delta/Diners/Eurocheque

The Mad Hatter

APPLIED

3-7 Stamford Street, London SE1 9NY
Tel: (0171) 401 9222
Fax: (0171) 401 7111
Waterloo/Blackfriars
Traditional English inn offering a high standard of accommodation with Fuller's Ale and Pie Bar restaurant on the ground floor. Opened in February 1998.
Bedrooms: 12 double, 18 twin
Bathrooms: 30 en suite
Credit Cards: Mastercard/Eurocard/Visa/Barclaycard/American Express/Switch/Delta/Diners/Eurocheque

Meadow Croft Lodge

COMMENDED

96-98 Southwood Road, New Eltham, London SE9 3QS
Tel: (0181) 859 1488
Fax: (0181) 850 8054
New Eltham
Small, family-run bed and breakfast hotel, between A2 and A20. Near New Eltham station for easy access to London.
Bedrooms: 4 single, 3 double, 9 twin, 1 family
Bathrooms: 1 private, 9 private showers, 4 public
Bed & Breakfast: single £21.00-£27.00, double £40.00-£45.00
Parking for: 9
Credit Cards: Eurocard/Visa/Barclaycard/American Express

Melrose House

COMMENDED

89 Lennard Road, London SE20 7LY
Tel: (0181) 776 8884/0956 357714
Fax: (0181) 776 8480
Pleasant, friendly accommodation with spacious en suite bedrooms. Good wholesome food and easy access to West End. Quiet, respectable and welcoming.
Bedrooms: 3 double, 1 twin, 1 family
Bathrooms: 4 en suite, 1 private
Bed & Breakfast: single £25.00-£30.00, double £40.00-£50.00
Parking for: 6
Credit Cards: Eurocheque

Novotel London Waterloo

COMMENDED

113 Lambeth Road, London SE1 7LS
Tel: (0171) 793 1010
Fax: (0171) 793 0202
Westminster, Waterloo
Three minutes from Waterloo station by car. Convenient location opposite Houses of Parliament and Big Ben. Good transport links. Hotel has 187 new rooms, all with air-conditioning and hairdryers.
Bedrooms: 187 double
Bathrooms: 187 en suite
Bed only: single £115.00-£135.00, double £135.00-£150.00
Evening meal: 1900 (l.o. 2400)
Parking for: 40
Credit Cards: Mastercard/Eurocard/Visa/Barclaycard/American Express/Switch/Delta/Diners/Eurocheque

Oakfield

HIGHLY COMMENDED

36 Southend Crescent, London SE9 2SB
Tel: (0181) 859 8989
Fax: (0181) 859 8989
E-mail: oakfield@dircon.co.uk
URL: www.users.dircon.co.uk/~oakfield
Eltham
Unique, elegant Victorian residence with spacious, comfortable, en suite guest rooms including one with four-poster bed. Cable TV. Excellent connections to central London, Kent and Europe by train, ferry or airports.
Bedrooms: 3 double
Bathrooms: 3 en suite, 1 public
Bed & Breakfast double £55.00-£80.00
Parking for: 5
Credit Cards: Mastercard/Visa/Barclaycard/Switch/Delta

The Plover

APPLIED

69 Plover Way, The Lakes, London SE16 1TS
Tel: (0171) 394 3326/0467 336386
Fax: (0171) 237 9656
E-mail: Niemoe1@Aol.com
Surrey Quays
Situated on a man-made lake next to Greenland Dock. Two miles from Greenwich and two miles from Tower Bridge.
Bedrooms: 3 double
Bathrooms: 3 en suite
Bed & Breakfast: double £75.00-£95.00
Parking for: 3
Credit Cards: Visa/Eurocheque

London's Country

Aaron (Wembley Park) Hotel Ltd

APPROVED

8 Forty Lane, Wembley, Middlesex HA9 9EB
Tel: (0181) 904 6329/(0181) 908 5711
Fax: (0181) 385 0472
Wembley Park
Small, family-run bed and breakfast hotel, close to Wembley Stadium and Conference Centre. Parking available.
Bedrooms: 4 single, 1 twin, 3 family
Bathrooms: 8 en suite, 1 public
Evening meal: 1800 (l.o. 2000)
Parking for: 12
Credit Cards: Mastercard/Visa/Barclaycard/American Express/Switch/Delta/Diners

Adelphi Hotel

APPROVED

4 Forty Lane, Wembley, Middlesex HA9 9EB
Tel: (0181) 904 5629
Fax: (0181) 908 5314
Wembley Park
Close to Wembley Stadium, Arena and Conference Centre. Ten minutes' walk from underground station. Ten minutes from the M1.

Bedrooms: 4 single, 4 double, 3 twin
Bathrooms: 7 en suite, 2 public
Bed only: single £28.00-£37.00, double £40.00-£45.00
Bed & Breakfast: single £30.00-£39.00, double £42.00-£49.00
Evening meal: 2000 (l.o. 2100)
Parking for: 12
Credit Cards: Mastercard/Eurocard/Visa/American Express/Switch/Delta/Diners/Eurocheque

Alpine Hotel
♛♛♛ APPROVED

16-22 Moreton Road, South Croydon, Surrey CR2 7DL
Tel: (0181) 688 6116
Fax: (0181) 667 1822
South Croydon
Family-run hotel, half a mile from central Croydon and rail stations. Convenient for access to Victoria, London Bridge, Charing Cross and Waterloo.
Bedrooms: 7 single, 5 double, 13 twin, 4 family
Bathrooms: 29 en suite, 1 public
Bed & Breakfast: single £45.00, double £60.00-£65.00
Evening meal: 1830 (l.o. 2130)
Parking for: 40
Credit Cards: Mastercard/Eurocard/Visa/Barclaycard/American Express/Switch/Delta/Diners/Eurocheque

Arena Hotel
♛♛ APPROVED

6 Forty Lane, Wembley, Middlesex HA9 9EB
Tel: (0181) 908 0670/(0181) 904 0019
Fax: (0181) 908 2007
Wembley Park
Friendly, private hotel with a large garden. Parking for 15 cars. Close to bus stops and underground. Convenient for Wembley Stadium, Arena and Conference Centre and within easy reach of the M1 and North Circular.
Bedrooms: 2 single, 2 double, 3 twin, 6 family
Bathrooms: 13 en suite, 1 public
Bed & Breakfast: single £41.00, double £51.00
Parking for: 15
Credit Cards: Mastercard/Eurocard/Visa/Barclaycard/American Express/Switch/Delta/Diners/Eurocheque

Ashdowne House
♛♛ COMMENDED

9 Pownall Gardens, Hounslow, Middlesex TW3 1YW
Tel: (0181) 572 0008
Fax: (0181) 570 1939
E-mail: ashhouse@aol.com
Hounslow Central
Comfortable, non-smoking, friendly guesthouse with all rooms en suite. Conveniently situated for travel to Heathrow or central London.
Bedrooms: 2 single, 3 double, 2 twin
Bathrooms: 7 en suite
Bed only: single £49.00, double £67.00
Bed & Breakfast: single £52.00, double £73.00
Parking for: 4
Credit Cards: Mastercard/Visa/Barclaycard/Delta

The Brands Hatch Thistle

Brands Hatch, Dartford DA3 8PE
Tel: (01474) 854900
Fax: (01474) 853220
Swanley
Set at the entrance to the world famous Grand Prix Circuit, the elegant Brands Hatch Thistle has wide appeal.
Bedrooms: 66 double, 51 twin, 4 family
Bathrooms: 121 en suite
Bed only: single £95.00-£180.00, double £112.00-£200.00
Bed & Breakfast: single £112.00-£196.00, double £136.00-£224.00
Evening meal: 1900 (l.o. 2200)
Parking for: 180
Credit Cards: Mastercard/Eurocard/Visa/Barclaycard/American Express/Switch/Delta/Diners/Eurocheque

Bridge Hotel

Western Avenue, Greenford, Middlesex UB6 8ST
Tel: (0181) 566 6246
Fax: (0181) 566 6140
Greenford
The Bridge Hotel has 68 bedrooms, each with hairdryer, trouser press and satellite TV. The lounge and bars have the original wood panelling and open fireplaces. Two bedrooms are specifically designed for the disabled.
Bedrooms: 24 double, 44 twin
Bathrooms: 68 en suite
Bed & Breakfast: single £55.00-£90.00, double £65.00-£100.00
Evening meal: 1900 (l.o. 2145)
Parking for: 68
Credit Cards: Mastercard/Visa/Barclaycard/American Express/Switch/Diners/Eurocheque

Channins Hounslow Hotel
APPLIED

41 Hounslow Road, Feltham, Middlesex TW14 OAU
Tel: (0181) 890 2358
Fax: (0181) 751 6103
Feltham
Hotel with 23 en suite rooms, convenient for Heathrow and Gatwick. Long term parking available. The hotel has restaurant and bar facilities.
Bedrooms: 14 single, 4 double, 2 twin, 3 family
Bathrooms: 23 en suite
Bed only: single £49.00-£51.00, double £56.00-£62.00
Bed & Breakfast: single £44.00-£54.00, double £65.00-£70.00
Evening meal: 1830 (l.o. 2115)
Parking for: 30
Credit Cards: Mastercard/Eurocard/Visa/Barclaycard/Switch/Delta/Diners/Eurocheque

The Chequers Thistle Hotel

Brighton Road, Horley, Surrey RH6 8PH
Tel: (01293) 786992
Fax: (01293) 820625
Horley
Modern hotel with some parts of building dating back to early 16th century. Courtesy coach to Gatwick Airport, which is only two miles away.
Bedrooms: 1 single, 33 double, 44 twin
Bathrooms: 78 en suite
Bed only: single £97.00-£108.00, double £108.00-£118.00
Bed & Breakfast: single £118.00, double £128.00
Evening meal: 1900 (l.o. 2145)
Parking for: 185
Credit Cards: American Express/Diners/Eurocheque

Cheshunt Marriott Hotel

Halfhide Lane, Turnford, Broxbourne, Hertfordshire EN10 6NG
Tel: (01992) 451245
Fax: (01992) 440120
Cheshunt
The Cheshunt Marriott offers peace and tranquility. Set in the beautiful Hertfordshire countryside, the hotel offers an ideal base for exploring the area, or for a weekend retreat.
Bedrooms: 105 double, 38 twin
Bathrooms: 143 en suite
Bed & Breakfast: single £75.00-£149.00, double £75.00-£149.00
Evening meal: 1830 (l.o. 2200)
Parking for: 200
Credit Cards: Mastercard/Eurocard/Visa/Barclaycard/American Express/Switch/Delta/Diners/Eurocheque

Civic Guest House

Listed Approved

87-89 Lampton Road, Hounslow, Middlesex TW3 4DP
Tel: (0181) 572 5107/(0181) 570 1851
Fax: (0181) 814 0203
Hounslow Central
Warm and friendly guesthouse conveniently located for Heathrow, 200 yards from Piccadilly line underground station. Twenty minutes from central London.
Bedrooms: 6 single, 3 double, 11 twin, 8 family
Bathrooms: 13 en suite, 1 private shower, 4 public
Bed & Breakfast: single £38.00-£43.00, double £50.00-£55.00
Parking for: 8
Credit Cards: Mastercard/Eurocard/Visa/Barclaycard/American Express/Eurocheque

Claremont Hotel

Applied

154 High Street, Wealdstone, Harrow, Middlesex HA3 7AT
Tel: (0181) 427 2738
Fax: (0181) 427 0181
Harrow & Wealdstone
Small friendly hotel. Off-street parking available. Easy access to central London and Wembley Conference Centre.
Bedrooms: 5 single, 5 double, 6 twin, 4 family
Bathrooms: 14 en suite, 3 private showers, 2 public
Parking for: 14
Credit Cards: Mastercard/Visa/Barclaycard/Switch/Delta/Eurocheque

Crescent Hotel

Commended

58-62 Welldon Crescent, Harrow, Middlesex HA1 1QR
Tel: (0181) 863 5491/(0181) 863 5163
Fax: (0181) 427 5965
E-mail: jivraj@crsnhtl.demon.co.uk
URL: www.crsnthtl.demon.co.uk
Harrow-on-the-Hill
Offering quality accommodation and a friendly atmosphere, within the heart of Harrow. Close to Wembley Conference Centre, the West End, Heathrow and motorways.
Bedrooms: 9 single, 3 double, 6 twin, 2 family
Bathrooms: 12 en suite, 3 public
Bed & Breakfast: single £45.00-£55.00, double £60.00-£70.00
Evening meal: 1900 (l.o. 2030)
Parking for: 7
Credit Cards: Mastercard/Eurocard/Visa/Barclaycard/American Express/Switch/Delta/Diners/Eurocheque

Crowne Plaza London Heathrow

Stockley Road, West Drayton, Middlesex UB7 9NA
Tel: (01895) 445555
Fax: (01895) 445122
West Drayton
Just ten minutes from Heathrow with coach service to and from hotel to Terminals 1,2,3. Thirty minutes from central London.
Bedrooms: 285 double, 173 twin
Bathrooms: 458 en suite
Bed only: single £169.00, double £179.00
Evening meal: 1730 (l.o. 2230)
Parking for: 400
Credit Cards: Mastercard/Visa/Barclaycard/American Express/Switch/Delta

Elm Hotel

Commended

1-7 Elm Road, Wembley, Middlesex HA9 7JA
Tel: (0181) 902 1764
Fax: (0181) 903 8365
Wembley Central
Close to Wembley Stadium, Arena and Conference Centre. Jet spa baths available.
Bedrooms: 5 single, 8 double, 8 twin, 5 family
Bathrooms: 26 en suite
Bed & Breakfast: single £36.00-£45.00, double £48.00-£58.00
Parking for: 7
Credit Cards: Mastercard/Visa/Barclaycard/Switch/Delta/Eurocheque

The Excelsior

Highly Commended

Bath Road, West Drayton, Middlesex UB7 0DU
Tel: (0181) 759 6611
Fax: (0181) 759 3421
Heathrow Terminals 1,2,3,
Hayes
On the A4 Bath Road opposite the main entrance to Heathrow. Three restaurants to choose from, ranging from under £10 to over £20.
Bedrooms: 5 single, 525 double, 278 twin, 19 family
Bathrooms: 828 en suite
Bed only: single £145.00-£175.00, double £155.00-£185.00
Bed & Breakfast: single £156.95-£186.95, double £177.95-£207.95
Evening meal: 1815 (l.o. 2300)
Parking for: 540
Credit Cards: Mastercard/Eurocard/Visa/Barclaycard/American Express/Switch/Diners

Forte Crest, Heathrow

Commended

Sipson Road, West Drayton, Middlesex UB7 0JU
Tel: (0181) 759 2323
Fax: (0181) 897 8659
Heathrow Terminals 1,2,3
A large, modern hotel close to the slip-road from the M4 motorway to Heathrow, offering an excellent choice of restaurants, bars and conference facilities.
Bedrooms: 343 double, 113 twin, 123 family
Bathrooms: 584 en suite
Bed only: single £75.00-£200.00, double £75.00-£200.00
Evening meal: 1830 (l.o. 2300)
Parking for: 400
Credit Cards: Mastercard/Visa/Barclaycard/American Express/Switch/Delta/Diners/Eurocheque

Foxley Mount

44 Foxley Lane, Purley CR8 3EE
Tel: (0181) 660 9751
Purley
Large Edwardian house. Family-run bed and breakfast. Close to 18 hole golf course. Walking distance to Purley station. Twenty minutes to Gatwick or central London.
Bedrooms: 1 single, 2 double, 1 twin, 1 family
Bathrooms: 1 public
Bed & Breakfast: single £20.00, double £40.00
Parking for: 3

The George

High Street, Crawley, West Sussex RH10 1BS
Tel: (01293) 524215
Fax: (01293) 548565
Crawley
Famous 17th century inn combining old world charm with modern amenities, including an up-to-date bedroom wing.
Bedrooms: 16 single, 21 double, 28 twin, 15 family
Bathrooms: 80 en suite
Bed only: single £50.00-£70.00, double £55.00-£80.00
Bed & Breakfast: single £60.00-£75.00, double £68.00-£95.00
Evening meal: 1900 (l.o. 2130)
Parking for: 95
Credit Cards: Mastercard/Visa/Barclaycard/American Express/Switch/Delta/Diners/Eurocheque

Glendevon House Hotel — APPROVED

80 Southborough Road, Bickley, Bromley BR1 2EN
Tel: (0181) 467 2183/(0181) 295 0701
Bickley
Family-run hotel with private car park, convenient for access to central London and Kent. Caters for tourists and businessmen.
Bedrooms: 2 single, 4 double, 3 twin, 1 family
Bathrooms: 10 en suite
Bed & Breakfast: single £28.00-£38.50, double £47.50-£51.50
Evening meal: (l.o. 2100)
Parking for: 7
Credit Cards: Mastercard/Eurocard/Visa/Barclaycard/Switch/Delta/Eurocheque

Grim's Dyke Hotel — COMMENDED

Old Redding, Harrow Weald, Harrow, Middlesex HA3 6SH
Tel: (0181) 954 4227/(0181) 385 3100
Fax: (0181) 954 4560
Stanmore
Former residence of WS Gilbert, set in 110 acres of magnificent gardens and woodland. A lovely Victorian country house.
Bedrooms: 30 double, 14 twin
Bathrooms: 44 en suite
Bed only: single £97.00-£180.00, double £107.00-£200.00
Bed & Breakfast: single £105.00-£250.00, double £115.00-£250.00
Evening meal: 1900 (l.o. 2130)
Parking for: 120
Credit Cards: Mastercard/Eurocard/Visa/Barclaycard/American Express/Switch/Delta/Diners/Eurocheque

Heathrow Marriott Hotel

Ditton Road, Langley, Slough SL3 8PT
Tel: (01753) 544244
Fax: (01753) 540272
Slough
Close to the M4 and the M25, with easy access to London and Heathrow. Well-appointed bedrooms, restaurant and leisure club.
Bedrooms: 254 double, 119 twin, 6 family
Bathrooms: 379 en suite
Bed & Breakfast: single £118.00-£148.00, double £126.00-£156.00
Evening meal: 1845 (l.o. 2230)
Parking for: 600
Credit Cards: Mastercard/Eurocard/Visa/Barclaycard/American Express/Switch/Delta/Diners/Eurocheque

Heathrow Park Hotel

Bath Road, Longford, West Drayton, Middlesex UB7 0EQ
Tel: (0181) 759 2400
Fax: (0181) 759 5278
Heathrow Terminals 1,2,3
Modern hotel with conference and training facilities for up to 700 people. Easy access to M3, M4 and M25. Airport transfer bus £2.00.
Bedrooms: 135 double, 119 twin, 56 family
Bathrooms: 310 en suite
Bed only: single £110.00-£130.00, double £130.00-£150.00
Bed & Breakfast: single £120.95-£140.95, double £151.90-£171.90
Evening meal: 1800 (l.o. 2330)
Parking for: 500
Credit Cards: Mastercard/American Express/Diners/Eurocheque

Hilton National Bracknell

Bagshot Road, Bracknell, Berkshire RG12 0QJ
Tel: (01344) 424801
Fax: (01344) 487454
Bracknell
Well situated in a thriving part of Berkshire.
Bedrooms: 22 single, 95 double, 50 twin
Bathrooms: 167 en suite
Bed & Breakfast: single £155.00-£165.00, double £165.00-£175.00
Evening meal: 1900 (l.o. 2200)
Parking for: 180
Credit Cards: Mastercard/Eurocard/Visa/Barclaycard/American Express/Switch/Delta/Diners/Eurocheque

Hilton National Cobham

Seven Hills Road South, Cobham, Surrey KT11 1EW
Tel: (01932) 864471
Fax: (01932) 868017
Cobham
Set in 27 acres of Surrey woodland, close to the M25. Traditional hotel with range of amenities.
Bedrooms: 102 double, 38 twin, 9 family
Bathrooms: 149 en suite
Bed only: single £160.00-£210.00, double £160.00-£210.00
Evening meal: 1700 (l.o. 2200)
Parking for: 300
Credit Cards: Mastercard/Eurocard/Visa/Barclaycard/American Express/Switch/Delta/Diners/Eurocheque

Hilton National Croydon

Waddon Way, Purley Way, Croydon, Surrey CR9 4HH
Tel: (0181) 680 3000
Fax: (0181) 681 6171
East Croydon

A modern 168-bedroomed hotel with excellent facilities including conference rooms, two restaurants and a well-equipped health club.
Bedrooms: 102 double, 66 twin
Bathrooms: 168 en suite
Bed & Breakfast: single £160.00-£200.00, double £175.00-£215.00
Evening meal: 1900 (l.o. 2200)
Parking for: 185
Credit Cards: Mastercard/Eurocard/Visa/Barclaycard/American Express/Switch/Delta/Diners/Eurocheque

Hilton National Watford

Elton Way, Watford WD2 8HA
Tel: (01923) 235881
Fax: (01923) 220836
URL: www.hilton.com.
Watford Junction
The hotel is just off the M1, 30 minutes from London and ten minutes from the M25.
Bedrooms: 104 double, 91 twin
Bathrooms: 195 en suite
Bed & Breakfast: single £135.00-£180.00, double £150.00-£200.00
Evening meal: 1900 (l.o. 2200)
Parking for: 350
Credit Cards: Mastercard/Eurocard/Visa/Barclaycard/American Express/Switch/Diners

Hilton National Wembley

Empire Way, Wembley, Middlesex HA9 8DS
Tel: (0181) 902 8839
Fax: (0181) 900 2201
Wembley Park, Wembley Stadium
Adjacent to the Wembley complex, this is the headquarters hotel for the conference centre. Within easy reach of major motorways. Free car parking available.
Bedrooms: 93 double, 194 twin, 16 family
Bathrooms: 301 en suite
Bed only: single £160.00-£180.00, double £160.00-£180.00
Evening meal: 1900 (l.o. 2200)
Parking for: 250
Credit Cards: Mastercard/Eurocard/Visa/Barclaycard/American Express/Switch/Delta/Diners/Eurocheque

Hindes Hotel

8 Hindes Road, Harrow, Middlesex HA1 1SJ
Tel: (0181) 427 7468
Fax: (0181) 424 0673
Harrow-on-the-Hill
Owner-run bed and breakfast hotel near the M1. Fifteen minutes to the West End by underground. Convenient for Wembley Stadium complex.
Bedrooms: 4 single, 4 double, 6 twin
Bathrooms: 7 en suite, 2 public
Bed & Breakfast: single £35.00-£42.00, double £47.00-£55.00
Evening meal: 1700 (l.o. 1900)
Parking for: 20
Credit Cards: Mastercard/Eurocard/Visa/Barclaycard/American Express/Switch/Diners/Eurocheque

Hotel Antoinette of Kingston

Approved

Beaufort Road, Kingston upon Thames, Surrey KT1 2TQ
Tel: (0181) 546 1044
Fax: (0181) 547 2595
E-mail: hotelantoinette@btinternet.com
Surbiton/Kingston
Close to Kew, Windsor, Hampton Court, Chessington World of Adventures and many famous sporting venues, with easy access to central London.
Bedrooms: 24 single, 8 double, 34 twin, 33 family
Bathrooms: 99 en suite
Bed & Breakfast: single £48.00-£56.00, double £58.00-£66.00
Evening meal: 1830 (l.o. 2115)
Parking for: 100
Credit Cards: Mastercard/Barclaycard/American Express/Switch/Delta/Eurocheque

Jarvis International Heathrow

Commended

Bath Road, Cranford, Hounslow, Middlesex TW5 9QE
Tel: (0181) 897 2121/(0181) 897 3079
Fax: (0181) 897 7014
Hounslow West
Modern hotel overlooking its own delightful English garden. Convenient for Heathrow and central London and nine miles from Windsor. Close to M25 and M4.
Bedrooms: 14 single, 27 double, 33 twin
Bathrooms: 74 en suite
Bed only: single £75.00-£120.00, double £85.00-£120.00
Bed & Breakfast: single £80.50-£130.95, double £91.00-£142.00
Evening meal: 1830 (l.o. 2200)
Parking for: 80
Credit Cards: Mastercard/Eurocard/Visa/Barclaycard/American Express/Switch/Delta/Diners/Eurocheque

Le Meridien London Gatwick

North Terminal, Gatwick Airport, Gatwick, West Sussex RH6 0PH
Tel: (01293) 567070
Fax: (01293) 567739
E-mail: 106571520@compuserve.co.uk
Gatwick
Modern hotel attached to North Terminal, Gatwick Airport.
Bedrooms: 229 double, 229 twin, 16 family
Bathrooms: 474 en suite, 5 public
Bed & Breakfast: single £166.00-£190.00, double £176.00-£200.00
Evening meal: 1830 (l.o. 2230)
Parking for: 100
Credit Cards: Mastercard/Eurocard/Visa/Barclaycard/American Express/Switch/Delta/Diners/Eurocheque

London Gatwick Airport Hilton

Gatwick Airport, Gatwick, West Sussex RH6 0LL
Tel: (01293) 518080
Fax: (01293) 528980
Gatwick
The only hotel linked by direct, covered walkway to South Terminal and by rapid transit system to North Terminal.
Bedrooms: 300 double, 220 twin, 30 family
Bathrooms: 550 en suite
Bed only: single £185.00-£187.00, double £185.00-£187.00
Evening meal: 1900 (l.o. 2300)
Parking for: 6000
Credit Cards: Mastercard/Eurocard/Visa/Barclaycard/American Express/Switch/Delta/Diners

London Heathrow Hilton

Terminal 4, Heathrow Airport, Hounslow, Middlesex TW6 3AF
Tel: (0181) 759 7755
Fax: (0181) 759 7579

E-mail: gm_heathrow@hilton.com
URL: www.hilton.com
Heathrow Terminal 4
Large hotel with three restaurants, cocktail lounge, leisure and conference facilities. Linked to Terminal 4 by a covered walkway.
Bedrooms: 231 double, 164 twin
Bathrooms: 395 en suite
Evening meal: 1600 (l.o. 2300)
Parking for: 250
Credit Cards: Mastercard/Barclaycard/American Express/Switch/Diners/Eurocheque

Madonna Halley's Hotel

88 Whitchurch Lane, Edgware, Middlesex HA8 6QN
Tel: (0181) 951 5959
Fax: (0181) 381 2493
Canons Park
Decorated by a Mediterranean ceramic artist. Quiet residential location with good motorway access.
Bedrooms: 2 single, 5 double, 1 twin, 12 family
Bathrooms: 20 en suite
Bed & Breakfast: single £58.00, double £69.00
Evening meal: 1730 (l.o. 2100)
Parking for: 8
Credit Cards: Mastercard/Eurocard/Visa/Barclaycard/Diners/Eurocheque

The Mary Rose Hotel

COMMENDED

40-50 High Street, St Mary Cray, Orpington, Kent BR5 3NJ
Tel: (01689) 871917/(01689) 875369
Fax: (01689) 839445
Saint Mary Cray
16th century buildings converted to an inn. Land traversed by the River Cray. Forty-five minutes from Hever Castle and Chartwell. Prices quoted are for 1998 and are subject to change during 1999.
Bedrooms: 5 single, 9 double, 8 twin, 18 family
Bathrooms: 27 en suite, 2 private, 2 public
Bed & Breakfast: single £34.50-£40.00, double £49.50-£75.00
Evening meal: 1900 (l.o. 2115)
Parking for: 50
Credit Cards: Mastercard/American Express/Switch/Delta/Diners/Eurocheque

Palms Hotel Piano Bar and Eating House

Southend Arterial Road, Hornchurch, Essex RM11 3UJ
Tel: (01708) 346789
Fax: (01708) 341719
Upminster
Modern hotel with good access to central London. Stylish restaurant and bar. Extensive conference facilities.
Bedrooms: 68 double, 68 twin, 1 family
Bathrooms: 137 en suite
Bed & Breakfast: single £70.95-£124.95, double £81.90-£135.90
Evening meal: 1900 (l.o. 2200)
Parking for: 200
Credit Cards: Mastercard/Eurocard/Visa/Barclaycard/American Express/Switch/Delta/Diners/Eurocheque

The Quality Harrow Hotel

COMMENDED

12-22 Pinner Road, Harrow, Middlesex HA1 4HZ
Tel: (0181) 427 3435
Fax: (0181) 861 1370
Harrow-on-the-Hill
Privately owned hotel. Professional and friendly service.
Bedrooms: 17 single, 19 double, 14 twin, 2 family
Bathrooms: 52 en suite
Bed & Breakfast: single £89.50-£99.00, double £119.90-£130.90
Evening meal: 1800 (l.o. 2230)
Parking for: 58
Credit Cards: Mastercard/Eurocard/Visa/Barclaycard/American Express/Switch/Delta/Diners/Eurocheque

Quinns Hotel

APPROVED

48 Sheen Road, Richmond, Surrey TW9 1AW
Tel: (0181) 940 5444
Fax: (0181) 940 1828
Richmond
Ideally located for business or pleasure, within easy reach of central London, airports and local places of interest.
Bedrooms: 6 single, 24 double, 7 twin, 1 family
Bathrooms: 23 en suite, 6 public
Bed & Breakfast: single £40.00-£75.00, double £60.00-£95.00
Parking for: 14
Credit Cards: Mastercard/Eurocard/Visa/Barclaycard/American Express/Switch/Delta/Diners/Eurocheque

Radisson Edwardian Hotel Heathrow

140 Bath Road, Hayes, Middlesex UB3 5AW
Tel: (0181) 759 6311
Fax: (0181) 759 4559
Heathrow Terminals 1,2,3
Award-winning hotel, with large atrium with pool and spa, opulent lounges and sumptuous restaurants.
Bedrooms: 3 single, 356 double, 86 twin, 14 family
Bathrooms: 459 en suite
Evening meal: 1900 (l.o. 2230)
Parking for: 242
Credit Cards: Mastercard/Eurocard/Visa/Barclaycard/American Express/Switch/Delta/Diners/Eurocheque

Richmond Gate Hotel and Gates on the Park Restaurant

HIGHLY COMMENDED

Richmond Hill, Richmond, Surrey TW10 6RP
Tel: (0181) 940 0061
Fax: (0181) 332 0354
Richmond
A country-house hotel, close to Richmond Park, renowned for its hospitality, service and food. Traditionally furnished rooms with modern facilities and leisure centre with pool and gym.
Bedrooms: 18 single, 32 double, 15 twin, 1 family
Bathrooms: 66 en suite
Bed & Breakfast: single £105.00-£144.00, double £130.00-£190.00
Evening meal: 1800 (l.o. 2200)
Parking for: 50
Credit Cards: Mastercard/Eurocard/Visa/Barclaycard/American Express/Switch/Diners/Eurocheque

The Royal Berkshire Hotel

London Road, Sunninghill, Ascot, Berkshire SL5 0PP
Tel: (01344) 623322
Fax: (01344) 627100

Queen Anne country mansion set in mature parkland.
Bedrooms: 6 single, 42 double, 9 twin, 6 family
Bathrooms: 63 en suite
Evening meal: 1930 (l.o. 2130)
Parking for: 250
Credit Cards: American Express/Diners

Selsdon Park
HIGHLY COMMENDED

Addington Road, South Croydon, CR2 8YA
Tel: (0181) 657 8811
Fax: (0181) 651 6171
East Croydon
Historic, country house hotel with sporting and leisure facilities, including golf course. Thirty minutes from London and Gatwick.
Bedrooms: 49 single, 84 double, 62 twin
Bathrooms: 199 en suite
Bed only: single £99.00-£110.00, double £145.00-£190.00
Bed & Breakfast: single £110.00-£125.00, double £160.00-£219.00
Evening meal: 1930 (l.o. 2200)
Parking for: 265
Credit Cards: Mastercard/Visa/Barclaycard/American Express/Switch/Delta/Diners

Shalimar Hotel
APPROVED

215-221 Staines Road, Hounslow, Middlesex TW3 3JJ
Tel: (0181) 572 2816/0500 238239
Fax: (0181) 569 6789
Hounslow Central
Family-run hotel close to Heathrow. Hounslow High Street, underground station and bus stop are all nearby.
Bedrooms: 12 single, 6 double, 11 twin, 4 family
Bathrooms: 23 en suite, 10 private showers
Bed & Breakfast: single £40.00-£45.00, double £50.00-£55.00
Evening meal: 1800 (l.o. 2000)
Parking for: 7
Credit Cards: Mastercard/Eurocard/Visa/Barclaycard/American Express/Switch/Delta/Diners/Eurocheque

Sheraton Heathrow Hotel

Colnbrook Bypass, West Drayton, Middlesex UB7 0HJ
Tel: (0181) 759 2424
Fax: (0181) 759 2091
Heathrow Terminals 1,2,3
A modern, comfortable hotel with an ideal location for Heathrow and London. Live entertainment on weekdays.
Bedrooms: 209 double, 181 twin, 34 family
Bathrooms: 424 en suite
Bed only: single £180.00-£200.00, double £190.00-£210.00
Evening meal: 1900 (l.o. 2330)
Parking for: 280
Credit Cards: Mastercard/Visa/Barclaycard/American Express/Diners

Sheraton Skyline Hotel and Conference Centre

Bath Road, Hayes, Middlesex UB3 5BP
Tel: (0181) 759 2535
Fax: (0181) 750 9150
URL: www.Sheraton.com
Heathrow Terminals 1,2,3
Located on the main Bath Road (A4) at Heathrow. Modern three-storey building with tropical garden feature.
Bedrooms: 163 double, 177 twin, 12 family
Bathrooms: 352 en suite
Evening meal: 1800 (l.o. 2300)
Parking for: 300
Credit Cards: Mastercard/Eurocard/Visa/Barclaycard/American Express/Diners/Eurocheque

The Ship Thistle Hotel

Monument Green, Weybridge, Surrey KT13 8BQ
Tel: (01932) 848364
Fax: (01932) 857153
Weybridge
Grade II Listed building which combines modern, comfortable facilities with traditional exterior. Excellent service and standards.
Bedrooms: 9 single, 10 double, 20 twin
Bathrooms: 39 en suite
Bed only: single £110.00-£120.00, double £125.00-£135.00
Bed & Breakfast: single £121.00-£131.00, double £147.00-£157.00
Evening meal: 1930 (l.o. 2145)
Parking for: 50
Credit Cards: Mastercard/Eurocard/Visa/Barclaycard/American Express/Switch/Delta/Diners/Eurocheque

Swallow Hotel

Old Shire Lane, Waltham Abbey, Essex EN9 3LX
Tel: (01992) 717170
Fax: (01992) 711841
Loughton
Innovatively designed, new property, off junction 26 of the M25. Two restaurants, cocktail bar, residents' lounge, leisure club and 163 bedrooms.
Bedrooms: 83 single, 27 double, 39 twin, 14 family
Bathrooms: 163 en suite
Bed & Breakfast: single £90.00-£105.00, double £110.00-£130.00
Evening meal: 1800 (l.o. 2300)
Parking for: 260
Credit Cards: Mastercard/Eurocard/Visa/Barclaycard/American Express/Switch/Delta/Diners/Eurocheque

APARTMENTS (SELF-CATERING)

51 Kensington Court

51 Kensington Court, London W8 5DB
Tel: (0171) 937 2030
Fax: (0171) 938 5312
E-mail: kencourt@btinternet.com
URL: www.demon.co.uk/hotel-net/kc1.html
Contact: Mr T Forester
Located in a quiet square just off Kensington High Street and a short stroll from Kensington Palace. Luxury apartments ideal for business travellers or holiday makers.
Units: 10 serviced apartments, sleeping a maximum of 6
Prices: £840.00-£1505.00 low season, £840.00-£1505.00 high season
LP

AAE Limited

1 Princess Mews, Belsize Crescent, London NW3 5AP
Tel: (0171) 794 1186
Fax: (0171) 433 3328
E-mail: aaeltd@globalnet.co.uk
Contact: Mrs G Davies

Fully equipped luxury apartments in Hampstead and St John's Wood areas.
Units: 25 self-contained flats, sleeping a maximum of 6
Prices: £260.00-£750.00 low season, £300.00-£800.00 high season
LP

Acorn Accommodation

PO Box 3031, Mill Hill, London NW7 4ZA
Tel: (0181) 905 3525
Fax: (0181) 905 3429
Contact: Ms M Withers
Self-contained, comfortably furnished, fully equipped apartments in central London near Bloomsbury, West End and the Florida State University London Study Centre in Great Russell Street.
Units: 88 self-contained flats, sleeping a maximum of 8
Prices: £265.00-£650.00 low season, £375.00-£785.00 high season
LP

Adelaide Marine Ltd

Adelaide Dock, Endsleigh Road, Norwood Green, Middlesex UB2 5QR
Tel: (0181) 571 5678
Fax: (0181) 571 5126
Contact: Mr P Woodley
Self-drive steel canal boats, from two-ten berth, fully equipped and with central heating. Cruise London and the countryside all year round.
Units: 12 stationary houseboats, sleeping a maximum of 12
Prices: £450.00-£700.00 low season, £700.00-£1200.00 high season
LP

Apartment Services London

2 Sandwich Street, London WC1H 9PL
Tel: (0171) 388 3558
Fax: (0171) 383 7255
Contact: Ms C Ayling
Self-contained, comfortably furnished, fully equipped apartments. Serviced weekly. Convenient for public transport, West End and theatres. Lets available from one week to a year.
Units: 100 self-contained flats, 1 self-contained house, sleeping a maximum of 7
Prices: £150.00-£1500.00 low season, £150.00-£1500.00 high season
LP

Aston's Budget & Designer Studios

39 Rosary Gardens, South Kensington, London SW7 4NQ
Tel: (0171) 370 0737
Fax: (0171) 835 1419
Contact: Mr M Cookson
Budget to luxury designer accommodation, with air-conditioning, in restored Victorian town houses in a centrally located, quiet, residential street. Very close to public transport, West End and theatres.
Units: 35 self-contained studio flats, 13 non-self-contained studio flats, sleeping a maximum of 4
Prices: £318.43-£999.93 low season, £318.43-£999.93 high season
LP

B & B Flatlets

72 Holland Park Avenue, London W11 3QZ
Tel: (0171) 229 9233
Fax: (0171) 221 1077
E-mail: HoteLondon@aol.com
Contact: Mr B McElhill
Small family-run guesthouse, in a pleasant central location. One minute from Holland Park underground station, buses and Airbus direct from Heathrow. All rooms have their own cable TV and cooking facilities. Breakfast served in bedrooms.
Units: 6 non-self-contained studio flats, sleeping a maximum of 5
Prices: £301.00-£350.00 low season, £350.00-£385.00 high season
LP

Beaufort House

HIGHLY COMMENDED

45-47 Beaufort Gardens, Knightsbridge, London SW3 1PN
Tel: (0171) 584 2600
Fax: (0171) 584 6532
Contact: Miss A Gledhill
Twenty-one, self-contained serviced apartments, two minutes' walk from Harrods.
Units: 21 serviced apartments, sleeping a maximum of 7
Prices: £1058.00-£2960.00 low season, £1110.00-£3400.00 high season
LP

Beaumont Apartments

HIGHLY COMMENDED

24 Combemartin Road, Southfields, London SW18 5PR
Tel: (0181) 789 2663/0956 545431
Fax: (0181) 265 5499
E-mail: afriat@mistral.co.uk.
URL: www.mistral.co.uk/afriat
Contact: Mr & Mrs A Afriat
Well-appointed flats in leafy suburb within 30 minutes of the West End. Close to underground, Wimbledon tennis, A3 and M4. Easy access to M25, Gatwick and Heathrow. Ideal for business or holiday.
Units: 2 self-contained flats, sleeping a maximum of 5
Prices: £390.00-£450.00 low season, £430.00-£650.00 high season
LP

Belgard

COMMENDED

PO Box 1026, London W2 1QE
Tel: (0171) 262 5273/(01865) 514199
Fax: (0171) 402 7173
Contact: Mrs N Reynish
A Victorian terraced house near Marble Arch, with self-contained one-bedroom flats.
Units: 4 self-contained flats, sleeping a maximum of 4
Prices: £350.00 low season, £475.00 high season
LP

The Birches

UP TO HIGHLY COMMENDED

7 The Birches, 22 Avenue Road, London SE25 4EF
Tel: 0410 403627
Fax: 0411 584261
URL: www.Chris.Birches@BTinternet.com
Contact: Ms C Heffernan
Attractive one- and two-bedroomed flats with luxury kitchen and bathroom, located in quiet, residential area, near a lake. One flat has a lake view.
Units: 2 self-contained flats, sleeping a maximum of 6
Prices: £350.00-£525.00 low season, £350.00-£525.00 high season
LP

Clarendon House Apartments

UP TO HIGHLY COMMENDED

48 Ranelagh Road, Ealing, London W5 5RJ
Tel: (01424) 212954
Fax: (01424) 212954

E-mail: clarendon.house@LineOne.net
URL: www.accomodata.co.uk
Contact: Mrs A Pedley
A spacious apartment in a Victorian house or a purpose-built ground floor apartment in a modern development. Both are in a pleasant residential area with easy access to the underground and are close to shops and restaurants.
Units: 2 self-contained flats, 2 non self-contained flats, sleeping a maximum of 6
Prices: £280.00-£650.00 low season, £320.00-£680.00 high season
LP

Clifton Lodge

45 Egerton Gardens, London SW3 2DD
Tel: (0171) 584 0099
Fax: (0171) 823 9194
Contact: Ms M Scovil
Nineteenth century town house of fully modernised serviced apartments, quietly situated in central London close to Harrods. Within walking distance of underground stations.
Units: 10 self-contained flats, sleeping a maximum of 3
Prices: £560.00-£910.00 low season, £560.00-£910.00 high season
LP

Craven Garden Lodge

5-10 Craven Hill Gardens, London W2 3ES
Tel: (0171) 402 0393/ (0171) 402 0396
Fax: (0171) 262 7179
URL: www.net-lettings.co.uk/lero
Contact: Mr M Wojtkiewicz
Modern self-catering units, near shops, bus routes, the underground and Hyde Park.
Units: 50 self-contained studio flats, 50 self-contained flats, sleeping a maximum of 10
Prices: £320.00-£700.00 low season, £350.00-£1000.00 high season
LP

Ealing Tourist Flats

UP TO COMMENDED

94 Gordon Road and 10 Hastings Road, London W13 8PT
Tel: (0181) 566 8187/ (01895) 233365
Fax: (0181) 566 7670
E-mail: holiday_apartments@bigfoot.com
URL: www.bigfoot.com/~holiday_apartments
Contact: Mr W G Smith
Attractive apartments for the business or holiday traveller. Close to underground, restaurants and shopping arcades. Ideal location, with good parking.
Units: 3 self-contained studio flats, 4 self-contained flats, sleeping a maximum of 7
Prices: £285.00-£545.00 low season, £290.00-£545.00 high season
LP

Eccleston House (Holiday Flatlets)

64 Eccleston Square, London SW1V 1PH
Tel: (0171) 834 0985
Fax: (0171) 373 6183
Contact: Miss Gomez
Comfortable serviced apartments with fully equipped kitchenettes or kitchens. Other accommodation available in the Victoria and Kensington areas.
Units: 13 serviced apartments, 4 self-contained flats, 3 non self-contained studio flats, sleeping a maximum of 5
Prices: £141.00-£300.00 low season, £141.00-£450.00 high season
LP

Elvaston Lodge

12 Elvaston Place, London SW7 5QG
Tel: (0171) 589 9412
Fax: (0171) 373 6183
Contact: Miss M O'Donnell
Comfortable serviced apartments in South Kensington, with fully equipped kitchenettes or kitchens. Other accommodation available in Kensington and Victoria areas.
Units: 16 self-contained studio flats, 6 non-self-contained studio flats, 10 serviced apartments, 4 self-contained flats, sleeping a maximum of 4
Prices: £141.00-£300.00 low season, £141.00-£350.00 high season
LP

Emperors Gate Short Stay Apartments

UP TO COMMENDED

8 Knaresborough Place, Kensington, London SW5 0TG
Tel: (0171) 244 8409/ (0171) 373 0323
Fax: (0171) 373 6455
Contact: Mr R G Arnold
Family-owned, centrally located apartments, close to Knightsbridge, Olympia and Earl's Court exhibition centres. Daily rates also available.
Units: 18 self-contained flats, sleeping a maximum of 4
Prices: £665.00-£1085.00 low season, £665.00-£1085.00 high season
LP

Glenthurston Holiday Apartments

COMMENDED

27 Canadian Avenue, London SE6 3AU
Tel: (0181) 265 5872
Fax: (0181) 265 5872
Contact: Miss S Halliday
Large Victorian house converted into seven flats with use of an indoor pool, sauna and steam room.
Units: 1 self-contained flat, sleeping a maximum of 4
Prices: £275.00 low season, £375.00 high season
LP

Grundy, Lytton & Partners

2 Violet Hill, St John's Wood, London NW8 9EB
Tel: (0171) 624 1165
Fax: (0171) 625 4552
Contact: Mr J Turner
Management of luxury holiday flats and houses (fully serviced) in central and north west London.
Units: 30 self-contained flats and houses
Prices: £200.00-£1000.00 low season, £200.00-£1000.00 high season

Hamlet UK Ltd

APPLIED

Burr Close and Nightingale House, St Katherine's Marina, London E1
Tel: (0181) 883 0024
Fax: (0181) 444 1118
E-mail: hamlet_uk@globalnet.co.uk
Contact: Miss R Naufal
Friendly and personal service. Very attractive surroundings. Comfortable and clean accommodation, close to public transport and supermarket. Prices quoted are not applicable between 17 December 1999 and 6 January 2000.

PARK WEST

ECONOMY AND LUXURY FLATS

FROM £275 - £900PW

Studio flats, 1-3 Bedrooms.
Within easy walking distance of the West End.
Ideal accommodation for leisure or business visitors - long-term flats available by arrangement.

24hr uniformed porters • Telex and Fax Services
Direct-Dial Telephones • Lifts • Servicing • Colour TV

THE PARK WEST RENTAL OFFICE

MAIN ENTRANCE,
1001 PARK WEST,
LONDON W2 2QL
TEL: 0171 724 1001
TELEX: 94013185
PARK G
FAX: 0171 724 7592
email:
info@parkwest.demon.co.uk

London Docklands Taeping Pavilion
Clippers Quay, London E14

Luxurious 2 Bed, 2nd floor Apartment situated in this award winning waterscaped development. A veritable oasis of peace and yet ten minutes from Central London (Docklands Railway 200m). Private parking, gardens, marina, walk to supermarket, shops, leisure centre, restaurant, pubs, park, Canary Wharf Business and Retail Centre.

7 nights £60 - £75 per night for apartment fully inc.
3 nights £72 - £85 per night for apartment fully inc.
Contact: John Graham, 22 Falcon Way, London E14 9UP
Tel/Fax: 0171 338 8980 Mobile: 0973 857187

English Tourist Board HIGHLY COMMENDED
LP
E ACCEPTED
YORKSHIRE MEMBER

APARTMENTS IN LONDON & EUROPE

EURACOM

TEL: 0171 436 3201
FAX: 0171 436 3203
e-mail: info@euracom.co.uk
www: euracom.co.uk

Q: What would the discerning visitor to London expect to pay for a fully serviced, furnished and equipped apartment in fashionable Chelsea?

A: From around £45 per day inc. VAT

We think you will agree, a very reasonable price to pay for the convenience and privacy of your own Chelsea home for a studio or 1-2 bedroom apartment. Direct-dial line, colour TV, maid service, 24 hour porterage, central heating. Parking and business facilities available.

☎ 0171 589 1105
FAX: 0171 589 9433
at Nell Gwynn House

NGH *APARTMENTS LTD*

SLOANE AVENUE LONDON SW3 3AX
http://www.demon.co.uk/hotel-net/ngh.html
E.MAIL 101562,1120@Compuserve.Com

COURT APARTMENTS

We have 35 tastefully furnished and standard apartments tailored to the needs of travellers, holidaymakers and business people alike. Ideally located, each self-contained apartment is spacious and distinctive.

- Selection of new luxury studios, 1 & 2 bedroom apartments all with fully equipped with high-spec Bosch kitchens, colour TV, direct-dial telephones, hairdryers etc.
- Selection of standard studios, 1 & 2 bedroom apartments all with fully equipped kitchen, marble bathroom, colour TVs, direct-dial telephone, hairdryer etc.
- Extra bed and cot facilities available
- Excellent security and entryphone systems
- Long, short or daily rentals from £60.00 per night, inclusive
- Breakfast on request at hotel

For reservations and enquiries, kindly contact:
Tel: 0171 370 0991 - Fax: 0171 3700994
www members.aol.com/capitalmayflhotel/private/MAY.HTM
26-28 Trebovir Road, London, SW5 9NJ

Units: 7 self-contained flats, sleeping a maximum of 6
Prices: £500.00-£650.00 low season, £560.00-£690.00 high season
LP

Harrington Gardens House

34 Harrington Gardens, London SW7 4LT
Tel: (0171) 373 2673/(0171) 589 2923
Fax: (0171) 373 6183
Contact: Mrs Gordon
Comfortable serviced apartments with fully equipped kitchens or kitchenettes. Other accommodation available in Kensington and Victoria areas.
Units: 14 serviced apartments, 7 non self-contained flats, sleeping a maximum of 4
Prices: £141.00-£300.00 low season, £141.00-£350.00 high season
LP

Holiday Serviced Apartments Limited

140 Cromwell Road, London SW7 4HA
Tel: (0171) 373 4477
Fax: (0171) 373 4282
E-mail: reservations@holidayapartments.co.uk
URL: www.holidayapartments.co.uk
Contact: Ms S Tamman
Specialising in advance bookings, serviced, non-serviced and privately owned apartments. Free fax from USA and Canada: 1-800 843 5287.
Prices: £400.00-£4000.00 low season, £400.00-£4000.00 high season

Hyde Park Residence Ltd

55 Park Lane, Mayfair, London W1Y 3DB
Tel: (0171) 409 9242/(0171) 409 9240
Fax: (0171) 493 4041
E-mail: lettings@hprapts.demon.co.uk
URL: www.hpr.co.uk/index.html
Contact: Ms S Farrero
Serviced apartments in Mayfair. Opposite Hyde Park and close to shops, theatres and historic sites and monuments. Easy access to airports.
Units: 100 serviced apartments, sleeping a maximum of 8
LP

Kensgate House

38 Emperor's Gate, London SW7 4HJ
Tel: (0171) 370 1040
Fax: (0171) 373 6183
Contact: Mr W Harris
Comfortable serviced apartments with fully equipped kitchens or kitchenettes. Other accommodation available in the Kensington and Victoria areas.
Units: 14 serviced apartments, 3 non-self-contained studio flats, sleeping a maximum of 5
Prices: £141.00-£300.00 low season, £141.00-£375.00 high season
LP

The Lexham

APPLIED

32-38 Lexham Gardens, London W8 5JE
Tel: (0171) 559 4444
Fax: (0171) 559 4400
E-mail: reservations@lexham.com
URL: www.lexham.com
Contact: Miss C Bucher
Units: 31 serviced apartments, sleeping a maximum of 5
Prices: £1145.63-£1498.13 low season, £1145.63-£1498.13 high season
LP

London Country Apartments Ltd

UP TO HIGHLY COMMENDED

121 Cherry Orchard Road, East Croydon, Croydon CR0 6BE
Tel: (0181) 686 8068/0961 300017
Fax: (0181) 686 0678
E-mail: 101327.1320@compuserve.com
Contact: Ms R Anselm
Superbly furnished, purpose-built apartments close to London. Ideal for families and tourists, or business relocations. Available all year. An excellent hotel alternative.
Units: 2 studio flats, 27 serviced apartments, sleeping a maximum of 7
Prices: £205.00-£885.00 low season, £205.00-£885.00 high season
LP

Moss Cottage

HIGHLY COMMENDED

2 Moss Lane, Pinner, Middlesex HA5 3AX
Tel: (0181) 868 5877
Contact: Mr and Mrs C Le Quesne
Wing of 17th century Grade II Listed building.
Units: 1 self-contained cottage, sleeping a maximum of 5
Prices: £700.00 low season, £800.00 high season
LP

NGH Apartments Ltd

Nell Gwynn House, Sloane Avenue, London SW3 3AX
Tel: (0171) 589 1105
Fax: (0171) 589 9433
E-mail: 101562.1120@compuserve.com
URL: www.demon.co.uk/hotel_net.html
Contact: Ms D Laughton
Situated in the heart of Chelsea, NGH offers 150 fully equipped and serviced studios, one- and two-bedroomed apartments. Close to Sloane Square and South Kensington underground. Many sights within easy reach.
Units: 150 serviced apartments, sleeping a maximum of 6
Prices: £310.00-£1170.00 low season, £310.00-£1350.00 high season
LP

Oakfield Estates

UP TO COMMENDED

107 South Eden Park Road, Beckenham, Kent BR3 3AX
Tel: (0181) 658 4441
Fax: (0181) 658 9198
E-mail: oakfield.co.uk
URL: www.oakfield.co.uk
Contact: Mr J E Deane
Victorian mansion with a large garden in a rural setting. Twenty-five minutes by rail to central London. Eight miles by road.
Units: 8 self-contained flats, 2 non self-contained flats, sleeping a maximum of 8
Prices: £200.00-£550.00 low season, £200.00-£550.00 high season
LP

Orion Barbican

COMMENDED

7-21 Goswell Road, London EC1M 7AH
Tel: (0171) 566 8000
Fax: (0171) 566 8130
Contact: Mrs H Bakker
A purpose-built apartotel located in the City of London and very near to the Barbican. All studios and apartments are well equipped and furnished. Good value for money. Rates quoted are from 1998 and are subject to change.

Units: 129 serviced apartments, sleeping a maximum of 4
Prices: £544.00 low season, £544.00 high season
LP

Orion Holborn/Covent Garden

94-99 High Holborn, London WC1V 6LF
Tel: (0171) 395 8800
Fax: (0171) 395 8799
Contact: Mr N Wallis
New apartotel, opened in June 1997, comprising 192 studios and apartments over six floors. Modern furnishing. Opposite Holborn underground station.
Units: 152 self-contained studio flats, 40 self-contained flats, sleeping a maximum of 4
Prices: £630.00-£875.00 low season, £630.00-£875.00 high season
LP

Orion Trafalgar Square

18-21 Northumberland Avenue, London WC2N 5BJ
Tel: (0171) 766 3700
Fax: (0171) 766 3766
E-mail: orionuk@ad.com
Contact: Mr G Bakker
Orion's latest Apartment-Hotel right in the heart of London, equipped to the latest standards for one day, one week, or more.
Units: 126 self-contained studio flats, 61 self-contained flats, sleeping a maximum of 6
Prices: £686.00-£1253.00 low season, £686.00-£1253.00 high season
LP

Park Lane Apartments

48 Curzon Street, Mayfair, London W1Y 7RE
Tel: (0171) 629 0763
Fax: (0171) 493 1308
URL: www.Parklane.co.uk
Contact: Ms K Neilson
Situated in a historically listed building, Park Lane Estates is in the heart of prestigious Mayfair.
Units: 101 self-contained flats, sleeping a maximum of 4
Prices: £700.00-£1850.00 low season, £850.00-£2150.00 high season
LP

Presidential Apartments

102 George Street, London W1H 5RJ
Tel: (0171) 486 0097
Fax: (0171) 487 3624
Contact: Mr M Bluston
Modern block with exclusive entrance and lift. Estate office on second floor.
Units: 12 self-contained flats, sleeping a maximum of 3
Prices: £425.00-£595.00 low season, £525.00-£795.00 high season
LP

Presidential Apartments

Presidential House, 1 University Street, London WC1E 6JQ
Tel: (0171) 486 0097
Fax: (0171) 487 3624
Contact: Mr M J Bluston
Modern block with exclusive entrance and lift to multi-bedroom, duplex apartments on the fifth and sixth floors.
Units: 20 self-contained studio flats, 12 self-contained flats, sleeping a maximum of 6
Prices: £325.00-£775.00 low season, £410.00-£1025.00 high season
LP

Royal Court Apartments

Up to Highly Commended

51-53 Gloucester Terrace, London W2 3DQ
Tel: (0171) 402 5077/0800 318798
Fax: (0171) 724 0286
Contact: Mr J S Gill
Studios and apartments with kitchenette, dining area, satellite TV and telephone. Located in central London, close to Paddington station and Lancaster Gate. Daily rates also available.
Units: 43 serviced apartments, 33 self-contained studio flats, sleeping a maximum of 7
Prices: £560.00-£1295.00 low season, £595.00-£1575.00 high season
LP

St James Court Hotel and Apartments

41-54 Buckingham Gate, London SW1E 6AF
Tel: (0171) 834 6655/ (0171) 963 8301
Fax: (0171) 630 7587
E-mail: Sales.sjc@stjamescourt.co.uk
Contact: Mr M Lamrani
Victorian-style apartments built in 1897 surrounding a central courtyard. Facilities include free health club, choice of three restaurants and cocktail bar.
Units: 83 self-contained flats, sleeping a maximum of 8
Prices: £1425.00-£4100.00 low season, £1511.00-£4100.00 high season
LP

Scala House

21 Tottenham Street, London W1P 9PD
Tel: (0171) 580 6644
Fax: (0171) 636 3405
E-mail: ken@scala-house.co.uk
URL: www.scala-house.co.uk
Contact: Mr and Mrs Palos
Family-run, central, comfortable apartments, in the heart of London. Goodge Street underground two minutes; British Museum six minutes.
Units: 34 serviced apartments, 34 self-contained flats, sleeping a maximum of 6
Prices: £535.00-£595.00 low season, £693.00-£770.00 high season
LP

Service Suites

Commended

4 Lower Sloane Street, and 11 Sloane Gardens, London SW1W 8BJ
Tel: (0171) 730 5766
Fax: (0171) 730 1261
Contact: Mr T Murkett
Two period properties just off Sloane Square. Some flats have two bathrooms and some have the use of private gardens.
Units: 12 self-contained flats, sleeping a maximum of 5
Prices: £822.00-£1762.00 low season, £900.00-£1938.00 high season
LP

Snow White Properties Ltd

Up to Highly Commended

55 Ennismore Gardens, London SW7 1AJ
Tel: (0171) 584 3307
Fax: (0171) 581 4686
E-mail: snowwhite-kensington@go-fax.com
URL: www.accomodata.co.uk/070396.htm
Contact: Miss M White
Close to Harrods, Hyde Park, South Kensington museums and public transport. Friendly atmosphere. Located in a garden square.

Units: 13 self-contained flats, sleeping a maximum of 4
Prices: £550.00-£900.00 low season, £640.00-£980.00 high season
LP

Vancouver Studios

30 Princes Square, Bayswater, London W2 4NJ
Tel: (0171) 243 1270
Fax: (0171) 221 8678
E-mail: hotels@vienna-group.co.uk
URL: www.vienna-group.co.uk
Contact: Ms J Boughton
Quality serviced studios at reasonable rates combining the convenience of a hotel with the privacy of an apartment. From a night to one month.
Units: 45 self-contained studio flats, sleeping a maximum of 4
Prices: £365.00-£850.00 low season, £365.00-£850.00 high season
LP

The Village Property Services

APPROVED

98 Dollis Hill Avenue, London NW2 6QX
Tel: (0181) 452 5327
Fax: (0181) 452 0903
E-mail: 113200.3015@compuserve.com
Contact: Mr M A Abeyakoon
Within easy reach of the West End and the City. Convenient for theatres, museums, shopping, parks and London Zoo.
Units: 1 self-contained flat, sleeping a maximum of 7
Prices: £150.00-£600.00 low season, £250.00-£900.00 high season
LP

Home Stay Agencies

At Home In London

70 Black Lion Lane, London W6 9BE
Tel: (0181) 748 1943
Fax: (0181) 748 2701
E-mail: athomeinlondon@compuserve.com
URL: www.athomeinlondon.co.uk
Contact: Ms Maggie Dobson
Minimum daily rate for single room: from £28.00
Minimum daily rate for double room: from £47.00
Minimum length of stay: 2 consecutive nights
Bed and breakfast in over 70 private homes in central locations, Knightsbridge, Chelsea and West London. Carefully chosen homes, close to underground stations. Established ten years. Small groups catered for.
Deposit: £7.50 per person per night
Areas covered: Central and West London

Best Bed & Breakfast London

PO Box 2070, London W12 8QW
Tel: (0181) 742 9123
Fax: (0181) 749 7084
E-mail: bestbandb@atlas.co.uk
URL: www.bestbandb.co.uk
Business hours: 0900-1800 hrs
Minimum rate for bed and breakfast: from £25.00
Minimum length of stay: 2 nights
Specialising in upmarket central London accommodation. Lovely private homes in Knightsbridge, Kensington, Chelsea, Mayfair, Belgravia and many other excellent locations.
Deposit: £6.00 per person per night
Areas covered: Inner and Greater London

Homes Away

3 Aldham Hall, New Wanstead, London E11 2SQ
Tel: (0181) 530 2271
Fax: (0181) 530 2271
Business hours: 0900-1800 hrs
Contact: Ms Elizabeth-Anne Garner
Minimum daily rate for a single room bed and breakfast: £20.00
Minimum daily rate for a double room bed and breakfast: £37.00
Minimum length of stay: 2 nights
Select home accommodation, pleasant area, clean and friendly homes offering bed and breakfast and half board. Within easy reach of the underground, direct access to the City and West End. Groups and vegetarians welcome. Handy for Stansted and City airports and Eurostar. Credit cards accepted.
Areas covered: East and North East London and parts of Essex.

Host And Guest Service

103 Dawes Road, London SW6 7DU
Tel: (0171) 385 9922/(0171) 385 3434
Fax: (0171) 386 7575
Business hours: 0900-1800 hrs (Monday-Friday)
Contact: Mrs Carol Rutter, Proprietor
Minimum daily rate for a single room bed and breakfast: from £16.50
Minimum daily rate for a twin/double room bed and breakfast: from £32.00
Minimum weekly rate for twin/double room bed and breakfast: from £80.00 per person
Minimum length of stay: 2 nights
Children catered for, no minimum age. Groups catered for. Long and short term accommodation can be arranged. Telephone and credit card bookings accepted. Price includes continental breakfast.
Deposit: Payment in advance
Areas covered: Greater London and UK

London Bed And Breakfast Agency Limited

71 Fellows Road, London NW3 3JY
Tel: (0171) 586 2768
Fax: (0171) 586 6567
E-mail: londonbb@dircon.co.uk
URL: www.dircon.co.uk/londonbb/
Business hours: 0800-1800 hrs Mon-Fri, 0900-1300 hrs Sat
Contact: Mrs Julia Stebbing
Minimum daily rate: from £19.00 per person per night
Minimum length of stay: 2 nights
Quality accommodation in lovely private homes in and around central London.
Areas covered: Central and Greater London (Zone 1/2/3)

London First Choice Bed And Breakfast

111 Hill Rise, Greenford, Middlesex UB6 8PE
Tel: (0181) 575 8877/0468 837728
Fax: (0181) 933 5778
E-mail: lfcaccom@bogo.co.uk
Contact: Mr M Whitlock
Minimum daily rate for a single room bed and breakfast: from £23.00 in outer London
Minimum daily rate for a single room bed and breakfast: from £50.00 in central London
Minimum daily rate for a double room bed and breakfast: from £42.00 in outer London
Minimum daily rate for a double room bed and breakfast: from £64.00 in central London
Minimum length of stay: 3 nights

Bed and breakfast in either a central London hotel or a well-appointed home in the London suburbs. All located near underground stations.
Deposit: 20%
Areas covered: Central and Greater London

London Homestead Services

Coombe Wood Road, Kingston upon Thames, Surrey KT2 7JY
Tel: (0181) 949 4455 (24 hrs)
Fax: (0181) 549 5492
Minimum daily rate for a single room bed and breakfast: £18.00
Minimum daily rate: for a twin/double room bed and breakfast: £32.00
Minimum length of stay: 3 nights
Children under 12 welcome.
Advance and same day reservations are accepted.
Deposit: 25%
Areas covered: Central and Greater London

Uptown Reservations

50 Christchurch Street, London SW3 4AR
Tel: (0171) 351 3445
Fax: (0171) 351 9383
E-mail: uptown@dial.pipex.com
URL: fenet.co.uk/uptown
Contact: Monica Barrington
Rates: £68.00 single room, £88.00 double or twin room, £115.00 family room per night
A bed and breakfast reservation service specialising in upmarket accommodation in private host homes in the fashionable areas of central London, primarily Kensington, Chelsea, Knightsbridge and Belgravia. Every room has a private bathroom and a full continental breakfast is provided. All major credit cards accepted.
Deposit: is required at time of booking £20.00 for a single, £25.00 for a double or twin and £32.00 for a family room
Areas covered: Central London

Welcome Assured Limited

1 Hillcrest Avenue, Edgware, Middlesex HA8 8NZ
Tel: (0181) 958 3996
Fax: (0181) 905 4747
Minimum daily rate bed and breakfast: £23.75
Minimum daily rate bed and breakfast and evening meal: £31.00
Minimum length of stay: 3 nights
Providing homestay accommodation in selected host families with a comprehensive programme of activities, transport and escorts for large groups, individual young people, adults and families throughout the year on 'paying guest basis'.
Deposit: £75.00 per person per booking if weekly, full amount in advance on other bookings
Areas covered: North West London and surroundings

WorldWide Bed & Breakfast Association (W.W.B.B.A.)

Suite 4, PO Box 2070, London W12 8QW
Tel: (0181) 742 9123 (24 hrs)
Fax: (0181) 749 7084
E-mail: bestbandb@atlas.co.uk
URL: www.bestbandb.co.uk
Business hours: 0900-1800 hrs
Minimum daily rate for bed and breakfast: £25.00
Minimum length of stay: 2 nights
Specialising in upmarket central London accommodation. Lovely private homes in Knightsbridge, Kensington, Chelsea, Mayfair, Belgravia and many other excellent locations.
Deposit: £6.00 per person per night
Areas covered: Central and Greater London

Group and Youth

SW1 Victoria/Westminster

Elizabeth House Hotel

118 Warwick Way, London SW1V 1SD
Tel: (0171) 630 0741
Fax: (0171) 630 0740
⊖/⇌ Victoria
Contact: Mr R Amin
Clean and secure basic bed and breakfast accommodation in central London for men, women and families. Garden available for guests' use. Five minutes' walk from Victoria coach and rail terminals.
Caters for: Males, Females, Individuals, Groups
Bedrooms: 10 single, 13 double, 1 triple, 3 family
Total no of bedspaces: 51
Bathrooms: 9 en suite, 8 public showers
Open over Christmas

Holland

53 Eccleston Square, London SW1V 1PG
Tel: (0171) 834 9104
⊖/⇌ Victoria
Contact: Mr T Perkins, Head of Personnel and Residential Services The London Hostels Association, 54 Eccleston Square, London SW1V 1PG
Contact Tel: (0171) 828 3263
Contact Fax: (0171) 834 7146
Budget accommodation in Victoria. Three-course evening meal included.
Caters for: Males, Females, Individuals, Groups
Bedrooms: 9 single, 13 double
Total no of bedspaces: 84
Bathrooms: 12 public showers
Bed only: single £16.00-£20.00, double £32.00-£40.00

University of Westminster

Wigram House, 84-99 Ashley Gardens, Thirleby Road, London SW1P 1HG
⊖/⇌ Victoria
Contact: Ms N Chanson, University of Westminster Commercial Services Luxborough Suite, 35 Marylebone Road, London NW1 5LS
Contact Tel: (0171) 911 5799
Contact Fax: (0171) 911 5141
Refurbished seven-storey mansion block in late-Victorian style, a few minutes' walk from Victoria station and next to the Westminster Roman Catholic Cathedral.
Caters for: Males, Females, Individuals, Groups
Bedrooms: 138 single, 28 double
Total no of bedspaces: 194
Bathrooms: 55 public showers
Bed only: single £19.50-£25.00, double £39.00-£50.00
Bed & Breakfast: single £22.50-£28.00, double £45.00-£56.00
Months open: July/August/ September

Wellington Hall

King's College London, 71 Vincent Square, London SW1P 2PA
Tel: (0171) 834 4740
Fax: (0171) 233 7709
⊖/⇌ Victoria, ⊖ Saint James Park
Contact: King's Campus Vacation Bureau
127 Stamford Street, Waterloo, London SE1 9NQ
Contact Tel: (0171) 928 3777
Contact Fax: (0171) 928 5777
Wellington Hall is delightfully situated in a quiet, green, central London square and combines modern facilities with traditional style. King's College has six additional halls of residences throughout central London.
Caters for: Males, Females, Individuals, Groups
Bedrooms: 39 single, 43 double
Total no of bedspaces: 125
Bathrooms: 17 public showers
Bed & Breakfast: single £21.94-£24.41, double £33.37-£37.08
Months open: January/April/June/July/August/September/December

W1
West End/Mayfair/ Oxford Street

Carr-Saunders Hall

18-24 Fitzroy Street, London W1P 5AE
Tel: (0171) 323 9712
Fax: (0171) 580 4718
⊖ Warren Street
Contact: Mr J F Ross
Central for the West End, including theatres, museums, parks, art galleries and shopping in Oxford Street and Covent Garden.
Caters for: Males, Females, Individuals, Groups
Bedrooms: 132 single, 12 double
Total no of bedspaces: 157
Bathrooms: 2 en suite, 35 public showers
Bed & Breakfast: single £20.50-£27.00, double £35.00-£45.00
Months open: January/March/April/July/August/September/December

International Students House

229 Great Portland Street, London W1N 5HD
Tel: (0171) 631 8300
Fax: (0171) 631 8315
E-mail: accom@ish.org.uk
URL: www.ish.org.uk
⊖ Great Portland Street
Contact: Ms M Downes
Ideally located hostel accommodation near Regent's Park, offering tourist accommodation, conference and meeting facilities and a full programme of social and recreational activities.
Minimum age: 5
Caters for: Males, Females, Individuals, Groups
Bedrooms: 169 single, 80 double, 8 triple, 40 family
Total no of bedspaces: 531
Bathrooms: 7 en suite, 95 public showers
Bed & Breakfast: single £28.00-£30.00, double £40.00-£44.00
Open over Christmas
Parking for: 10

Oxford Street YHA

14-18 Noel Street, London W1V 3PD
Tel: (0171) 734 1618
Fax: (0171) 734 1657
⊖ Oxford Street
Contact: Ms D Bader
In the heart of Soho and near Oxford Street, this hostel is a good sightseeing base for individual travellers. Sleeping accommodation is in small bedrooms with individual security lockers. Rates are subject to change.
Minimum age: 6
Caters for: Males, Females, Individuals
Bedrooms: 24 double, 5 triple, 3 family
Total no of bedspaces: 75
Bathrooms: 11 public showers
Bed only: single £15.90-£21.10
Open over Christmas

University of Westminster

Wells Street Halls of Residence, 32-38 Wells Street, London W1R 8AL
⊖ Oxford Circus
Contact: Ms N Chanson, University of Westminster Commercial Services Luxborough Suite, 35 Marylebone Road, London NW1 5LS
Contact Tel: (0171) 911 5799
Contact Fax: (0171) 911 5141
Small hall of residence attached to one of the University's teaching blocks, offering spacious bedrooms in central London, on a self-catering basis.
Caters for: Males, Females, Groups
Bedrooms: 31 single
Total no of bedspaces: 31
Bathrooms: 13 public showers
Months open: July/August/September

WC1/WC2
Bloomsbury/Strand/ Leicester Square

Astors Museum Inn

27 Montague Street, Bloomsbury, London WC1B 5BH
Tel: (0171) 580 5360
Fax: (0171) 636 7948
E-mail: AstorHostels@msn.com
URL: www.scoot.co.uk/astorhostels/
⊖ Russell Square/Tottenham Court Road
The Museum Inn is located next to the British Museum and within walking distance of Soho, Covent Garden and Oxford Street.
Caters for: Males, Females, Individuals, Groups
Bedrooms: 2 double, 5 family
Total no of bedspaces: 70
Bathrooms: 7 public showers
Bed & Breakfast: single £13.00-£16.00
Open over Christmas

The Florida State University London Study Centre

100-103 Great Russell Street, London WC1B 3LA
Tel: (0171) 813 3223
Fax: (0171) 813 3270
⊖ Tottenham Court Road
Contact: Mr I Watkins, Acorn PO Box 3031, Mill Hill, London NW7 4ZA
Contact Tel: (0181) 905 3525
Contact Fax: (0181) 905 3429
Self-contained, comfortably furnished, fully equipped apartments, classrooms, offices, computer lab and lecture theatre.
Caters for: Males, Females, Individuals, Groups

Bedrooms: 4 single, 31 double, 14 triple, 7 family
Total no of bedspaces: 136
Bathrooms: 36 public showers
Open over Christmas

Generator

Macnaghten House, Compton Place, London WC1H 9SD
Tel: (0171) 388 7666/ (0171) 388 7655
Fax: (0171) 388 7644
Euston/King's Cross
Contact: Mr K Duffy
Contact Tel: (0171) 388 7666
Contact Fax: (0171) 388 7644
Budget accommodation with an exciting futuristic design theme. Extensive communal areas including bar, restaurant and games area.
Minimum age: 10
Caters for: Males, Females, Individuals, Groups
Bedrooms: 27 double, 38 triple, 115 family
Total no of bedspaces: 813
Bathrooms: 70 public showers
Bed & Breakfast: single £36.00-£40.00, double £46.00-£54.00
Open over Christmas

John Adams Hall (Institute of Education)

15-23 Endsleigh Street, London WC1H 0DP
Tel: (0171) 387 4086
Fax: (0171) 383 0164
E-mail: jah@ioe.ac.uk
Euston
Contact: Mr M Lam-Hing
John Adams Hall is an assembly of elegant Georgian houses.
Caters for: Males, Females, Individuals, Groups
Bedrooms: 127 single, 22 double
Total no of bedspaces: 171
Bathrooms: 2 en suite, 26 public showers
Bed & Breakfast: single £21.00-£23.10, double £36.75-£39.90
Months open: January/March/April/July/August/September/December

LSE Residence High Holborn

High Holborn Residence, 178 High Holborn, London WC1V 7AA
Tel: (0171) 379 5589
Fax: (0171) 379 5640
Holborn
Contact: Ms S Jons
Modern, self-catering flats situated in the heart of London.
Caters for: Males, Females, Individuals, Groups
Bedrooms: 310 single, 94 double, 4 triple
Total no of bedspaces: 496
Bathrooms: 20 en suite, 114 public showers
Bed & Breakfast: single £28.00-£32.00, double £44.00-£65.00
Months open: July/August/September

Passfield Hall

1 Endsleigh Place, London WC1H 0PW
Tel: (0171) 387 7743/ (0171) 387 3584
Fax: (0171) 387 0419
Euston
Contact: Ms J Martin
A conversion of Georgian houses in a quiet, central location. Well served by both train and underground stations. Meals provided for groups.
Minimum age unaccompanied: 15
Caters for: Males, Females, Individuals, Groups
Bedrooms: 100 single, 34 double, 10 triple
Total no of bedspaces: 198
Bathrooms: 36 public showers
Months open: March/April/May/July/August/September

W2 Paddington/Bayswater

Astors Quest Hotel

45 Queensborough Terrace, Bayswater, London W2 3SY
Tel: (0171) 229 7782
Fax: (0171) 727 8106
E-mail: AstorHostels@msn.com
URL: **www.scoot.co.uk/astorhostels/**
Queensway/Bayswater
A fun and friendly hostel located close to Hyde Park and Kensington Palace, with lots of restaurants, cafés and pubs in the area.
Caters for: Males, Females, Individuals, Groups
Bedrooms: 2 double, 6 family
Total no of bedspaces: 90
Bathrooms: 4 en suite, 7 public showers
Bed & Breakfast: single £13.00-£16.00
Open over Christmas

Leinster

46 Leinster Gardens, London W2 3AT
Tel: (0171) 723 7803
Fax: (0171) 262 3794
Bayswater
Contact: Mr T Perkins, Head of Personnel and Residential Services The London Hostels Association, 54 Eccleston Square, London SW1V 1PG
Contact Tel: (0171) 828 3263
Contact Fax: (0171) 834 7146
Budget accommodation near Paddington. Three-course evening meal included.
Caters for: Males, Females, Individuals, Groups
Bedrooms: 14 single, 32 double
Total no of bedspaces: 198
Bathrooms: 15 public showers
Bed only: single £16.00-£20.00, double £32.00-£40.00
Open over Christmas

London House Hotel

81 Kensington Gardens Square, London W2 4DJ
Tel: (0171) 727 0696
Fax: (0171) 243 8626
E-mail: hotels@vienna-group.co.uk
URL: **www.vienna-group.co.uk**
Bayswater
Contact: Miss J Boughton
16 Leinster Square, London W2 4PR
Contact Tel: (0171) 221 1400
Contact Fax: (0171) 229 3917
Friendly, comfortable budget hotel, convenient for shops, theatres and sightseeing.
Caters for: Males, Females, Individuals, Groups
Bedrooms: 3 single, 40 double, 6 triple, 16 family
Total no of bedspaces: 220
Bathrooms: 41 en suite, 14 public showers
Bed & Breakfast: single £41.00, double £54.00
Open over Christmas

London House

13 Craven Hill, London W2 3EN
Tel: (0171) 402 9155
Fax: (0171) 723 8303
Paddington
Contact: Mr T Roberts
Budget accommodation near Paddington.
Caters for: Males, Females, Individuals, Groups
Bedrooms: 6 single, 19 double, 10 triple
Total no of bedspaces: 80
Bathrooms: 35 en suite
Bed & Breakfast: double £50.00-£55.00
Open over Christmas
Parking for: 8

Lords Hotel

20-22 Leinster Square, London W2 4PR
Tel: (0171) 229 8877
Fax: (0171) 229 8377
E-mail: lords@netcomuk.co.uk
Bayswater/Queensway
Contact: Mr N G Ladas
Bed and breakfast accommodation in the heart of London. TV in rooms. Most rooms with private facilities.
Minimum age unaccompanied: 10
Caters for: Males, Females, Individuals, Groups
Bedrooms: 9 single, 27 double, 11 triple, 17 family
Total no of bedspaces: 175
Bathrooms: 55 en suite, 7 public showers
Bed & Breakfast: single £30.00-£48.00, double £44.00-£60.00
Open over Christmas

New Atlantic Hotel

1 Queen's Gardens, London W2 3BB
Tel: (0171) 262 4471
Fax: (0171) 706 8548
E-mail: hotels@vienna-group.co.uk
URL: www.vienna-group.co.uk
Paddington
Contact: Ms J Boughton
16 Leinster Square, London W2 4PR
Contact Tel: (0171) 221 1400
Contact Fax: (0171) 229 3917
Budget hotel in Bayswater, ideal for youth groups.
Caters for: Males, Females, Individuals, Groups
Bedrooms: 37 single, 99 double, 11 triple, 37 family
Total no of bedspaces: 462
Bathrooms: 94 en suite, 34 public showers
Bed & Breakfast: single £41.00-£45.00, double £54.00-£66.00
Open over Christmas

New Mansion

38 Lancaster Gate, London W2 3AT
Tel: (0171) 723 4421
Fax: (0171) 262 3797
Lancaster Gate
Contact: Mr T Perkins, The London Hostels Association
54 Eccleston Square, London SW1V 1PG
Contact Tel: (0171) 834 7146
Contact Fax: (0171) 834 7146
Single, double and dormitory rooms available. Price for dormitories includes bed, breakfast and a three-course evening meal.
Caters for: Males, Females, Individuals, Groups
Bedrooms: 18 single, 38 double
Total no of bedspaces: 89
Bathrooms: 15 public showers
Bed only: single £16.00-£20.00, double £32.00-£40.00
Open over Christmas

The Porchester Hotel

33 Princes Square, London W2 4NJ
Tel: (0171) 221 2101
Fax: (0171) 727 9976
E-mail: hotels@vienna-group.co.uk
URL: www.vienna-group.co.uk
Bayswater
Contact: Miss J Boughton
16 Leinster Square, London W2 4PR
Contact Tel: (0171) 221 1400
Contact Fax: (0171) 229 3917
Ideal for youth groups, the Porchester has its own passenger lift and offers rooms with private facilities. The hotel provides affordable accommodation.
Caters for: Males, Females, Individuals, Groups
Bedrooms: 6 single, 17 double, 11 triple, 21 family
Total no of bedspaces: 175
Bathrooms: 31 en suite, 10 public showers
Bed & Breakfast: single £41.00, double £54.00-£63.00
Open over Christmas

Railton

10 Craven Hill, London W2 3DT
Tel: (0171) 723 5643
Paddington
Contact: Mr T Perkins, Head of Personnel and Residential Services
The London Hostels Association, 54 Eccleston Square, London SW1V 1PG
Contact Tel: (0171) 828 3263
Contact Fax: (0171) 834 7146
Self-catering hostel.
Caters for: Males, Females, Individuals, Groups
Bedrooms: 14 single, 40 double
Total no of bedspaces: 142
Bathrooms: 9 public showers
Bed only: single £13.00-£17.00, double £26.00-£34.00

Sandeman Allen

40 Inverness Terrace, London W2 3JB
Tel: (0171) 727 2719
Fax: (0171) 229 2526
Bayswater
Contact: Mr T Perkins, Head of Personnel and Residential Services
The London Hostels Association, 54 Eccleston Square, London SW1V 1PG
Contact Tel: (0171) 828 3263
Contact Fax: (0171) 834 7146
Budget accommodation in Paddington. Three-course evening meal included.
Caters for: Males, Females, Individuals, Groups
Bedrooms: 29 single, 36 double
Total no of bedspaces: 122
Bathrooms: 15 public showers
Bed only: single £16.00-£20.00, double £32.00-£40.00

SW3/5/7/10 Chelsea/Earl's Court/South Kensington

Belvedere

6 Grenville Place, London SW7 4RT
Tel: (0171) 373 5701
Fax: (0171) 370 7556
Gloucester Road
Contact: Mr T Perkins, Head of Personnel and Residential Services
The London Hostels Association, 54 Eccleston Square, London SW1V 1PG
Contact Tel: (0171) 828 3263

Contact Fax: (0171) 834 7146
A self-catering hostel.
Caters for: Males, Females, Individuals, Groups
Bedrooms: 23 single, 52 double
Total no of bedspaces: 271
Bathrooms: 17 public showers
Bed only: single £13.00-£17.00, double £26.00-£34.00
Open over Christmas

Curzon House Hotel

58 Courtfield Gardens, London SW5 0NF
Tel: (0171) 581 2116
Fax: (0171) 835 1319
⊖ Gloucester Road
Contact: Mr C A Otter
Curzon House Hotel offers budget accommodation; guests have free use of the kitchen and dining room. Reduced weekly rates available from October to June.
Caters for: Males, Females, Individuals, Groups
Bedrooms: 2 single, 4 double, 2 triple
Total no of bedspaces: 62
Bathrooms: 1 en suite, 5 public showers
Bed & Breakfast: single £15.00-£28.00, double £35.00-£42.00
Open over Christmas

Earl's Court YHA

38 Bolton Gardens, London SW5 0AQ
Tel: (0171) 373 7083
Fax: (0171) 835 2034
⊖ Earl's Court
Contact: Mr D Green
Victorian town house in a residential area, close to shops, restaurants, nightlife and major tourist attractions. Comfortable dormitory accommodation.
Minimum age: 5
Caters for: Males, Females, Individuals
Bedrooms: 2 triple, 4 family
Total no of bedspaces: 155
Bathrooms: 22 public showers
Bed & Breakfast: single £16.45-£18.70
Open over Christmas

Halpin

97 Queen's Gate, London SW7 5AB
Tel: (0171) 373 4180
Fax: (0171) 370 7606
⊖ South Kensington
Contact: Mr T Perkins, Head of Personnel and Residential Services
The London Hostels Association, 54 Eccleston Square, London SW1V 1PG
Contact Tel: (0171) 828 3263
Contact Fax: (0171) 834 7146
Self-catering accommodation situated in South Kensington and convenient for museums.
Caters for: Males, Females, Individuals
Bedrooms: 23 single, 68 double
Total no of bedspaces: 145
Bathrooms: 14 public showers
Bed only: single £13.00-£17.00, double £26.00-£34.00

Hunters Lodge Hotel

38 Trebovir Road, London SW5 9NJ
Tel: (0171) 373 7331/0956 238277
Fax: (0171) 460 3524
⊖ Earl's Court
Contact: Mr S Tayeb
A family-run budget bed and breakfast, with all basic facilities, within walking distance of Earl's Court underground station.
Caters for: Males, Females, Individuals, Groups
Bedrooms: 6 single, 7 double, 6 triple, 2 family
Total no of bedspaces: 60
Bathrooms: 3 en suite, 8 public showers
Bed & Breakfast: single £25.00-£42.00, double £32.00-£55.00
Open over Christmas

Imperial College

Vacation Accommodation Office, Watts Way, Prince's Gardens, London SW7 1LU
Tel: (0171) 594 9507/(0171) 594 9511
Fax: (0171) 594 9504
E-mail: vacation.accommodation@ic.ac.uk
⊖ South Kensington
Contact: Ms L Carrington, Imperial College, Conference Office
Watts Way, Prince's Gardens, London SW7 1LU
Contact Tel: (0171) 594 9525
Contact Fax: (0171) 594 9504
University accommodation overlooking attractive gardens in South Kensington. Museums, Royal Albert Hall, Hyde Park and Harrods located nearby.
Minimum age: 10
Caters for: Males, Females, Individuals, Groups
Bedrooms: 700 single, 24 double
Total no of bedspaces: 748
Bathrooms: 140 public showers
Bed & Breakfast: single £29.50-£47.00, double £47.00-£75.00
Months open: March/April/June/July/August/September
Parking for: 200

Lightfoot Hall

King's College London, Manresa Road, London SW3 6LX
Tel: (0171) 333 4898
Fax: (0171) 333 4901
⊖ Sloane Square
Contact: King's Campus Vacation Bureau
127 Stamford Street, Waterloo, London SE1 9NQ
Contact Tel: (0171) 928 3777
Contact Fax: (0171) 928 5777
A modern, ten-storey building in the famous King's Road, Chelsea, in the heart of London. Other halls of residence in Westminster, Wandsworth, Denmark Hill, Hampstead and Kensington.
Caters for: Males, Females, Individuals, Groups
Bedrooms: 174 single, 24 double
Total no of bedspaces: 222
Bathrooms: 30 public showers
Months open: June/July/August/September

Regina

110 Gloucester Road, London SW7 4RJ
Tel: (0171) 373 5151
Fax: (0171) 370 7580
⊖ Gloucester Road
Contact: Mr T Perkins, The London Hostels Association
54 Eccleston Square, London SW1V 1PG
Contact Tel: (0171) 828 3263
Contact Fax: (0171) 834 7146
Single, double and dormitory rooms available. Prices for dormitory rooms include bed, breakfast and a three-course evening meal.
Caters for: Males, Females, Individuals, Groups
Bedrooms: 12 single, 26 double
Total no of bedspaces: 105

Bathrooms: 10 public showers
Bed only: single £16.00-£20.00, double £32.00-£40.00

EC1/2/3/4 CITY OF LONDON

City of London YHA

36 Carter Lane, London EC4V 5AB
Tel: (0171) 236 4965
Fax: (0171) 236 7681
St Paul's, Blackfriars
Contact: Mr P Clarke
In the centre of the City of London, in an area of winding narrow streets, this hostel is a former school for choirboys of St Paul's Cathedral. Prices to be advised on application.
Minimum age unaccompanied: 14
Caters for: Males, Females, Individuals, Groups
Bedrooms: 3 single, 7 double, 7 triple, 10 family
Total no of bedspaces: 193
Bathrooms: 2 en suite, 10 public showers
Bed & Breakfast: single £20.00-£26.00, double £40.00-£52.00
Open over Christmas

Finsbury Residences City University

Bastwick Street, London EC1V 3PE
Tel: (0171) 477 8811
Fax: (0171) 477 8810
URL: www.city.ac.uk/conference
Angel, Old Street
Contact: Mrs S Arbos
Finsbury Residences comprise two modern halls built in the mid-70s. They are close to the Barbican Arts Centre and Upper Street.
Minimum age: 7
Caters for: Males, Females, Individuals, Groups
Bedrooms: 320 single
Total no of bedspaces: 320
Bathrooms: 52 public showers
Bed & Breakfast: single £19.00-£35.00, double £38.00-£50.00
Months open: January/March/April/July/August/September/December

Rosebery Avenue Hall

90 Rosebery Avenue, London EC1R 4TY
Tel: (0171) 278 3251
Fax: (0171) 278 2068
Angel, King's Cross
Contact: Ms M Zanfal
Modern hall of residence convenient for Oxford Street and the West End. Every room with washbasin. Lift. TV and meals available.
Minimum age unaccompanied: 15
Caters for: Males, Females, Individuals, Groups
Bedrooms: 159 single, 107 double, 13 triple
Total no of bedspaces: 448
Bathrooms: 18 en suite, 70 public showers
Months open: March/April/July/August/September

W8/11/14 KENSINGTON/NOTTING HILL GATE HOLLAND PARK

Bowden Court

24 Ladbroke Road, London W11 3NN
Tel: (0171) 727 5665
Fax: (0171) 229 2534
Notting Hill Gate
Contact: Mr T Perkins, Head of Personnel and Residential Services
The London Hostels Association, 54 Eccleston Square, London SW1V 1PG
Contact Tel: (0171) 828 3263
Contact Fax: (0171) 834 7146
Single, double and dormitory rooms available. Dormitory prices include bed, breakfast and a three-course evening meal.
Caters for: Males, Females, Individuals, Groups
Bedrooms: 62 single, 122 double
Total no of bedspaces: 450
Bathrooms: 21 public showers
Bed only: single £16.00-£20.00, double £32.00-£40.00

Holland House YHA

Holland Walk, Kensington, London W8 7QN
Tel: (0171) 937 0748
Fax: (0171) 376 0667
High Street Kensington
Contact: Mr A Lamb
Modern hostel incorporating part of a Jacobean mansion, set in a park with woodland, lawns and playing field. Prices to be advised on application.
Minimum age: 5
Caters for: Males, Females, Individuals, Groups
Bedrooms: 1 single, 1 double, 1 triple, 1 family
Total no of bedspaces: 201
Bathrooms: 38 public showers
Open over Christmas

Queen Elizabeth Hall

King's College London, Campden Hill Road, London W8 7AH
Tel: (0171) 333 4255
Fax: (0171) 333 4401
High Street Kensington
Contact: King's Campus Vacation Bureau
127 Stamford Street, Waterloo, London SE1 9NQ
Contact Tel: (0171) 928 3777
Contact Fax: (0171) 928 5777
On a self-contained campus near Kensington High Street, convenient for shopping, sightseeing and London's theatres. Groups of ten or more only accepted.
Caters for: Males, Females, Groups
Bedrooms: 36 single, 102 double
Total no of bedspaces: 240
Bathrooms: 28 public showers
Bed & Breakfast: single £20.85-£23.20, double £32.45-£36.10
Months open: June/July/August/September
Parking for: 20

W3/4/5/6/7/12 ACTON/CHISWICK/EALING/HAMMERSMITH

Tent City – Acton

Old Oak Common Lane, East Acton, London W3 7DP
Tel: (0181) 743 5708
Fax: (0181) 749 9074
E-mail: tentcity@btinternet.com
URL: www.btinternet.com/~tentcity
East Acton
Contact: Ms M Lambert
A tented hostel in a large park, providing cheap, simple accommodation for group and individual summer visitors to London. Sociable, cosmopolitan atmosphere. Also a campsite.
Minimum age unaccompanied: 15
Caters for: Males, Females, Individuals, Groups

Total no of bedspaces: 448
Bathrooms: 24 public showers
Months open: June/July/August/September
Parking for: 30

North West London

Belsize

40 Belsize Park Gardens, London NW3 4NA
Tel: (0171) 722 8131
Fax: (0171) 483 0889
⊖ Belsize Park
Contact: Mr T Perkins, Head of Personnel and Residential Services
The London Hostels Association, 54 Eccleston Square, London SW1V 1PG
Contact Tel: (0171) 828 3263
Contact Fax: (0171) 834 7146
Hostel offering budget accommodation near Belsize Park station. Three-course evening meal included in the price.
Caters for: Males, Females, Individuals, Groups
Bedrooms: 19 single, 48 double
Total no of bedspaces: 144
Bathrooms: 16 public showers
Bed only: single £16.00-£20.00, double £32.00-£40.00

Hampstead Heath YHA

4 Wellgarth Road, Golders Green, London NW11 7HR
Tel: (0181) 458 7196/(0181) 458 9054
Fax: (0181) 209 0546
⊖ Golders Green
Contact: Ms B Robinson
Attractive building in well-kept gardens in an area of architectural and natural beauty. Good value accommodation just 20 minutes by underground from central London.
Minimum age unaccompanied: 14
Caters for: Males, Females, Individuals, Groups
Bedrooms: 14 double, 9 triple, 14 family
Total no of bedspaces: 199
Bathrooms: 24 public showers
Bed only: single £13.35-£15.60, double £26.70-£38.50
Bed & Breakfast: single £18.55, double £37.10-£38.50
Open over Christmas
Parking for: 14

King's College London Hampstead Campus

Kidderpore Avenue, London NW3 7ST
Tel: (0171) 435 3564
Fax: (0171) 431 4402
⊖ Finchley Road
Contact: King's Campus Vacation Bureau
127 Stamford Street, Waterloo, London SE1 9NQ
Contact Tel: (0171) 928 3777
Contact Fax: (0171) 928 5777
University campus offering single and twin rooms in modern and turn-of-the-century buildings. Function rooms available.
Caters for: Males, Females, Individuals, Groups
Bedrooms: 252 single, 124 double
Total no of bedspaces: 500
Bathrooms: 40 public showers
Bed only: single £13.60-£16.00, double £23.20-£27.50
Bed & Breakfast: single £17.30-£20.35, double £30.45-£35.80
Months open: June/July/August/September

Regents College

Inner Circle, Regent's Park, London NW1 4NS
Tel: (0171) 487 7495
Fax: (0171) 487 7425
E-mail: markhamt@regents.ac.uk.
URL: www.regents.ac.uk.
⊖ Regent's Park
Contact: Ms T Markham
International college and affiliated teaching organisations on central London campus, with one large hall of residence: Reid Hall.
Caters for: Males, Females, Individuals, Groups
Bedrooms: 22 single, 78 double, 16 triple
Total no of bedspaces: 226
Bathrooms: 5 en suite, 40 public showers
Months open: January/May/June/July/August
Parking for: 45

St Pancras YHA

79-81 Euston Road, London NW1 2QS
Tel: (0171) 388 9998
Fax: (0171) 388 6766
⊖/≹ Euston/King's Cross
Contact: Ms J Bancroft
New YHA hostel, near to stations. Ideal for staying in London. Short walk to Camden Market.
Minimum age unaccompanied: 14
Caters for: Males, Females, Individuals
Bedrooms: 11 double, 13 family
Total no of bedspaces: 150
Bathrooms: 33 en suite, 14 public showers
Bed & Breakfast: single £22.50-£25.40
Open over Christmas

University of Westminster

Marylebone Road Hall of Residence, 35 Marylebone Road, London NW1 5LS
⊖ Baker Street
Contact: Ms N Chanson, University of Westminster Commercial Services
Luxborough Suite, 35 Marylebone Road, London NW1 5LS
Contact Tel: (0171) 911 5799
Contact Fax: (0171) 911 5141
Student residence in central London, offering well-appointed, single study-bedrooms, on a self-catering basis or with meals.
Caters for: Males, Females, Individuals, Groups
Bedrooms: 220 single
Total no of bedspaces: 220
Bathrooms: 84 public showers
Bed & Breakfast: single £22.50-£28.00
Months open: July/August/September

North London

Kent House

325 Green Lanes, London N4 2ES
Tel: (0181) 802 0800/(0181) 802 5100
Fax: (0181) 802 9070
E-mail: Kenthall@dircon.co.uk
URL: www.users.dircon.co.uk/~Kenthall
⊖ Manor House
Special off-season and weekly rates. Groups and school parties welcome. Facilities for self-catering available.
Minimum age unaccompanied: 16
Caters for: Males, Females, Individuals, Groups
Bedrooms: 3 single, 13 double

Total no of bedspaces: 34
Bathrooms: 6 public showers
Bed only: single £14.00-£16.00, double £32.00
Bed & Breakfast: single £22.00-£25.00, double £32.00-£36.00
Open over Christmas
Parking for: 4

University of Westminster Alexander Fleming Halls of Residence

3 Hoxton Market, London N1 6HG
Old Street
Contact: Ms N Chanson, University of Westminster Commercial Services Luxborough Suite, 35 Marylebone Road, London NW1 5LS
Contact Tel: (0171) 911 5799
Contact Fax: (0171) 911 5141
Situated on the edge of the City, the halls offer good quality single study-bedrooms in self-contained units of four to eight. The halls are well served by public transport and are ideal for sightseeing.
Caters for: Males, Females, Individuals, Groups
Bedrooms: 186 single
Total no of bedspaces: 186
Bathrooms: 62 private bathrooms
Bed & Breakfast: single £22.50-£28.00
Months open: July/August/September
Parking for: 5

University of Westminster

Furnival House, Chomeley Park, Highgate, London N6 5EU
Highgate/Archway
Contact: Ms N Chanson, University of Westminster Commercial Services Luxborough Suite, 35 Marylebone Road, London NW1 5LS
Contact Tel: (0171) 911 5799
Contact Fax: (0171) 911 5141
Refurbished Edwardian hall of residence in Highgate Village, situated in its own grounds, within walking distance of Waterlow Park and Hampstead Heath. Good quality accommodation on a self-catering or bed and breakfast basis.
Minimum age: 12
Caters for: Males, Females, Individuals, Groups
Bedrooms: 113 single
Total no of bedspaces: 113
Bathrooms: 16 public showers
Bed & Breakfast: single £22.50-£28.00
Months open: July/August/September
Parking for: 6

Walter Sickert Hall City University

Graham Street, London N1 8LA
Tel: (0171) 477 8822
Fax: (0171) 477 8823
Angel
Contact: Ms M Preston
Hall of residence with all en suite rooms, close to Angel underground station and Camden Market, with easy access to the West End.
Minimum age: 7
Caters for: Males, Females, Individuals, Groups
Bedrooms: 226 single, 8 double
Total no of bedspaces: 242
Bathrooms: 234 en suite
Bed & Breakfast: single £32.00-£40.00, double £52.00-£57.00
Months open: July/August/September
Parking for: 6

South West London

The New Ark Floating Hostel

Adrenalin Village, Queenstown Road, London SW8 4NP
Tel: (0171) 498 7337/(0171) 720 9496
Fax: (0171) 627 8861
Battersea Park
Contact: Miss S Curtis
The only floating accommodation on the River Thames. Converted barge, ideal for travellers. Fun, lively atmosphere. Home of the UK Bungee Club.
Caters for: Males, Females, Individuals, Groups
Bedrooms: 10 family
Total no of bedspaces: 40
Bathrooms: 4 public showers
Open over Christmas

East London

Claredale House

Claredale Street, Bethnal Green, London E2 6PE
Tel: (0171) 739 7440
Fax: (0171) 729 5570
E-mail: enquiries@claredalehouse.demon.co.uk
Bethnal Green
Contact: Mr J Edwards
Student halls offering comfortable, self-catering accommodation in flats, during vacation times. Close to the City of London.
Caters for: Males, Females, Individuals
Bedrooms: 267 single
Total no of bedspaces: 267
Bathrooms: 70 public showers
Months open: June/July/August
Parking for: 20

Sir John Cass Hall

150 Well Street, London E9 7LQ
Tel: (0181) 533 2529
Fax: (0181) 525 0633
E-mail: sirjohncass.demon.co.uk.
Bethnal Green
Contact: Ms A Young
Claredale House, Claredale Street, Bethnal Green, London E2 6PE
Contact Tel: (0171) 739 7440
Contact Fax: (0171) 729 5570
Student halls offering comfortable accommodation during vacation times. Close to the City. Reasonable rates for individuals and groups.
Minimum age unaccompanied: 16
Caters for: Males, Females, Individuals, Groups
Bedrooms: 102 single
Total no of bedspaces: 102
Bathrooms: 12 public showers
Months open: March/April/July/August/September
Parking for: 20

South East London

Bankside House

24 Sumner Street, London SE1 9JA
Tel: (0171) 633 9877
Fax: (0171) 574 6730
Blackfriars/Waterloo
Contact: Mr F Anderson
Situated on the South Bank next to the Globe Theatre. Bankside House provides modern, en suite bed and breakfast accommodation, with a restaurant, TV, bar and good facilities.
Caters for: Males, Females, Individuals, Groups
Bedrooms: 290 single, 227 double, 14 triple, 4 family

Total no of bedspaces: 833
Bathrooms: 308 en suite, 25 public showers
Months open: June/July/August/September
Parking for: 30

Butlers Wharf Residence

Butlers Wharf Residence, 11 Gainsford Street, London SE1 2NB
Tel: (0171) 407 7164
Fax: (0171) 403 0847
London Bridge
Contact: Mr G Kane
Within one minute's walk of Tower Bridge. The residence has 275 bedspaces in self-catered cluster flats of five, six or seven beds.
Caters for: Males, Females, Individuals, Groups
Bedrooms: 253 single, 12 twin
Total no of bedspaces: 277
Bathrooms: 94 public showers
Months open: July, August, September

Great Dover Street Apartments

165 Great Dover Street, London SE1 4XA
Tel: (0171) 407 0069
Fax: (0171) 378 7973
Borough, London Bridge
Contact: King's Campus Vacation Bureau
127 Stamford Street, London SE1 9NQ
Contact Tel: (0171) 928 3777
Contact Fax: (0171) 928 5777
A modern residence built around a courtyard and located in a historic area of London.
Caters for: Males, Females, Individuals, Groups
Bedrooms: 700 single
Total no of bedspaces: 700
Bathrooms: 700 en suite
Months open: July/August/September

King's College Hall

King's College London, Champion Hill, London SE5 8AN
Tel: (0171) 733 2166
Fax: (0171) 737 0235
Denmark Hill
Contact: King's Campus Vacation Bureau
127 Stamford Street, London SE1 9NQ
Contact Tel: (0171) 928 3777
Contact Fax: (0171) 928 5777
Set in pleasant, quiet grounds this hall offers budget accommodation. Three miles from Westminster and the City.
Caters for: Males, Females, Groups
Bedrooms: 450 single
Total no of bedspaces: 450
Bathrooms: 70 public showers
Bed & Breakfast: single £16.25-£18.00
Months open: January/April/June/July/August/September/December
Parking for: 60

Rotherhithe YHA and Conference Centre

Salter Road, London SE16 1PP
Tel: (0171) 232 2114
Fax: (0171) 237 2919
Rotherhithe
Contact: Mr R E Stackhouse
Purpose-built hostel offering modern furnishings, central heating and privacy. All bedrooms have en suite facilities. Sleeping accommodation is mainly in small bedrooms with modern bunks and security lockers.
Caters for: Males, Females, Individuals, Groups
Bedrooms: 22 double, 16 family
Total no of bedspaces: 320
Bathrooms: 70 en suite
Bed & Breakfast: single £17.80-£21.30, double £41.00-£49.00
Open over Christmas

St Christophers Inn

121 Borough High Street, London Bridge, London SE1 1NP
Tel: (0171) 407 1856
Fax: (0171) 403 7715
London Bridge, Borough
Contact: Mr R Bradford
Three minutes' walk from London Bridge underground station. Grade I Listed building with an amazing history. Late-licensed pub within the building, with a chill-out room open 24 hours.
Caters for: Males, Females, Individuals, Groups
Bedrooms: 1 triple, 7 family
Total no of bedspaces: 48
Bathrooms: 8 public showers
Bed & Breakfast: single £10.00-£14.00
Open over Christmas
Parking for: 3

Stamford Street Apartments King's Campus Vacation Bureau

127 Stamford Street, Waterloo, London SE1 9NQ
Tel: (0171) 873 2960/ (0171) 873 2962
Fax: (0171) 873 2964
Waterloo
Contact: King's Campus Vacation Bureau
A modern residence with 560 single bedrooms arranged in units of four-nine rooms. All rooms are en suite with shower.
Caters for: Males, Females, Individuals, Groups
Bedrooms: 558 single
Total no of bedspaces: 558
Bathrooms: 558 en suite
Months open: July/August/September

University of Greenwich

Avery Hill Campus, Southwood Site, Avery Hill Road, London SE9 2UG
Tel: (0181) 331 8121
Fax: (0181) 331 8114
New Eltham
Contact: Mr K Humphrey, University of Greenwich Southwood Site, Help Desk, The Dome, Henry Tudor Court, Avery Hill Road, London SE9 2PQ
Contact Tel: (0181) 331 7543
Contact Fax: (0181) 331 9492
Four educational campuses in south London and north Kent.
Caters for: Males, Females, Groups
Bedrooms: 2000 single, 8 double
Total no of bedspaces: 2016
Bathrooms: 270 public showers
Bed only: single £16.00-£18.00, double £32.00-£36.00
Bed & Breakfast: single £18.50-£22.50, double £37.00-£45.00
Months open: April/July/August/September
Parking for: 775

University of Westminster

International House, 1-5 Lambeth Road, London SE1 6HU
⊖ Lambeth North, ⊖/⇌ Waterloo
Contact: Ms N Chanson, University of Westminster Commercial Services Luxborough Suite, 35 Marylebone Road, London NW1 5LS
Contact Tel: (0171) 911 5799
Contact Fax: (0171) 911 5141
Small hall of residence, 15 minutes from the Houses of Parliament, offering good quality accommodation in single or twin rooms on self-catering or bed and breakfast basis.
Caters for: Males, Females, Individuals, Groups
Bedrooms: 63 single, 9 double
Total no of bedspaces: 81
Bathrooms: 18 public showers
Bed only: single £19.50-£25.00, double £39.00-£50.00
Bed & Breakfast: single £22.50-£28.00, double £45.00-£56.00
Months open: July/August/September
Parking for: 2

London's Country

Brunel University College

300 St Margaret's Road, Twickenham TW1 1PT
Tel: (0181) 891 0121
Fax: (0181) 891 8270
⊖/⇌ Richmond, ⇌ St Margaret's
Contact: Mrs Oprey
This pleasant campus is on the Thames near Richmond, within easy reach of Heathrow and central London.
Caters for: Males, Females, Groups
Bedrooms: 314 single, 15 double
Total no of bedspaces: 344
Bathrooms: 60 public
Bed & Breakfast: single £22.00
Months open: January, March, April, July, August, September, December

Brunel University Conference Centre

Conference Office, Brunel University, Uxbridge UB8 3PH
Tel: (01895) 238353
Fax: (01895) 203142
E-mail: conference@brunel.ac.uk
⊖ Uxbridge
Contact: Mrs Tomlinson
En suite and standard bedrooms, cafeteria or silver service meals, purpose-built theatres and classrooms, audio and visual aids and sports facilities all available.
Caters for: Males, Females, Individuals, Groups
Bedrooms: 695 single
Total no of bedspaces: 695
Bathrooms: 464 en suite, 85 public
Bed & Breakfast: single £35.00, double £67.00
Months open: June, July, August, September

University of Westminster

Harrow Hall of Residence, Watford Road, Harrow, Middlesex HA1 3TP
Tel: (0171) 911 5986
Fax: (0171) 911 5967
⊖ Northwick Park
Contact: Ms Corbishley
Newly redeveloped campus, offering comfortable en suite bedrooms, bright and spacious meeting rooms, modern auditorium/lecture theatres and good quality catering.
Caters for: Males, Females, Individuals, Groups
Bedrooms: 450 single, 10 double
Total no of bedspaces: 470
Bathrooms: 460 en suite
Bed only: single £22.00-£27.50, double £43.00-£55.00
Bed & Breakfast: single £25.00-£30.50, double £50.00-£61.00
Months open: July, August, September

Caravan and Camping Parks

Crystal Palace Caravan Club Site ✓✓✓✓✓

Crystal Palace Parade, London SE19 1UF
Tel: (0181) 778 7155
Fax: (0181) 676 0980
⇌ Crystal Palace
Contact: The Warden
Busy site on A212, off A205 South Circular Road. Good transport links to London.
Total no of pitches: 150
Daily Prices: Prices on application
Open: All year

Lee Valley Campsite ✓✓✓✓✓

Sewardstone Road, Chingford E4 7RA
Tel: (0181) 529 5689
Fax: (0181) 559 4070
Contact: Mr D S Pegg
⇌ Chingford
Spacious park with well-planned facilities on the A112 between Chingford and Waltham Abbey, 12 miles from central London. Wide range of recreational activities in the surrounding area of the Lee Valley Park.
Total no of pitches: 200
Daily Prices: Prices on application
Open: April-October

Lee Valley Leisure Centre ✓✓✓✓

Meridian Way, London N9 OAS
Tel: (0181) 345 6666/ (0181) 803 6900
Fax: (0181) 884 4975
⇌ Edmonton Green
Contact: Ms V Blacker
This site is part of Lee Valley Leisure Centre with a wide range of sporting and leisure activities. Fast train service to central London within a short bus ride, and the countryside of Epping Forest and Lee Valley nearby.
Total no of pitches: 160
Daily Prices: £10.40 per pitch, £2.25 electrical hook up
Open: All year

Lee Valley Park, Eastway Cycle Circuit ✓✓

Temple Mills Lane, Leyton, London E15 2EN
Tel: (0181) 534 6085
Fax: (0181) 536 0959
⊖ Leyton
Contact: Mr S G Turner
Part of the 40-acre landscaped park which is the home of the unique Eastway Cycle circuit only four miles from the city of London. Well-maintained surroundings and a wide range of modern facilities. Prices quoted per person per night.
Total no of pitches: 100
Daily Prices: £10.40 per pitch
Open: March-October

Tent City – Hackney

Millfields Road, Hackney, London
E5 0AR
Tel: (0181) 985 7656
Fax: (0181) 749 9074
E-mail: tentcity@btinternet.com
URL: www.btinternet.com/~tentcity/
⊖ Leyton
Contact: Ms M Lambert
London's most central campsite and tented hostel. Canal-side site in nature reserve. Friendly and peaceful atmosphere. Run by international staff. Profits to charity.
Total no of pitches: 200
Daily Prices: £5.00 per person
Open: June-August

ADVERTISERS' INDEX